PASTORS IN TRANSITION

PULPIT & PEW

Jackson W. Carroll, series editor

Pulpit & Pew is a major research project whose purpose is to describe as comprehensively as possible the state of Protestant and Catholic pastoral leadership in the U.S. What are the trends, and what issues do clergy face? The project also aims to contribute to an understanding of excellent pastoral leadership and how it can be called forth and supported. Undertaken by Duke University Divinity School, the project is supported by a grant from Lilly Endowment, Inc. For further information, see *www.pulpitandpew.duke.edu.*

Pastors in Transition

Why Clergy Leave Local Church Ministry

Dean R. Hoge *&* Jacqueline E. Wenger

WILLIAM B. EERDMANS PUBLISHING COMPANY
GRAND RAPIDS, MICHIGAN / CAMBRIDGE, U.K.

© 2005 Wm. B. Eerdmans Publishing Co.
All rights reserved

Wm. B. Eerdmans Publishing Co.
255 Jefferson Ave. S.E., Grand Rapids, Michigan 49503 /
P.O. Box 163, Cambridge CB3 9PU U.K.

Printed in the United States of America

09 08 07 06 05   7 6 5 4 3 2 1

ISBN 0-8028-2908-2

www.eerdmans.com

Contents

Foreword

In our society, work is for many a core aspect of personal identity. This is especially true for those in the professions, who typically undergo a long and intensive socialization into their chosen field and often consider their work to be a life calling. Their work is central to how they think of themselves and relate to others, and it is also central to how others relate to them. Thus, when one of these individuals leaves his or her profession, the change is often a difficult, sometimes traumatic one, even if the leaving was voluntary.

If this is true for most professionals, it is especially true for clergy — the subject of this book — who are particularly likely to think of themselves (and be considered by others) as having been called by God to ordained ministry. When I left pastoral ministry after five quite happy and rewarding years to accept a call to be a campus minister (and later to become a seminary professor), many friends, especially clergy friends, asked why I was leaving the ministry. Being a campus minister obviously didn't count with them, and, to varying degrees, they began to relate to me differently. I was no longer considered "one of them." Although I thought of my new position as an equally valid way of fulfilling my calling as a minister and was excited about the challenges it afforded, my friends' response was disconcerting and troubling. And I am not alone in experiencing such change in this way. Yet, my experience with change was mild when compared with that of those who have left pastoral ministry involuntarily (or even voluntarily) because of some difficulty that has prevented them from functioning effectively. For such persons, leaving can be an extremely tough experience. And it is also difficult for their friends, families, congregations, and denominations.

This is a book about such change, about those who leave pastoral ministry, whether for another form of ministry outside the local congregation or for a secular occupation. Are clergy leaving local church ministry today more frequently than in the past? Is being a pastor more difficult today than previously, or is it just different? Why do clergy choose to leave the pastorate? What can be done to prevent them from leaving, or if they choose to leave either voluntarily or involuntarily, what can be done to make their leaving a less painful experience for them and their congregations? These are the important questions that Dean Hoge and Jacqueline Wenger set out to answer in their research.

Their work is part of *Pulpit & Pew*, a multi-year research project on Protestant and Catholic pastoral leadership underway at Duke University Divinity School with support from Lilly Endowment, Inc. A major goal of *Pulpit & Pew* is to answer these questions: What is the current state of pastoral leadership at the beginning the 21st century? What are factors affecting pastoral leadership today, and what do current trends portend for the future? Clearly questions about clergy who leave pastoral ministry and the reasons for their leaving are of considerable concern in assessing the state of pastoral leadership today; thus we asked Hoge and Wenger to seek to answer them for us. Their focus is on Protestant clergy. In two earlier books prepared for *Pulpit & Pew*, one by Hoge and the other by Hoge and Wenger, their concern was with issues facing the Catholic priesthood, including priests' decisions to leave the priesthood.[1] Although some of the issues facing Catholic priests are markedly different from those facing Protestant clergy, Protestant readers will greatly benefit from these earlier books. But they will be especially helped by the insights gained from this book's research on clergy in five Protestant denominations who have left pastoral ministry either voluntarily or involuntarily.

The book is filled with poignant stories of clergy who have left

---

1. Dean R. Hoge, *The First Five Years of Priesthood: A Study of Newly Ordained Priests* (Minneapolis: Liturgical Press, 2002); and Dean R. Hoge and Jacqueline E. Wenger, *Evolving Vision of the Priesthood: Changes from Vatican II to the Turn of the New Century* (Minneapolis: Liturgical Press, 2003).

and of the impact that their leaving has had on them personally and on their family, friends, congregations, and denominations. The stories offer important insights into why they left — either, as I did, to change from ministry in a local church to some other form of ministry, or to leave ordained ministry altogether for a secular occupation. The authors surveyed a broad sample of clergy who have left parish ministry and analyzed responses to questionnaires and personal interviews to discern the complex, multifaceted reasons that have led clergy to leave. In organizing the book according to the various reasons for leaving, the authors help us gain greater clarity about those reasons and to see the implications for congregations, denominations, and for the clergy themselves. They also add important insights from interviews and focus groups conducted with denominational leaders.

Who will benefit from this book? Clearly current parish clergy, especially those who entertain thoughts of leaving or are discouraged in their work, will find the book helpful in clarifying their thinking and in seeing possibilities for renewing and fulfilling their calling where they are or in some other ministry setting. Those considering becoming ordained ministers or who are currently in seminary will also find much to ponder in the chapters and the stories they contain. But the book, I believe, is absolutely essential reading for seminary faculty who prepare pastors for church leadership; for denominational leaders who help to select, deploy, counsel, and support the clergy in their care; and for the lay leaders of congregations who work with their pastors on a day-to-day basis. To be sure, many of the reasons that lead to leaving local church ministry lie with the clergy themselves, especially in cases where misconduct or poor performance was at issue. But many ex-pastors speak with considerable passion about inadequacies in their seminary education and of the insensitivity and lack of support that they received from their denominational officials and the lay leaders of their churches. These groups, especially, come in for substantial and serious criticism, and they will be challenged and instructed by the insights of the book.

To be sure, not all cases of clergy leaving pastoral ministry are necessarily bad for the clergy or for the church. Some have always entertained fulfilling their calling to ministry in some other position than as pastor of a congregation. Others discover that they were mistaken in believing that they were called to ordained ministry, and they and the church are better served when they find fulfillment in ministry as laity. For both of these groups, there is a great need to find ways of making their transition both caring and positive. But we especially need to find ways of stanching the outflow of those who do feel called to serve as local church pastors, who have the requisite gifts for doing so, but who, for whatever reason, see leaving the pastorate as their only option. Taking seriously the insights from Hoge and Wenger's research will be enormously helpful in addressing both of these issues.

JACKSON W. CARROLL
Director, Pulpit & Pew:
Research on Pastoral Leadership

Introduction

Local church ministers in Protestant denominations today feel many pressures. This is evident in the numerous paperback books being sold to help them analyze church conflicts and to give them "survival skills." The Pulpit and Pew Project at Duke University Divinity School is analyzing the life situations of local church ministers, and as part of this endeavor it decided to launch a study of men and women who left local church ministry.

The Duke research team did not assume that life for local church ministers is harder today than it was in the past, and it did not assume that conditions are inherently unfair to those ministers. But it did make these two assumptions: that conditions of ministry have changed in the last three or four decades, and that too many local church ministers leave. This situation is not new; the number leaving has always been too high. The Duke team believes that the outflow is partly preventable and that reducing it would be good for the God-given ministries of all American denominations.

In early 2001 the *Pulpit & Pew* committee, headed by Dr. Jackson Carroll, commissioned us to study former local church ministers who have left parish ministry. Our main purpose was to describe as accurately as possible the situation in several denominations and to gather feedback and recommendations from ministers and judicatory officers as to how policies might be updated. There was no assumption that the rate of departures from local church ministry has increased recently or that it is now in crisis; probably the situation has been stable in the last decade. A secondary purpose was to gather information on changes that have occurred since the 1960s and 1970s — changes in church life, in seminaries, in the candidates for ministry, and in the religious orientations of Protestants. This information has the potential to help everyone involved understand what has changed and why, and it could upgrade today's debates about how to prepare for the future.

After three years of work we are presenting our findings in this book. We describe our research methods in Appendix B, but it may be useful to say a few words about them here. The process began with two meetings of an advisory committee, one in January 2001 and another a year later in January 2002. During 2001 we investigated sampling problems and pretested our instrument. In January 2002 we defined the categories of persons we wanted to study:

> We are interested in everyone who was ordained in the past, who served in parish ministry full-time or part-time, and within the last eight years has left parish ministry in either of two ways: (1) left parish ministry for non-parish ministries recognized by their ordinations, especially hospital chaplaincies, military chaplaincies, campus ministers, teachers, and professors; or (2) left church ministry entirely. It does not matter whether the persons, when serving in parish ministry in the past, were the senior pastor or not, whether or not they define their current non-parish jobs as their "ministry," or whether or not they have given up their ordination. It does not matter if the departure was voluntary or involuntary. It does not matter if the persons were seminary graduates.

> We will not study (1) persons temporarily without a job who are now actively seeking a parish ministry job, (2) persons who have retired or who have moved from full-time to part-time parish ministry, (3) persons who have switched denominations but have remained in local church ministry, and (4) persons who left the parish to take denominational jobs such as presbytery staff or district superintendent.

During 2001 we enrolled five denominations: the Assemblies of God, the Evangelical Lutheran Church in America, the Lutheran Church–Missouri Synod, the Presbyterian Church (U.S.A.), and the United Methodist Church. Each agreed to use its denominational database to gather a random sample of about two hundred ministers fitting our definition. In summer and fall 2002 we gathered question-naire data from all five. (Fortunately, the Pulpit and Pew Project provided us a control group of active ministers in three of the denominations, taken from its comprehensive survey of American clergy.) Also during 2001 and 2002 we carried out focus groups and interviews with judicatory leaders in all five denominations, we interviewed ninety ex-pastors by phone, and we researched morale in other professions, mainly law, medicine, and social work.

By the end of 2002 the data were collected. We put together a research team at the Life Cycle Institute at Catholic University to analyze the data, identify the principal motivations and categories of parish-leavers, transcribe the taped phone interviews, and interpret the results. Our purpose has always been to portray today's situation as reliably as possible and to feed back the principal viewpoints and recommendations voiced by the people we surveyed. In the chapters below, all names of individuals, cities, and states have been changed.

We found that many pastors left local church ministry for preventable reasons and that denominations can learn a good bit from those who left. Much can be done to assist these people, and we hope it will be done. Church leaders need both an interpretation of the situation today and specific ideas about improvements.

A project of this size depends on help from many people. We have been blessed with helpful and insightful advisors and collaborators. We wish to thank our initial advisors, including Becky McMillan, Adair Lummis, Jack Marcum, Marcia Myers, Robert Kohler, Gary Allen, Craig Settlage, Martin Smith, James Miley, Michael Ross, Brooks Faulkner, John Dever, Bruce Hartung, Houston Hodges, William McAtee, Edward White, and Jane Wick. We thank the denominational staff who took charge of sampling, mailing, and leading focus groups: Keith Wulff, Jack Marcum, Gary Allen, Jack Roulier, Art Gafke, Martin Smith, and John O'Hara. We thank our research staff, especially Kathleen Pluth, Rosalind Grigsby, Ismail Demirezen, Florence Cole, and Sarina Ward. We also thank Andrew Hoogheem, our editor at Eerdmans.

Above all, we thank Jackson Carroll and John James of the Pulpit and Pew Project at Duke Divinity School for their patience, assistance, and encouragement.

D.H. AND J.W.
March 2004

1 *The Setting*

Ministers who leave local church ministry do so for very diverse reasons — so diverse that we need to separate them into categories at the outset. For example, some leave voluntarily while others do so involuntarily. Consider the cases of Pastor Rowan and Pastor John.

Rowan left local church ministry voluntarily. He entered the ELCA ministry with a strong interest in ministry in higher education, and he understood the denominational rule that pastors are required to spend at least three years in a parish before going into a specialized ministry, and so he accepted a call to a church. His anticipated three years were happy and stretched into eighteen, during the last years of which he taught courses as an adjunct at a nearby Lutheran college. This reawakened his desire to devote himself to higher education, so when an opening occurred at another Lutheran college, he applied. He is now the college chaplain there.

For Rowan there were "push" factors as well as "pull" factors. He felt during his last years of parish ministry that he had hit a plateau and needed a new challenge. He considered taking another parish call and negotiated with two other churches, but for various reasons decided not to pursue those calls. At the same time some tensions had built up among staff members of his church, making him unexcited about the prospect of continuing in ministry there. So when the opportunity came to be a college chaplain, he took it. He was 44 at the time.

Pastor John, on the other hand, exemplifies a minister who left involuntarily. He was the senior pastor of a thousand-member United

1

Methodist church in the American West when it became known that he was having an affair with a woman in another church. When their relationship was uncovered, the woman's family filed charges and contacted the bishop, who in turn called John in. The bishop gave John a choice between surrendering his orders and undergoing a church trial. Since John knew he was guilty, he surrendered his orders there on the spot.

John reflected with us that his marriage had been unhappy for many years before this event, but for various reasons he hadn't wanted a divorce. He and his wife had been in marital counseling for a long time, and the affair happened at a time when they were thinking about separating. He was then 51. Now he works for an environmental organization and wishes he could re-enter ministry.

Some pastors no longer in local church ministry left for organizational reasons; others did so for personal reasons. Take the cases of Pastor Barbara and Pastor Allen. Barbara got caught up in organizational problems — specifically, conflicts in her congregation. She accepted a call as associate in a Presbyterian church when she finished seminary in her early forties. The senior pastor at that church had been there for 25 years and was eager to have an associate to do youth work, expand mission work, and reach out to young adults. But before long Barbara was frustrated by the indifference of many members to the church's program. She found that people voiced interest in new ideas but seemed unwilling to expend any time or effort helping her implement those ideas. For example, she became involved at the local homeless shelter, but nobody else in the church joined her. The senior pastor was too tired to take any initiative at all, and the lay leaders seemed to be continually protecting him. Barbara felt betrayed, and soon she began to feel blamed for the tensions. It was so dispiriting that she took a job working full-time in the health field. She left at 46.

Allen is an example of a pastor who left for a very personal reason: his marriage fell apart. He was the solo pastor in a new Lutheran Church–Missouri Synod congregation, and both he and his wife found their situation stressful. He felt entrapped in his role as pastor, and his wife did not feel comfortable playing the role of pastor's wife. They had very few close friends from whom to derive support, and eventually their marriage ended in separation and divorce. In the

LCMS, if a pastor divorces it is up to the district president to decide whether he (the LCMS does not ordain women) can continue in ministry. But in most cases the individual is forced at least to move to a different congregation some distance away. Allen did not want to move because of the burden doing so would put on his children, so he resigned. He was 35.

Allen still lives in the metropolitan area where he was a pastor, and he is now remarried to a woman from the Brethren denomination. He talked with us at length, pondering what had happened. He guessed that parishioners' expectations of him and his wife, expectations not openly expressed, contributed to their marital problems, but that, more importantly, he and his wife were slowly growing farther and farther apart. Now he works for a non-profit substance abuse organization.

These cases demonstrate how diverse the ex-pastors in our target group are. The first task in our research was therefore to distinguish the main types, to "map the territory," since pastors leave for many reasons. A second task was to try to assess motivations, since it is atypical for any pastor to leave for a single clear-cut reason. Fathoming the conditions and motivations for leaving was our main challenge in the study. In Chapter 2 we describe our methods of analysis.

To understand the situation today, one needs to understand the setting in which these pastors worked. The remainder of this chapter will describe trends in pastoral ministry in recent decades and give specific information about the five denominations.

Changes in the Protestant Ministry since the Sixties

One of the basic assumptions motivating the Duke Divinity School to undertake our project is that social change in the last four decades has put new pressures on the ministry, requiring an evaluation of today's structures to see if they are still serving well. This is a hypothesis on the minds of many church officials today, but to be truly useful it needs to be stated in more specific terms. That is, exactly *what* has changed? *What* are the pressures on today's structures? *How* do we know the structures are not performing well? To introduce the topic, we recall recent changes in the Protestant ministry.

3

Research on changes in the ministry typically uses the 1950s or 1960s as a starting point. There is no compelling reason for doing this except that most social science research on ministry dates back only to the 1950s, making that decade a convenient benchmark for measuring change. But there is a risk in doing this, since the fifties decade was atypical relative to the decades before it. In the 1950s all indicators of church involvement rose above levels prior to World War II and remained high until the middle or late 1960s.[1] During those years, more people were coming to church, shopping for churches, and committing themselves to church life than had been the case for a long time, and it pleasantly surprised Protestant leaders. It was a story of growth, growth, growth, especially in the new suburbs. When the surge subsided, Protestants felt that something had been lost and wondered what they were doing wrong. It is entirely possible that they were doing nothing at all wrong, but rather that the ground was shifting beneath them.

The research on Protestant ministry in the 1960s was dominated by the secularization theory, which asserted that long-term secularization trends in the United States were pushing steadily onward and in the process changing the role and identity of the Protestant minister. A second assumption was that the ideal of professionalism was growing among Protestant clergy, moving ministry from an earlier self-understanding as a religious vocation based on lifelong calling, self-sacrifice, and personal holiness to a new professional ideal stressing learning, certification, and identity.[2]

From the vantage point of the year 2005 these earlier assumptions cannot be accepted. America did not become secularized as some predicted it would in the last decades of the twentieth century, and the putative advance in professionalism has not been apparent. American society is as religious and nonsecular today as it was in the 1960s, and talk of the growing professionalism of the Protestant ministry has subsided. Our approach in this study is less defined by such overarching theories, and more inductive and concrete. So we will compare

1. Robert Wuthnow, *The Restructuring of American Religion: Society and Faith since World War II* (Princeton, N.J.: Princeton University Press, 1988), ch. 3.
2. The secularization assumption is clear in the writings of the 1960s. See Edgar W. Mills, "The Sacred in Ministry Studies," in *The Sacred in a Secular Age*, ed. Phillip E. Hammond (Berkeley: University of California Press, 1985), pp. 167-86.

specifics between today and the 1960s while remembering the uniqueness of that earlier period. We can speak confidently of four trends in the Protestant ministry.

More Educated Laity

First, without doubt, Protestant ministers serve a more educated laity than they did a half-century ago. In the entire adult American population in 1970, 10.7 percent had attended four or more years of college; in 2000 it was 24.2 percent.[3] Cultural diversity has also increased in the United States since the sixties.[4] International travel skyrocketed after the 1960s; in 1960 about 2 million Americans went abroad (not counting trips to Canada or Mexico); in 1997 it was 22 million.[5] A more educated, more cosmopolitan laity will have higher expectations of the performance of clergy; thus, what would have been an acceptable quality of preaching, teaching, and leadership in 1960 is less so today.

Less Trust in Centralized Authority

Second, since the 1960s numerous studies in the United States have demonstrated a decrease of trust in centralized institutions. This is true of the federal government as well as mass media, large corporations, national labor leaders, and national professional associations.

3. Theodore Caplow, Louis Hicks, and Ben J. Wattenberg, *The First Measured Century* (Washington, D.C.: American Enterprise Press, 2001); U.S. Bureau of the Census, *Educational Attainment: 2000* (Washington, D.C., 2003), available online at http://www.census.gov/2000pubs.

4. A far-reaching event took place in the 1960s that has not been fully appreciated by researchers: the U.S. Immigration and Naturalization Act of 1965. Before that year, immigration had been restricted to annual quotas based on the national origins of the U.S. population in 1880 — mainly northern and western Europe. But in 1965 the quotas for other nations were vastly increased, ushering in a second wave of immigration largely from Latin America and Asia. See Roger Finke and Rodney Stark, *The Churching of America, 1776-1900: Winners and Losers in Our Religious Economy* (New Brunswick, N.J.: Rutgers University Press, 1992).

5. Caplow, *First Measured Century*, p. 130.

The change is seen vividly in opinion polls. A question in numerous American surveys asked, "How much of the time do you trust the government in Washington to do the right thing?" The percentage saying "Just about always" or "Most of the time" dropped from 76 in 1964 to 25 in 1995. Another often-used question asked the respondent to choose between two options: "Most people can be trusted," and "You can't be too careful in dealing with people." In 1964, 54 percent said that most people can be trusted, and in 1995, 35 percent did.[6] Americans today reserve their trust for local institutions that they know more personally. For example, national philanthropic organizations have been forced to decentralize their actions to more local levels, and Protestant mission programs have had to build networks of local relationships rather than depend on national appeals from national offices. The downturn in trust is most dramatic among the young.[7]

Decreased Denominational Commitment

Third, identification with specific Protestant denominations is lower in 2003 than it was several decades earlier. When, for example, a Presbyterian family moves to a different town, they will start their church-shopping by visiting the Presbyterian churches nearby; then they will branch out to other denominations, ultimately making their choice based on what the church offers in programs, inspiration, like-minded people, and convenience. Typically they will say, "Denominational differences don't matter, and we felt more at home in the other church." A partial exception may be found in denominations with a strong ethnic identity. For example, Lutherans whose Scandinavian or German heritage is important to them would not think of joining a church without such a heritage.

Robert Wuthnow argues that mainline denominationalism went into decline after the 1960s because of several factors: the ecumenical movement; attitudes of greater tolerance, fostered by a growing num-

6. Richard Morin and Dan Balz, "Americans Losing Trust in Each Other and Institutions," *Washington Post*, January 28, 1996, pp. A1, A6.
7. Robert D. Putnam, *Bowling Alone: The Collapse and Revival of American Community* (New York: Simon & Schuster, 2000), ch. 7.

ber of Americans with higher education; the displacement of denominational seminaries by university-based religious studies departments as the arena for teaching theology; and increasing intermarriage between adherents of different faiths.[8] Central denominational structures have been gradually losing their authority as church members pay more attention to their local churches and less to the denomination to which they belong. Local churches, in turn, are less willing to go along with denominational directives or to buy into denominational programs in youth ministry, Sunday school curricula, missions, and the like. It is telling that the fastest growth in Protestant churches in the last two decades has been in nondenominational churches and in those that de-emphasize their denominational ties.[9]

Lower Clerical Authority

Fourth, the authority and esteem accorded to clergy by Protestants in America has changed. Two explanations are commonly asserted to explain a perceived decline in the esteem of ministers in recent decades: the loss of social functions that the clergy once held (when social work, counseling, and welfare were church functions) and the ambiguities of theological authority in a pluralistic and relativistic culture. Regardless of the power of these proposed explanations, the amount of public confidence placed in religious leaders is a measurable entity, and it is monitored by public opinion polls. Figure 1.1 on page 8 shows trends of confidence in American institutions since 1973. Confidence in most institutions, with the exception of the military, has declined. Organized religion has enjoyed a high level of public confidence the whole time, but its rating did drop modestly after the early 1980s. Though these polls do not show confidence specifically in *clergy* — as

8. Robert Wuthnow, *The Struggle for America's Soul: Evangelicals, Liberals, and Secularism* (Grand Rapids: Eerdmans, 1989), p. 15.

9. Donald E. Miller, *Reinventing American Protestantism* (Berkeley: University of California Press, 1997). Also see Christian Smith, *American Evangelicalism: Embattled and Thriving* (Chicago: University of Chicago Press, 1998); Kimon H. Sargeant, *Seeker Churches* (New Brunswick, N.J.: Rutgers University Press, 2000); and Milton Coalter, John M. Mulder, and Louis B. Weeks, *Vital Signs: The Promise of Mainstream Protestantism* (Grand Rapids: Eerdmans, 1996).

Figure 1.1
How much confidence do you, yourself, have in each of these
institutions in American Society? Gallup polls, 1973-2000.
(Percent saying "a great deal" or "quite a lot")

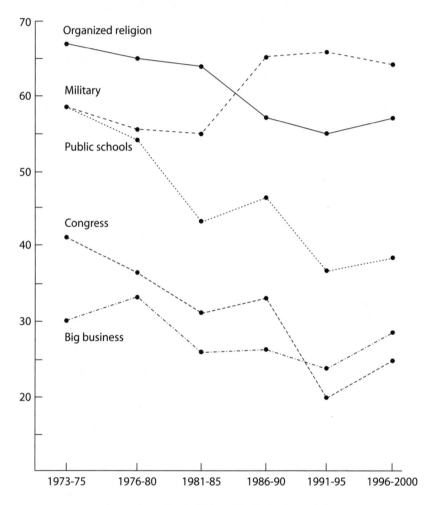

Source: *Sourcebook of Criminal Justice Statistics,* 2000.

opposed to the institutional church — the trends would probably be similar. Regardless, the basic point is this: the esteem of *most* leaders of institutions has declined since the 1970s. Relative to the average decline, the decline for religious leaders has been smaller. That is, everybody went down, but the clergy went down less than others. Thus, theories about how the ministry has changed due to alleged loss of esteem of clergy in America have little explanatory power.

Have there been changes in the acceptance of *styles* of clerical leadership? We believe that authoritarian leadership by church leaders is less acceptable in 2005 than it was in 1960. The leveling between clergy and laity in education and training results in church members today demanding a more collaborative and less arbitrary leadership style.[10] The level of respect accorded a clergyperson solely due to his or her status as clergy is lower today. Clergy who are new to a given community need to prove their wisdom and leadership through their actions; they cannot expect to be accepted as community leaders *a priori*.

Can we conclude that the Protestant ministry is more difficult than it was four decades ago? We put this question to a panel of veteran ministers and concluded, from what they said, that no such conclusion is warranted. Past research also contains no evidence. The job is *different* today, to be sure, but whether it is more difficult is not easy to know. Anyone trying to understand the ministry today should not assume that it has become more difficult in the last three or four decades — but they should assume that it is different. Today's pastors are shepherds to a more educated and cosmopolitan flock whose denominational loyalty has diminished along with its overall trust in institutions.

Changes in Seminary Graduates

Apart from the question of changes in the Protestant ministry, have the graduates of seminaries changed over three or four decades? Yes. The

---

10. Jackson W. Carroll, *Mainline to the Future: Congregations for the 21st Century* (Louisville, Ky.: Westminster John Knox Press, 2000). Also see Jackson W. Carroll, *As One with Authority: Reflective Leadership in Ministry* (Louisville, Ky.: Westminster John Knox Press, 1991).

research clearly shows that seminary students today differ from those of yesteryear in three significant ways: more are women, more are older, and fewer have had church experience in their own denomination.

More Seminary Graduates Are Women

The arrival of women seminary graduates to ordained ministry is one of the most consequential changes of the past half-century. In 1950, almost none of the Protestant students studying for the ministry in American seminaries were women; in 1977 12 percent were; and in 2002 36 percent were.[11] The percentage of women in four of the denominations in our study ranged from 14 to 22.[12] Women were ordained in the Assemblies of God as evangelists and missionaries in 1914, and in 1935 ordination to all ministry categories was extended to them. In the United Methodist Church women were first ordained in 1956, in the Presbyterian Church (U.S.A.) in 1956, and in the ELCA in 1970.[13] Today, women seminary students are more likely to be single than men students; they also tend to be older.[14] Are the women graduates as capable of doing ministry as the men? This is a difficult question to test, but researchers have found that women are equal to men in academic performance and that more women prefer a democratic

11. Daniel O. Aleshire, "Who Is Going to Seminary? A Look at Students in Theological Schools," in *Fact Book on Theological Education 2002-2003* (Pittsburgh: Association of Theological Schools, 2003), pp. 15-23. Aleshire adds a comment: "Women are not enrolled in theological schools to the extent that they are present in American law schools (just over 50% in 2000) or medical schools (just under 50%)," p. 18. Available online at http://www.ats.edu.

12. The research on women ministers is voluminous. The best recent review is by Edward C. Lehman Jr., *Women's Path into Ministry: Six Major Studies* (Durham, N.C.: Duke University Pulpit and Pew Project, 2002). Foremost research studies are Jackson W. Carroll, Barbara Hargrove, and Adair T. Lummis, *Women of the Cloth: A New Opportunity for Churches* (New York: Harper & Row, 1983); Edward C. Lehman Jr., *Gender and Work: The Case of the Clergy* (Albany, N.Y.: State University of New York Press, 1993); and Barbara Brown Zikmund, Adair T. Lummis, and Patricia Mei Yin Chang, *Clergy Women: An Uphill Calling* (Louisville, Ky.: Westminster John Knox Press, 1998).

13. Mark Chaves, *Ordaining Women: Culture and Conflict in Religious Organizations* (Cambridge, Mass.: Harvard University Press, 1997), p. 17.

14. Zikmund, *Clergy Women*, p. 27.

and collaborative leadership style than do men.[15] Still, women have a harder time in the Protestant ministry, and more women than men leave the ministry after a few years.[16] Women are as easily placed as men in initial and second placements after ordination, but after that they are harder to place since most larger Protestant congregations still prefer men as senior ministers.[17]

More Seminary Graduates Are Older

Whereas most seminarians in the 1950s and 1960s were young men right out of college, today the majority are older persons. The average age of students in Master of Divinity programs in the U.S. rose from 25 in 1962 to 34 in 1991.[18] In a 1999 survey the average age was 37. Today, seminary graduates range in age from 25 to over 50. Older graduates are commonly called "second career," since most come to seminary after some years in another profession. Research on seminary students has found that the older students have generally poorer pre-seminary academic records than do students who come to seminary immediately after college. They are more diverse racially and ethnically, they include a higher percentage of women, and they are more inclined to enter congregational ministry.[19]

How does this change affect their ministry? The experts we consulted agreed that older ordinands are by and large more practical, less academic, and more ready for the everyday challenges of church leadership. Older ministers also attract more older parishioners, just as younger ministers attract more of the young; thus denominations with younger ministers are more likely to draw young adults. Evangelical denominations benefit in this regard from the greater numbers of under-35 ministers serving their churches.[20]

15. Zikmund, *Clergy Women*, p. 60.

16. Zikmund, *Clergy Women*, p. 7.

17. Paula D. Nesbitt, *Feminization of the Clergy in America: Occupational and Organizational Perspectives* (New York: Oxford University Press, 1997), p. 67.

18. Study by Larsen, reported in Nesbitt, *Feminization*, p. 92.

19. Aleshire, "Who Is Going to Seminary?" p. 17.

20. Hillary Wicai, "Clergy by the Numbers: Statistics Show It's Not a Youthful Picture," *Congregations*, March-April 2001, pp. 6-9.

Financial difficulties often beset older seminary students who, upon graduation, find that their incomes as pastors will be less — in some cases much less — than what they earned in their prior occupations. Since most of them are married and have children this is especially unwelcome news, and it influences many of the newly ordained to refuse to go to small parishes that can afford to pay only low salaries.

Fewer Seminary Graduates Have Church Experience in Their Denominations

A third shift is that fewer of today's seminarians had long histories of involvement in their denominations, and fewer came to seminary after exercising leadership in youth groups, college groups, or denominational programs. To use one observer's phrase, they did not come up "through the farm clubs" of the denomination. More often they pursued a call to ministry after a conversion experience or inspiration in a spiritually powerful church or movement. Half switched denominations at least once before enrolling in seminary.[21] A corollary of this is another intriguing trend: that fewer today are "PKs" (preachers' kids). Veteran church observers told us that the newly ordained are less familiar with the cultures of their denominations and with basic knowledge regarding how to handle practical situations like visiting the sick, conducting funerals, and presiding at civic events.

Seminary admissions today are not competitive. Some seminaries admit the vast majority of the applicants, and 90 percent of theological students today report that they are attending their first-choice institution. Two-thirds of the entering students report that they applied to only one theological school — the one they are attending. By contrast, more than 85 percent of law students made multiple applications, and only 46 percent of law students are attending their first choice of school.[22] Very few theological students today are dismissed during seminary training.

Defenders of the new generation of seminary graduates argue that

---

21. Barbara G. Wheeler, "Fit for Ministry? A New Profile of Seminarians," *Christian Century*, April 11, 2001, pp. 16-23 at 16.

22. Wheeler, "Fit for Ministry?" p. 17.

the newly ordained, being less submerged in traditional church life, are a source of innovation and new inspiration. We have come across many cases during our research showing that this is true. The downside, of course, is that not every local church is interested in that kind of innovation and inspiration — in spite of what they might say when searching for a new pastor. This leaves thousands of new pastors frustrated at how immovable and resistant their parishioners turn out to be. We found many cases where new pastors committed to turning around small dying churches found their ideas blocked and their inspiration wrung dry.

Comparisons with Other Professions

How do Protestant ministers compare with individuals in other professions in terms of their level of satisfaction and in the factors that induce some to leave? Are Protestant ministers happier, or less happy, than the others? What can we learn from comparisons?

After searching for comparative research, we are forced to conclude that no studies exist that report clearly the relative levels of morale and satisfaction in Christian ministry and in professions such as law, medicine, and social work. The research necessary to answer the question has not been done. Furthermore, comparative studies of retention and resignation rates in the professions have not been done. Our impression, based on the studies that have been done, is that the differences among the four are not great.

An important study of satisfaction in four different professions (but not including Christian ministry) by Cary Cherniss found that levels of satisfaction varied *within* professions more than *between* professions.[23] Cherniss concluded that satisfaction comes from meaning, recognition, autonomy, and remuneration. The work must be *meaningful if members of any profession are to be satisfied and committed.* Cherniss asked people what "meaningful" meant in daily, concrete terms, and most defined it as seeing that they "are making a difference in other people's lives." He quoted Viktor Frankl, who said that people "can

23. Cary Cherniss, *Beyond Burnout: Helping Teachers, Nurses, Therapists, and Lawyers Recover from Stress and Disillusionment* (New York: Routledge, 1995).

find meaning in activities done for the sake of a cause, for the sake of a loved one, or for the sake of a higher being."[24] Professionals, like all human beings, crave self-transcendence even more than self-fulfillment and find their deepest meaning in devotion to a truly valuable cause or to truly beloved people. If a sense of meaninglessness persists over time, members of any profession will look for ways to change jobs or even to change professions. They will wonder if the money they are making — even if they are making a lot of it — is worth it. Cherniss found that lawyers more than health professionals lamented a lack of meaning in their work; they frequently noted a feeling of being burdened with "piddly" work and routine tasks, and they often saw little real human value in what they did.

Other cravings Cherniss found were for recognition and autonomy, both of which made professionals feel gratified. They felt alienation, on the other hand, when others showed a lack of respect for them and when their supervisors told them precisely what to do and how to do it. Within as well as between each profession, levels of satisfaction could be explained in terms of whether a given individual experienced meaning, recognition, autonomy, and adequate remuneration.

The value of the Cherniss study for us is that it puts the rewards of professional life — meaning, recognition, autonomy, and money — in perspective. Christian ministry scores high on some rewards, low on others. It is high in meaning and autonomy, and relatively low on money. But what is important to any given person? Meaning? Money? We should expect to find the incumbents of any profession to be reflecting day by day on the tradeoffs. Is the money worth it? Worth the "piddly work"? Or is the meaning they derive worth the low pay or the tedium?

Cherniss also found that professional people forced to do tasks outside their chosen fields of expertise (for example, physicians forced to do bureaucratic tasks) were more unhappy than those doing what they had chosen to do and did best. This pattern we should expect to find among ministers also. A brief look at three other professions — law, medicine, and social work — alongside ministry will show us how satisfactions and dissatisfactions develop in concrete professional life.

24. Cherniss, *Beyond Burnout*, p. 186.

Lawyers, Doctors, and Social Workers

Of the four professions, two typically pay well and two do not. Lawyers, according to recent government statistics, earn on average about $80,000 to $100,000 per year. Physicians earn on average $120,000 to $200,000, depending on their specialty (and certain specialties are higher). By contrast, social workers average about $40,000 to $50,000 annually.[25]

Clergy tend to have incomes a bit higher than social workers'. Looking at the five denominations in our study, United Methodist ministers in 2001 had an average annual income, including benefits, of about $49,000. Presbyterian ministers earned an average of $48,000 (including housing) in 2003, plus pension and benefits (increasing this figure by an additional 29.5 percent). In the ELCA, the average was about $49,000 plus pension and benefits (amounting to an additional 33 percent). In the LCMS the average was about $47,000 plus benefits (which averaged $14,000). The Assemblies of God national office does not keep records of such data, but our advisors agreed that the figure would be notably lower than those of the other four denominations.[26]

Remuneration aside, lawyers have experienced a gradual diminution in career satisfaction over the last two decades. Though most are paid well, many find a lack of meaning in their work. They also complain of excessive pressure to compete, a lack of collegiality among their peers, and a poor public image. But their greatest grievance is increasingly long workdays, with decreasing time for personal and family life.[27] Lawyers are typically pressured to bill so many hours that they must work six days per week. The issue of time is especially im-

25. U.S. Bureau of Labor Statistics, 2001; available online at http://www.bls.gov. Additional data from the General Social Survey published by the National Opinion Research Center.

26. We may note that Jewish rabbis are similar to Protestant ministers in the characteristics of their profession. Like Protestant ministers they serve constituencies who hire and fire them, and they are constantly preoccupied with the commitment and unity of their flocks. Their professional training is similar. They differ in that beginning rabbis earn twice as much as beginning ministers. See Wheeler, "Fit for Ministry."

27. Patrick J. Schiltz, "On Being a Happy, Healthy, and Ethical Member of an Unhappy, Unhealthy, and Unethical Profession," *Vanderbilt Law Review* 52 (May 1999): 871-951, at 890.

portant to women, who make up an increasing percentage of the profession; many women practicing law have expressed a preference to work part-time.[28] Despite these concerns, the number of people fighting their way into law school is considerably greater than those applying to a seminary.

Lawyers and ministers are opposites in one important sense: lawyers are paid well but often find their work meaningless, while ministers consistently find meaning in their work but tend to be poorly paid. Having said this, at least two trends are the same in both professions: more women are entering the profession and there is growing resistance to long work hours.

Physicians in recent years are also decreasingly satisfied with their profession. Their typical priorities are to provide quality care and ongoing wellness to their patients. But the trend toward managed care and HMOs has reduced doctors' autonomy and has pressured them to spend less time with their patients.[29] Medicine has shifted from being a traditional profession to being a business, guided by market forces and profit margins. Thus physicians today no longer enjoy the same deference and esteem from non-physicians as they did in years past; under present-day managed care programs they tend to be viewed as engineers and technicians more than as personal counselors and confidants. This deflates their feelings of satisfaction. Physicians, like lawyers and ministers, are concerned about the need to be constantly on call and the resulting invasion of personal time. "On-call cooperatives" are being developed to alleviate the pressure of around-the-clock patient care.[30] This issue has grown more relevant with the influx of women into the profession, in that women commonly express more concern about family time than men do.

Three similarities exist between today's physicians and today's ministers: Both have experienced a moderate loss of professional prestige; both must reconcile a 24-hour on-call expectation with the

28. Deborah L. Rhode, *Balanced Lives: Changing the Culture of Legal Practice* (Chicago: American Bar Association, 2001), p. 11.

29. Donald E. Pathman et al., "Physician Job Satisfaction, Job Dissatisfaction, and Physician Turnover," *The Journal of Family Practice* 51 (July 2002): 1-9 at 2.

30. V. Swanson, K. G. Power, and R. J. Simpson, "Occupational Stress and Family Life: A Comparison of Male and Female Doctors," *Journal of Occupational and Organizational Psychology* 71 (September 1998): 237-60 at 242.

realities of personal and family life; and (as with lawyers) more women are entering the profession.

Social workers, like ministers, typically find their work meaningful despite relatively low pay. Social work is more stressful than most other professions, largely because of the clientele with whom social workers are faced and because of value conflicts resulting from discrepancies between clients' needs and institutional demands.[31] Social workers are most satisfied when they have autonomy in their jobs, when they are not troubled by conflicts in their work places, when they find their work intellectually challenging, when job stress is kept to a manageable level, and when they receive support and esteem from fellow workers. In our study we will see that three of these factors hold true for ministers as well: congregational conflicts, job stress, and a lack of support contribute significantly to ministers' dissatisfaction.

So we see that Christian ministry is unique in a few ways, but not unique in many others. We cannot conclude that ministers' morale is higher, the same, or lower, than that of lawyers, physicians, or social workers. The scattered evidence we do have indicates that the morale of ministers is similar to other professionals'.[32] Probably the variations in morale *within* segments of each profession are greater than overall variation *between* them.

Again, the sources of deep, sincere satisfaction in professional life can roughly be summarized as meaning, recognition, autonomy, and money. Any organization that wants to increase the satisfaction of its professionals should search for ways to maximize all four. We look next at organizational factors.

---

31. Chris Lloyd, Robert King, and Lesley Chenoweth, "Social Work, Stress and Burnout: A Review," *Journal of Mental Health* 11:3 (2002): 255-65. Also see Marit Soderfeldt, Bjorn Soderfeldt, and Lars-Erik Warg, "Burnout in Social Work," *Social Work* 40:5 (1995): 638-46.

32. John H. Beck, "The Effects of the Number of Roles, the Time Spent in Different Roles, and Selected Demographic Variables on Burnout and Job Satisfaction among Iowa Lutheran Clergy" (Ph.D. diss., University of Iowa, 1997).

Structures of the Five Denominations

Ministers live and work in specific denominations, and the denominational context in many ways defines their work and their careers. All ministers know the rules and institutional cultures of their denomination, but few know much about others. We gathered comparative data on the five denominations under study, some of which are important to mention here.

Characteristics of Members

The denominations we studied have different memberships. Table 1.1 below shows nationwide survey data describing a random sample of Americans who say they belong to one of them. The five are arranged in the table in a way that seems intuitive to us, from most to least hierarchical. So the United Methodist Church (UMC), which is the most structured of the five and which maintains the highest level of institutional direction, is at one end, and the Assemblies of God (A/G), which is the least centralized of the five, at the other. In the middle are the three denominations whose polities are roughly similar — the Presbyterians (PCUSA), Evangelical Lutheran Church in America (ELCA), and the Lutheran Church–Missouri Synod (LCMS). From the table we can see that the Presbyterian Church has the most affluent

---

Table 1.1

Characteristics of Adherents of the Five Denominations, 1988-2000 National Data

	UMC	PCUSA	ELCA	LCMS	A/G
N =	1531	669	717	338	134
Family Income (mean)	$39,800	$46,900	$40,200	$40,900	$31,900
Of Persons 20 Years or Older, Percent with a Four-Year College Degree or More	23	35	23	20	8

Source: General Social Survey, combined data from 1988 to 2000. Based on self-identified religious preference, not formal membership.

---

and most educated members of the five. The Assemblies of God, by contrast, has the least affluent and least educated. (Despite being the least affluent, the Assemblies of God has a relatively high level of commitment of members as measured by attendance and financial contributions. Past research has shown that evangelicals and Pentecostals in general have higher levels of financial giving, as a percent of family income, than mainline Protestants.[33]) The other three are arrayed between, with little difference among them. This alerts us that the five institutions serve different populations and probably have evolved structures and policies accordingly. The Assemblies of God, for example, was organized as recently as 1914, and it grew partly in opposition to traditional denominations, from which many of its early leaders had come. Thus the Assemblies of God today is careful to describe itself as a "movement" and not a "denomination." (In this book we use phrases such as "all five denominations" simply for the sake of simplicity.)

Deployment of Clergy

Table 1.2 on page 20 provides additional information about the five denominations. Median church size is similar for the United Methodists, Presbyterians, and Assemblies of God churches, but larger for the two Lutheran bodies. The percent of clergy who are women is similar in the United Methodist Church, Presbyterian Church, and ELCA, but it is lower for the Assemblies of God. The Lutheran Church–Missouri Synod does not ordain women clergy.

The last three lines in Table 1.2 summarize how the five denominations handle the placement of clergy. These five represent a continuum from a highly centralized system (United Methodist) to a free-market one with minimal denominational authority (Assemblies of God). The Presbyterian Church, ELCA, and LCMS are grouped in the middle. Here we will add a few words about all five, beginning with the Presbyterians and Lutherans, which are similar in how they place clergy.

33. Dean R. Hoge, Charles Zech, Patrick McNamara, and Michael J. Donahue, *Money Matters: Personal Giving in American Churches* (Louisville, Ky.: Westminster John Knox Press, 1996).

Table 1.2

Structures of the Five Denominations

	UMC	PCUSA	ELCA	LCMS	A/G
Number of congregations	35,900	11,142	10,766	6,150	12,133
Median size of congregations	112	117	314	268	100[a]
Percent women in the clergy	18[b]	18	22	0	14
Who selects clergy for local churches?	Bishop	Local Congregation	Congreg. and Bishop[c]	Local Congregation	Local Congregation
Who has final authority in hiring and firing clergy?	Annual Conf.	Presbytery	Mixed	Mixed	Local Congregation

a Estimate. The Assemblies of God has a unique definition of "member" which is not compara-
ble to that of other denominations. Median church *attendance* on Sunday is 70. We know
from other research that Assemblies of God churches are smaller than Presbyterian
churches.

b The 18% figure is for all six levels of credentialing; for ordained elders and deacons in full
connection the figure is 16%.

c The system in the ELCA is mixed, in that the process of selecting clergy is heavily guided by
bishops, but with some input from local lay committees.

The Presbyterians and Lutherans give most, but not all, power to
congregations for selecting their pastors; indeed the leaders of the
Presbyterian Church and the LCMS emphasized repeatedly that clergy
choice is up to the local church. The ELCA has a system that does not
lend itself to succinct description, but in it, too, the congregation has
a great influence in selecting a pastor — even if he or she is from a
limited list provided by the bishop. All three denominations have
safeguards at higher levels than the local church to limit the power of
local committees.

The three denominations vary in the details. The Presbyterian
Church has an open matching system of jobs and candidates, in which
any ordained Presbyterian pastor or candidate may participate. In the
ELCA bishops maintain some control over the selection process; a
pastor is not free to candidate for a different job unless the bishop approves. In the LCMS a minister desiring a new call announces his
availability, and his name then typically goes on the "call list" of one

or more districts. When he receives a call from a church's search committee, the district president will generally go along with the committee's choice.

The United Methodist Church is unique in that the bishop of each annual conference has full responsibility for placing all licensed and ordained clergy in his or her conference. Lay committees in the local churches have limited input regarding candidates for their churches, but the bishop is clearly responsible for final decisions. Indeed, the bishop is obligated to find full-time employment for all "fully itinerant" clergy throughout their careers. No other denomination in our study has this level of centralization, supervision, and commitment to its clergy. But the job security of United Methodist ministers is bought at a price: they are not free to change churches or to accept any other outside employment without the permission of the bishop if they want to continue in it. United Methodist clergy may, of course, voice their opinions about churches and appointments to the bishop. They may even express their desire for an appointment or their objections to being appointed to a particular place, but in the end they are required to accept their assignment by the bishop or to withdraw from the itinerant ministry of the church.

The Assemblies of God has two kinds of churches: "self-governing" (which comprise 56 percent of the total) and "district-supervised." The latter are smaller and many do not have full-time pastors. For self-governing churches, the A/G uses a free-market system for selecting clergy. When an opening occurs in a church, the laity elect a committee which has the power to select the pastor of their choice, so long as the candidate is credentialed in the Assemblies of God. In the small, district-supervised churches, the situation differs in that the district superintendent has the power to select and dismiss pastors.

Denominational structures have decisive influence on clergy for obvious reasons. In a centralized system each clergyperson desiring a successful career must constantly look upward on the organizational chart to remain in good relations with the bishop and the bishop's staff. The specific tastes and preferences of bishops and district superintendents influence each person's career and thus become a focus of ministers' attention. Of course, if things do not go to a minister's liking it is easy for him or her to complain that "the bishop doesn't like me." By contrast, in a less hierarchical system each person's future ministry is determined by laypersons in that church and by fellow ministers in the district. Each minister succeeds or fails in a competitive free market of leadership. Leaders in the Assemblies of God told us they prefer their system because it increases ministers' innovativeness and dedication.

United Methodist Ordination Among the five denominations, the United Methodist system is unique. Whereas the Presbyterians and Lutherans require seminary training and have a single category of ordained minister, the United Methodists have six categories of clergy. The largest by far is "ordained elder in full connection," of whom there are about 32,600. These persons are typically seminary graduates who have served in a probationary status for at least three years. Once ordained, they are guaranteed ministerial employment until retirement, and in return they are obligated to serve where the bishop puts them.

A similar category is "ordained deacon in full connection," of which there are about 1000. Ordained deacons in full connection must find their own employment in local churches or in other ministries. Two other categories are mainly temporary — "probationary member" and "associate member." They number about 4,400. They are not ordained, but most of them aspire to eventual ordination. The final two categories are "full-time local pastor" and "part-time local pastor," totaling together about 6,000. These persons have been received into membership in the annual conference, but they are not ordained. Seminary training is not required of them, though most have gone through a denominational training program called the "Local Pastor Course of Study." Local pastors must serve where they are sent by the bishop, but they are not guaranteed continuous employment. In interviews we conducted, some of them expressed frustration at sometimes being treated like second-class clergy.

Ordained United Methodist clergy are under the authority of bishops. All appointments of ministers are year-to-year, and ministers are moved every three to six years on average. Ministers are not free to search for a new appointment on their own, and lay committees in vacant churches are not free to interview candidates on their own. If lay committees are unhappy with their ministers, they must convince their bishop or district superintendent that a change is needed.

All this means that United Methodist ministers concerned about their futures must pay constant attention to their district superintendents, and in turn, the district superintendents must plan ahead so that all of the ordained elders in their district have employment. It is certainly understandable how sensitive the relationships between ministers and district superintendents become.

The Assemblies of God Organization   The Assemblies of God is unique in several ways. Its structure is flatter and looser than the others in our study, with very little central authority. As one expert said, "Power flows up, not down." Local churches (except for small district-supervised churches) are autonomous. They own their buildings, hire and fire their own ministers, and run their own affairs. Each of the 58 districts in the U.S. has its own constitution. The Assemblies of God puts more emphasis on local church growth than the other denominations in our project, and it invests more money and energy in church growth programs and new church planting. Also, because Assemblies of God churches tend to be smaller than in the other four denominations, there are more part-time ministers.

Districts are headed by superintendents elected by a voting constituency of licensed and ordained ministers and one lay delegate from each General Council–affiliated church. Below the district level are "sections," normally composed of 8 to 16 churches, each headed by an elected presbyter and a "sectional committee" of two or three pastors. Credentialed ministers in local churches are classified as certified, licensed, or ordained. To be certified or licensed, a person must demonstrate that he or she has had a conversion experience and possesses knowledge of the Bible. A candidate for licensing must take correspondence courses and be interviewed several times by the sectional committee. If approved, the candidate is given a one-year, renewable license. After two years of ministry the licensed minister is eligible for ordination. If a self-governing local church needs a pastor, its committee may pick any credentialed candidate. (If the preferred candidate is not credentialed, he or she is often hired anyway, provided that he or she agrees to become credentialed as soon as doing so is feasible.)

Clergy-Related Issues

A comparison of our five denominations' stances on a few key issues relating to ministers is crucial to our study. Those issues are divorce, sexual misconduct, open homosexuality, specialized ministries, and new church development. We will consider each briefly here.

Clergy Divorce   All five denominations face the reality of clergy divorcing. In the United Methodist, Presbyterian, and ELCA bodies, divorce is ordinarily not detrimental to the pastor's position. In the LCMS, the district president decides what level of action needs to be taken when a divorce occurs; such action ranges from mild penalties that allow for continuance in ministry for pastors not seen as being "at fault" all the way to removal from the roster for clear cases of adultery.

In the Assemblies of God, ministers who divorce after credentialing may or may not lose their positions, depending on the judgment of their local lay committee. If the pastor is perceived as not having been at fault in the divorce, nothing is done. If the pastor's behavior was questionable, he or she is commonly dismissed from the church. Probably more important, the Assemblies of God has a rule that a divorced person cannot remarry and continue as a pastor, based on a New Testament passage in the book of 1 Timothy, unless the divorce occurred prior to conversion or the minister qualifies for an ecclesiastical annulment. Of course, in reality there is some flexibility in enforcing this.

Clergy Sexual Misconduct   Sexual misconduct is troubling for all five denominations. It most commonly takes the form of a heterosexual extramarital affair; other forms — sexual abuse of children, for example — are much less common but remain a concern for everyone. In the Assemblies of God, viewing pornography is also viewed as sexual misconduct. Each denomination has developed a clear set of procedures to deal with these problems. Depending on the severity of the misconduct, penalties can range from a brief suspension to the surrendering of credentials.

Open Homosexuality of Ministers   The United Methodist Church officially permits no "self-avowed, practicing homosexual" to be appointed or ordained. Anyone who professes or is discovered to be in a sexual relationship with someone of the same sex loses his or her ordination. Having a homosexual *orientation,* on the other hand, is viewed as a private matter and is not grounds for dismissal. The task of identifying and defining disallowed behavior is left to bishops, and in reality the practices vary regionally. We were told that on the West Coast there is more leniency about homosexual behavior than in the rest of the nation.

The Presbyterian Church is similar to the United Methodist except that enforcement of the rule about open homosexual practice varies greatly and the rule itself has been under constant debate for the last decade. Due to strong feelings in the denomination on both sides of the issue, practice has been allowed to vary from presbytery to presbytery, depending on local attitudes. Of the five denominations in our study the Presbyterian Church is probably the most open to homosexuality; still, plenty of gay and lesbian clergy confided to us that they experienced discrimination in different forms.

The ELCA is similar to the United Methodist Church in its decisions about homosexual clergy. Open homosexual behavior by an ELCA minister is supposed to lead to loss of ordination, yet actual practice varies from region to region, with greatest tolerance again being on the West Coast.

The LCMS rule about homosexuality is similar in turn to that of the ELCA, but discipline is much stricter. No open homosexuality is tolerated, and violations lead to quick loss of credentials. The same is true in the Assemblies of God.

Specialized Ministry All denominations consider certain non-parish ministries as valid and worthy of credentialing. An unavoidable issue in every system is *which* jobs constitute valid Christian ministry. For example, is a chaplaincy in a retirement home a valid ministry for an ordained person? Is teaching in a denominational college? In a public university? Financial administration for a denominational pension fund? What if a person in one of these positions is also serving a local church part-time?

In the United Methodist Church, any minister wanting to move to a specialized ministry outside the structure of the church while retaining membership in the annual conference must convince the bishop and the board of ordained ministry that the specialized ministry is an appropriate expression of the church's ministry. Normally the bishop approves such positions as professor at a seminary or chaplain of a hospital. But some positions may not be approved, and the clergyperson may need to surrender conference membership. However, even when a person discontinues conference membership, there is provision for retaining ordination status. All non-parish positions requiring denominational certification (such as hospital or military chaplaincies) are open to fully ordained persons only. Thus it is not uncommon that some new ordinands serve in local churches a few years until ordination, hoping to move to specialized ministries as soon as they can. The Assemblies of God has a similar system, requiring license or ordination for any person in a specialized ministry needing denominational certification.

The Presbyterian Church allows ministers to take any ministerial or secular job they want, but whether they can thereafter maintain ordination depends on the nature of the job — mainly on how much Christian ministry and involvement with local churches it entails. Final decisions depend on a vote of the presbytery. In the ELCA and LCMS, the system is very similar to the Presbyterian one, with an exception: in the ELCA an ordained minister is normally not eligible for a call to specialized ministry until he or she has served three years in congregational ministry.

We stumbled into some sensitivity among United Methodists and Lutherans about the questionnaire we sent out, which carried the title on the front page, "Study of Local Church Ministers Who Change Careers." Several persons felt strongly that a move to a non-parish ministry was not at all a change of careers and that they were ministers in non-parish settings as much as they ever were in parish ones. The strength of the reaction surprised us and let us know that we had accidentally touched a nerve. Later, while conducting phone interviews, we heard numerous complaints from ministers in non-parish positions that they were not taken seriously by denominational leaders and by other ministers, that they were not included in clergy mailing lists, for example. They felt they were receiving little respect.[34] Such sensitive feelings seem to exist in many contexts about the status of non-parish ministers.

34. Other researchers have found the same. Apparently feelings that non-parish ministers are not "real clergy" are widespread. See Zikmund, *Clergy Women*, p. 114.

New Church Development   The development of new churches is important to our study because of the many former pastors we encountered who had failed in their attempts at doing so. They were mainly Assemblies of God pastors, and they felt they had not been supported in their high-risk ministries. As we will see, the Assemblies of God is unique in its new church development program.

The United Methodist Church has several ways of planting new churches, but most often it is done by an annual conference. Typically the conference appoints a church development pastor and gives him or her a salary for several years to get a new church going. There is no guarantee that these ventures will succeed, and many in fact do fail. In the Presbyterian Church, starting new churches is a project of presbyteries. A presbytery will typically call a minister to start the church and pay him or her a full-time salary for a few years, gradually decreasing it over time, making decisions year by year based on the growth of the church and its ability to support a pastor financially. A certain percentage of these new church starts fail; for example, only 44 percent of new starts begun in 1992-96 were officially recognized congregations in 2002. The ELCA process of new church development is similar to the Presbyterian one. In the LCMS, all new church starts are sponsored by districts, not by a national program. As in the ELCA, the district pays a new church development pastor a full-time salary for four or five years, after which the support decreases annually. One denominational official estimated the success rate in new church starts at 75 percent.

The Assemblies of God is more aggressive and more entrepreneurial than the others in planting new churches. Recognizing the riskiness of this job, it sponsors a special training program annually for new church development pastors. New church starts are either sponsored by districts or by strong local churches called "mother churches." They often — though certainly not always — recruit new church pastors and pay them full-time salaries for a year or two, and when a mother church is involved the pastor also usually persuades some of its members living near the new church to transfer to it. Church planters are under great pressure to grow the new church, yet many fail. A rule of thumb among Assemblies of God leaders is that a new church needs 75 to 100 members to be "viable." Using this definition, during the 1990s 50 percent of new churches became viable and the others closed down, often inducing a sense of failure among all those involved. When this happened, the Assemblies ministers often complained that they had not been provided with any kind of safety net.

How Many Ministers Are Leaving Local Church Ministry?

For the sake of perspective, we need some more general information on how many ministers leave ministry after ordination. Past research is uneven. Several studies have examined how many have left parish ministry, how many remain in some other form of Christian ministry, and how many remain in parish ministry. One United Methodist study found that 59 percent of ministers were still in parish ministry ten years out from ordination, but only 42 percent remained after 20 years.[35] Despite this movement away from parish ministry, 93 percent were still in *some* form of Christian ministry.

A 1998 study surveyed 5,000 ordained clergy in 15 denominations.[36] It found that by age 45 or 50, 67 percent remained in local church ministry but that more women had left than men (59 percent of the women and 75 percent of the men remained). More women than men were serving in non-parish settings.[37]

The ELCA studied its 1988 ordination class and found that 15 percent resigned or were removed from the roster in the following 13 years. Again, women left more often than men.[38]

A 1998 Presbyterian study estimated that between 11 and 13 percent of ministers ordained in 1990-92 who had served in a local church had left the Presbyterian ministry entirely.[39]

35. Rolf Memming, "United Methodist Ordained Ministry in Transition," in *The People(s) Called Methodist*, edited by William B. Lawrence, Dennis M. Campbell, and Russell E. Richey (Nashville: Abingdon Press, 1998). Available from *Pulpit & Pew*, Duke Divinity School.

36. Zikmund, *Clergy Women*, ch. 6.

37. Zikmund, *Clergy Women*, p. 118.

38. Private communication from Martin Smith, Department of Research and Evaluation of the Evangelical Lutheran Church in America, June 2002.

39. Presbyterian Church (U.S.A.) Research Services, "Ministers Ordained in the 1990s: A Look at Clergy Who Have Left the Ministry" (Louisville, Ky.: Presbyterian Church [U.S.A.], 1999).

Why did ministers in the various denominations leave? Three summary statements are supported by the research. (See Appendix A for a review of studies.) (1) Conflict was the main reason ministers left — conflict with parishioners, with other staff members, or with denominational officials. Many ministers felt blocked or frustrated in their efforts to bring new life to their congregations, and this led to disillusionment with their members and with their denominations. (2) Women left local church ministry more often than men. Often this was due to family responsibilities, especially the needs of their children. Women also left because of disillusionment with denominational systems and continuing resistance to women clergy in some local churches and among some district superintendents. (3) More clergy left due to institutional or interpersonal problems than due to loss of faith or financial need. The greatest interpersonal problems were feelings of loneliness, isolation, and inadequate boundaries between ministry and family life.

Supply and Demand of Clergy

The question of supply and demand has been discussed in numerous articles in the last four years. Our conclusion, after reviewing the evidence, is that the cries of alarm about looming shortages are exaggerated. Some specific shortages exist — specific to region and to type of church — but there is not a general shortage of clergy.

A recent ELCA study found that synods with smaller congregations have the most trouble filling pastorates, while those with larger ones have an oversupply.[40] Patricia Chang, in an article reviewing recent clergy supply-and-demand research, reaches the same conclusions:[41] in general there is no clergy shortage in mainline Protestant denominations. The shortages, when they appear, are only in specific

40. Evangelical Lutheran Church in America, Division for Ministry, *Ministry Needs and Resources in the 21st Century* (Chicago: Evangelical Lutheran Church in America, 2000).

41. Patricia Mei Yin Chang, "Pulpit Supply: A Clergy Shortage?" *Christian Century*, November 29, 2003, 28-32. On the Evangelical Lutheran Church in America, see *Ministry Needs*. On the Presbyterian Church (U.S.A.), see Jack Marcum, "Parsing the Pastor 'Shortage,'" *Monday Morning*, September 3, 2001, pp. 1-3.

types of churches. Mainly these are small, rural churches, especially those not paying a full-time salary; they experience a shortage because many ordained clergy prefer not to serve in them. Second-career pastors are often constrained in their place of ministry by the necessity of finding jobs for working spouses, and many have educational debts to pay off. Many unmarried women ministers hesitate to locate in small towns where they foresee loneliness and the lack of a network of support. As a result, small churches cannot find the ministers they need. For some denominations the problem may be worsening. The ELCA study, for example, found that the number of smaller congregations is increasing while the number of ordained ministers serving is decreasing.

There are some variations by denomination. The Assemblies of God has an oversupply of ministers, and the LCMS has an undersupply. In the case of the LCMS, women are not eligible for ordination, and denominational supervision of seminary students is relatively rigid, both factors limiting the number of candidates.

For some reason the media have recently carried several stories about shortages of clergy in Protestant denominations. They are overstated. Unlike the Roman Catholic Church, the Protestants do not have a clergy shortage in general.

With this background we can better comprehend the findings in our new survey in 2002-2003. We turn in Chapter 2 to a description of the former pastors.

2 Pastors Who Left Local Church Ministry

When you're a one-person operation, and you're trying not only to build the congregation, you're building budget, you're driving capital campaigns, you're looking at staff, program, seven days a week and seventeen hours a day, it takes its toll. Even though you may love every minute of it, the reality is, you have to come up for some air.

A 60-year-old ELCA man

We come now to the heart of our inquiry: why did pastors leave local church ministry? We asked numerous questions in order to discern their motives. A basic finding of our study is that motivations are multiple: there were many reasons pastors left, and usually more than one came into play in each pastor's decision to leave. Any change as momentous as a pastor's to leave local church ministry can be expected to be motivated by more than one force, and this is clearly the case. Our task as researchers was to discern the most important influences on the ex-pastors, and then to interpret these influences comprehensively.

We gathered our data through questionnaires and telephone interviews with a random sample of persons who fit the definition (described in the Introduction) that we set for the project.[1] Table 2.1 on

1. We had good initial samples in the five denominations, but the response rates varied, with low response from United Methodist and Assemblies of God ex-pastors. From our phone interviews we gleaned that, of all the persons who left parish ministry,

page 33 shows the overall characteristics of those who responded. Both men and women were present in the sample (it is worth noting that while women comprise 18 percent of active clergy in the Presbyterian Church, they have left local ministry in disproportionately large numbers).[2] In every denomination except the Assemblies of God, the vast majority graduated from seminary, and most had been fully ordained. Average age of full ordination was between 29 and 34 in all five denominations, and the vast majority of respondents were senior or solo pastors in their last ministry position. Few had been serving more than one congregation in their last position, but many had been part-time pastors, working at another job in addition to their ministry.

The percentage of part-time pastors was by far the highest in the Assemblies of God, a reflection of the smaller size of Assemblies of God congregations. The most common supplementary jobs in all five denominations were other religious ministries, sales, teaching in elementary or high school, and general labor. Most respondents said that their last congregation was in a suburb or small town, with little variation from denomination to denomination. Table 2.2 on page 34 compares the former local church ministers with current senior or solo pastors in three of the denominations. (Our control group had members of only three of the five denominations, and it included only senior or solo pastors, hence for purposes of comparison the former pastors in the table are also limited to senior or solo pastors.) It tells us that former pastors were neither younger nor older than the average for current pastors, and that the number of years they served was similar. Thus we cannot say that younger or older ministers were especially likely to leave local church ministry; those who left were of all ages.

The percentage of women who left was much higher than the percentage in active service among the Presbyterians, but not among the United Methodists and Lutherans. Marital status of former pastors and current pastors was similar, except that few of the United Methodists who left are still in their first marriage and more are now remarried after a divorce. (More of the former United Methodist pastors

the ones who were angry, hurt, or alienated from their denomination were less likely to cooperate with our research. Thus we believe our questionnaire survey overrepresents happy ex-pastors and underrepresents unhappy ones, at least in these two groups.

2. No significance tests are shown in this and subsequent tables, but differences between denominations of 8 percentage points are significant at .05.

Table 2.1
Characteristics of Sample Members

	UMC	PCUSA	ELCA	LCMS	A/G
Percent female	29	41	17	0	5
What is the highest level of theological training you have obtained?					
Percent Master of Divinity, Bachelor of Divinity, or more	94	100	100	99	27
Were you ever ordained (credentialed) as a minister?					
Percent Yes	90	99	100	100	95
If yes, how old were you when you received full ordination as minister or pastor?					
Average (years)	34	31	29	32	29
How would you describe your last local church ministry position?					
Percent senior or solo pastor	79	52	68	83	64
Percent assistant or associate pastor	14	28	16	13	25
At the same time did you serve another congregation in addition to this one?					
Percent Yes	25	10	11	17	2
While serving in your last position, did you work at any job other than as minister of that congregation (or congregations)?					
Percent Yes	18	22	21	20	49

Table 2.2
Characteristics of Former and Current Senior Pastors

		UMC	PCUSA	ELCA
	No. of former	177	106	221
	No. of current	171	416	357
Average age when left (years)	Former	46	46	45
Average age at the same time (years)	Current	47	50	46
Percent female	Former	27	32	13
	Current	24	18	15
Were you ever ordained? Percent Yes	Former	90	100	100
	Current	86	100	100
If ever ordained, for how many years?	Former	12	15	16
Average at the same time the former				
pastors left	Current	13	18	16
Marital status				
Percent never married	Former	7	6	6
	Current	6	7	6
Percent in first marriage	Former	36	62	54
	Current	61	67	74
Percent remarried after divorce	Former	29	16	18
	Current	22	19	12

are currently divorced or separated — 20 percent, contrasted to 7 percent of the current pastors.) To this point the only clear demographic difference we found between pastors who left and currently active pastors was on marital status among the United Methodists.

Table 2.3 on page 35 gives us the histories of the former pastors. They began local church ministry at an average age of about 30 years (younger for the Assemblies of God — 25 years), and they left at an average of about 45 (again, younger for the Assemblies of God — 41 years). During this time they served an average of three congregations (more for the United Methodists). The Assemblies of God pastors were more often in their first marriage than those in the other denominations, less often divorced, and less often remarried. They also had

Table 2.3

Personal and Professional History of Sample Members

	UMC	PCUSA	ELCA	LCMS	A/G
Age when began local church ministry					
Average (years)	30	30	28	31	25
Age when left local church ministry					
Average (years)	45	44	45	45	41
(If ever ordained or credentialed) How many different positions did you serve as a paid local church minister?					
3 or more	72%	46%	57%	37%	61%

more children living at home, probably a reflection of their younger average age. (For the complete data, see Table C.1 in Appendix C.)

Why Did They Leave Local Church Ministry?

We asked in our questionnaire, "Please describe your main feelings and motivations when you decided to, or were required to, leave local church ministry," and invited up to a half page of written-in comments. We identified sixteen topics in the answers to the question and entered up to three of them in the data set.[3] The top ten responses are shown in Table 2.4 on page 36. (For all sixteen see Table C.3 in Appendix C.)

The most common explanation, mentioned by about one-third of the respondents, was that an opportunity arose for new ministry. This was reported more often by the LCMS respondents than by the others. Second most common, important to about 26 percent of the ministers,

---

3. Ninety-one percent of the respondents wrote in comments, and we coded up to three ideas, with a mean of 1.9 per questionnaire.

Table 2.4
**Reported Feelings When Deciding to Leave Church Ministry:
Ideas in Open-Ended Comments (in Percents)**

Opportunity came for a new ministry 32

Denomination not supportive or conflict with denominational officials 26

Burned out, discouraged, stressed, overworked 21

Needs of family and children 11

Conflicts with church members 9

Domination by senior pastor; conflicts in staff 8

Doctrinal conflicts (service to the poor, homosexuality, women's issues, spirituality) 7

Unreasonable expectations from church members 7

Felt constrained by staff or members; church resisted change 7

Marital difficulties or divorce 6

was the feeling that denominational leaders were not supportive or that there was conflict with denominational officials. Third most common was a feeling of being burned out, discouraged, stressed, or overworked, mentioned by 21 percent. These top three were far ahead of all the others.

Fourth came the needs of children and family, stated by 11 percent. The rest of the motivations were stated by one-tenth of the sample or less: conflicts with parishioners; conflicts among church staff; unreasonable expectations from church members; doctrinal conflicts; marital difficulties or divorce; and a feeling of being constrained by staff or church members. Six other reasons not in Table 2.4 occurred much less frequently: financial difficulties; sexual misconduct; health issues; a desire to pursue further study; coming out as gay or lesbian; and difficulties co-pastoring with a spouse.

We then presented the respondents with twelve possible reasons for leaving local church ministry, reasons which we had collected from past research and from our pretests. The top six responses are graphed in Table 2.5 on p. 37. (See Table C.4 in Appendix C for the complete list of responses.) The first three are reports of personal

Table 2.5

How important was each of the following possible reasons why you left your position in local church ministry?
(Percent "Great importance" or "Somewhat important")

I felt drained by the demands on me.	58
I felt lonely or isolated.	51
I felt bored or constrained in the position.	43
I was not supported by denominational officials.	43
I found a better job outside of congregational work.	38
I had marital or personal relationship problems.	27

feelings more than of particular events: "I felt drained by the demands on me," "I felt lonely or isolated," and "I felt bored or constrained in the position." The sources of these feelings were mainly conflicts in the congregation, conflicts among the staff, or conflicts with denominational leaders. In some cases family problems and marital problems added to the stress. (See Table C.5 in Appendix C for additional data.)

Based on this information we identified the seven main motivations for leaving local church ministry, then reviewed all of our surveys to identify which of those was the most prominent motivation in each. This method, though simple to describe, was not easy to carry out due to the multiple motivations reported by most of the respondents. It introduces an element of approximation into our report, a result of our research team needing to make judgments regarding which of several motivations was the most significant in each case. We were hampered by incomplete information. In unclear cases we relied on judgments by two or three members of our research team. If we had too little to go on in any case, or if the respondent emphasized a motivation not in our top seven, we categorized that case as "inadequate data or other." The results are in Table 2.6 on page 38, a central table for conveying our study's findings.

Note, at the bottom of the table, the 18 percent in the "inadequate data or other" category. In about half of these cases we could not tell what the main motivation was, often because the information given was brief and vague. Written-in comments on some questionnaires in-

Table 2.6

Seven Main Motivations for Leaving Local Church Ministry

	Total (%)	Men (%)	Women (%)
Voluntary			
1. Preference for other ministry	27	28	21
2. Need to care for family or children	4	2	15
Involuntary or Partly Involuntary			
3. Conflict in congregation (with staff or laity)	17	16	21
4. Conflict with denominational officials or disillusionment with denomination	10	10	10
5. Burnout; frustration; feeling of constraint; sense of inadequacy	14	13	16
6. Allegations of sexual misconduct	6	7	1
7. Problems in family; divorce	5	6	1
Inadequate data or other	18	19	15

dicated to us that important information was being withheld. This 18 percent would be much smaller if the persons returning questionnaires had been more forthright. This means that the estimates of the seven motivations in Table 2.6 should be seen as minimums. For example, the third category, "conflict in the congregation," is estimated to have been the main motivation for 17 percent, but that should be understood as 17 to 19 percent. Similarly the sixth category, "sexual misconduct," is reported as 6 percent, but a more accurate estimate would be 6 to 8 percent.

Table 2.6 is divided into two categories, voluntary and involuntary. Some ex-pastors were "pulled" out and others were "pushed" out against their will. We need to assess both positive "pulls" toward decisions to leave (voluntary reasons) and negative "pushes" away (involuntary reasons). We will discuss these distinctions more fully below.

The first line in Table 2.6 identifies the percentage of ministers who left because they preferred another form of ministry — usually specialized ministry such as chaplaincy, administration, social work, or teaching. This was the primary motivation for an estimated 27 percent. It was often difficult to determine whether the pull toward a different kind of ministry was the main motivation, or whether the push of frustration with their present job was foremost. Actually more than 27 percent left for non-parish ministries, but we judged that 27 percent were primarily motivated by voluntary pull factors. Women were less likely than men to have preference for another ministry as their main motivation.

The need to care for family and children was a primary motivation for about 4 percent, most of whom were women. Ministers who left for this reason did so more voluntarily than involuntarily.

The other five motivations in the table describe ministers who left involuntarily or in part involuntarily. The third and fourth types have to do with conflict, which we divided into two types — conflict within the congregation and conflict with denominational officials. The two when combined add up to 27 percent. We can therefore say that preference for a specialized ministry and conflict (of one kind or another) are the main two reasons the ministers left local church ministry. Conflict, obviously, takes several forms, especially within the congregation, where we distinguished conflict with other staff from conflict with laity; the former occurs only in congregations that employ multiple staff members. Conflict within the congregation pushed more ministers out of local church ministry than did conflict with denominational leaders.

The fifth type in the table describes a motivation that varies in how it is described by the ministers we surveyed, but includes burnout, resignation, and frustration. It is an emotional state whose sources are not clear in every instance, but it is very often caused by failures to achieve goals or to convince other individuals in the church to contribute time and energy. Pastors talking about their burnout often complained that the laity are not committed to the faith or are opposed to new ideas, or that they themselves feel blocked by senior staff or lay leaders from taking any initiative. Some talked about declining church attendance, saying they had tried their best to stem the tide, but to no avail.

The sixth and seventh motivations in Table 2.6 are smaller, and both are matters of personal life. About 6 percent of the ministers left due to allegations of sexual misconduct, and about 5 percent left after divorce or marital problems. We can summarize, in general, that personal problems are less important than professional and institutional problems in pushing ministers out of the pastorate. Problems *in the ministry,* and usually *interpersonal* problems, are the main reason why ministers leave local church ministry.

The last line in Table 2.6, as noted above, reports that in 18 percent of the cases the person gave us too little information or told about an uncommon motivation. In these cases four less common motivations were visible: (a) financial pressures; (b) difficulties relating to being openly gay or lesbian while in the ministry; (c) health problems; and (d) loss of Christian faith. These last four motivations push some ministers away from the local church, but they are not nearly as widespread as the top seven. We estimate that the four together would add up to about half of the 18 percent.

We encountered a small number of persons who left local church ministry out of a feeling that they had outgrown it. One left to become a writer, and another left to establish a women's spiritual growth center. Two others left to head up programs to aid pastors or missionaries. They struck us as successful pastors now restless for new challenges, in some cases hoping for more personal recognition. Also, remember that at the outset of our study we decided to exclude persons from the sample if they had left local church ministry due to a "promotion" to an office in the denomination such as presbytery executive or bishop. Such persons were easy to identify, and we took them out of the sample. But several others we encountered left for jobs that were not clearly promotions in that sense, and so we left them in the sample. They left voluntarily, but they are not now clearly in ministry as their denominations define it. They do not fit our seven main types. We did not single them out as a separate category due to their small number — about one or two percent of the total. They are included in the "other" category in the table.

Table 2.6 contains two columns contrasting men and women. Two of the motivations are found almost exclusively among the men: (1) allegations of sexual misconduct and (2) problems in the family, including divorce. One motivation is found almost exclusively among women: leaving due to a need to care for family or children. This motivation is so common among women ministers that it is almost as important as the top motivations in the table.

We also compared the five denominations to see if they varied in their motivations for leaving. (The data are not shown here.) Three patterns appeared. First, the Presbyterian ministers reported a higher level of conflict within the congregation than ministers of the other four denominations. Second, they also included more persons (mostly women) who left local church ministry to take care of family or children. This is partly a reflection of the higher percentage of women in the Presbyterian sample, but probably it is a result of other factors as well. Third, the United Methodist ministers reported more conflict with denominational officials.

Our questionnaire included other items, and the respondents expressed three other concerns which add perspective to the main reasons for leaving. Fifty-four percent agreed with the statement, "I felt the demands of laity were unrealistic." The Assemblies of God ministers agreed less than the others — 43 percent. Second, on the statement, "I felt I could not speak openly and honestly with denominational officials," 51 percent agreed. The United Methodist ministers agreed more than the others — 63 percent. Third, on the statement, "I was troubled by marital problems," 29 percent of the currently married ministers agreed, and the percentages of respondents in all five denominations were similar. (See Table C.5 in Appendix C.) In sum, problems with laity generally were more common than problems with denominational leaders, as we suggested earlier, and marital problems were somewhat less common reasons for leaving.

We asked about levels of satisfaction in ministry felt by the former ministers, and the same questions were put to active ministers in three denominations in the control group. Table 2.7 on page 42 summarizes the responses, arranged from the sources of highest satisfaction to the ex-pastors down to the sources of least satisfaction. (For more details see Table C.6 in Appendix C.)

Housing arrangements, relations with other clergy, and relations with lay leaders in the congregation were clearly sources of satisfaction, while (at the bottom) the amount of support from denominational officials, spiritual life, and salary were areas of dissatisfaction. Ministers in the three denominations were remarkably similar in their

Table 2.7

Levels of Satisfaction in Ministry Reported by
Former and Current Senior Pastors (Percent "Very Satisfied")

At present (in the final years of your last local church ministry position), what is (was) your level of satisfaction with the following? "Very satisfied"

		UMC	PCUSA	ELCA
Housing or living arrangements	Former	50	57	54
	Current	63	68	66
	Difference	13	11	12
Relations with other clergy	Former	27	44	42
	Current	34	34	43
	Difference	7	-10	1
Relations with lay leaders in your congregation	Former	31	31	29
	Current	56	57	56
	Difference	25	26	27
Your overall effectiveness as a pastoral leader	Former	36	30	32
	Current	44	45	42
	Difference	8	15	10
Your ministry position	Former	36	29	30
	Current	52	57	62
	Difference	16	28	32
Your family life	Former	30	27	31
	Current	54	58	54
	Difference	24	31	23
Your salary and benefits	Former	25	23	26
	Current	44	41	45
	Difference	19	18	19
Spiritual life	Former	23	18	23
	Current	28	24	22
	Difference	5	6	-1
Support from your denominational officials	Former	9	21	24
	Current	39	38	40
	Difference	30	17	16

ratings, except for lower satisfaction derived by United Methodists from their relations with other clergy.

The table also compares those who left with current senior or solo pastors, and shows the difference between the two. (The difference score is the percentage for current ministers minus the percentage for former ministers.) Three items in the table show the greatest differences: "Relations with lay leaders in your congregation," "Your ministry position," and "Your family life." These three appear to be more consequential for the ministers' lives than anything else in the table — with the exception of dissatisfaction with denominational support among United Methodists (last item in Table 2.7).

Table 2.7 gives us more evidence that difficulties in the congregation were the greatest sources of stress impelling ministers to leave local church ministry, and that problems in family life were nearly as great. By contrast, problems in the ministers' spiritual lives, their relations with other clergy, and their housing were less consequential. Problems of finances and lack of support from denominational officials were secondary problems (except for United Methodists), not main ones.

Voluntary or Involuntary Leaving?

Past researchers have often tried to distinguish ex-pastors who left voluntarily from those who left involuntarily. But to force a clear-cut distinction between voluntary and involuntary would be simplistic, and such a distinction should be discarded. The problem is not only that motivations for leaving local church ministry are multiple, but also that the voluntarily-versus-involuntary distinction is really a matter of more or less, with no clear line of demarcation. A more adequate categorization distinguishes three overall types.

The first is an "involuntary leaver." The clearest example of someone in this category would be a pastor forced out entirely against his or her will. This might occur if the pastor was found to be guilty of prohibited behavior, such as an extramarital sexual affair, and forced to resign. Another example would be divorce in a denomination that forbids clergy divorces: as soon as the divorce becomes known, the pastor is removed regardless of whether he or she wants to continue in ministry.

The second type is the polar opposite, what might be called the "voluntary leaver due to pull factors." A pull factor, as we mentioned earlier, is a motivation pulling the pastor into a new occupation entirely apart from conditions in his or her present situation. A clear example would be an ELCA pastor who had always wanted to be a hospital chaplain. Following ELCA rules, this individual would spend the requisite three years in local church ministry before being eligible for such a specialized ministry, but when the three years are over he or she would leave local church ministry because of the pull of the other position — independent of his or her experiences as a local church minister.

The crucial characteristic of the voluntary leaver due to pull factors is that no discernible push factor constitutes a part of his or her decision to leave. This is easily stated but difficult to discern, because any given ex-pastor may not divulge all the factors contributing to the decision to leave; indeed, he or she may not even be fully conscious of all of them. Thus in the research setting it is impossible to be sure that absolutely no push factors influenced the decision.

The third type we can call "voluntary leaver including push factors." It falls between the other two types, denoting an individual who was not forced to leave; the decision to do so was at least partly voluntary although, by his or her own account, push factors were clearly present. The minister in such a situation ponders the pull and push factors and makes his or her decision based on the influence of both. We decided that if in our questionnaire sample or phone interviews we saw or heard any evidence of noteworthy push factors at work, we would put the person citing them in this third category.

Making that call, however, was not always easy. Consider an example: an ex-pastor may tell us simply that she left local church ministry because a good position as hospital chaplain opened up nearby. Were push factors also present? Was she exasperated with stubborn or contentious congregants? Had she long been seeking an escape to a different type of ministry? Without more information we cannot be completely certain whether this person should be categorized as the second or the third type. But, given the other information in the questionnaire and in comments, we have made what we think are intelligent judgments in the majority of the cases. (One could attempt to further subdivide this third type into one having push factors that outweigh pull factors and another in which the opposite is the case. Either definition is logically possible, but the task of estimating the weight of the factors simply would not be feasible in many cases.)

In the end, then, we can identify three types of voluntary or involuntary departures. All or almost all of the first type — the involuntary leavers — are no longer in church ministry at all. Ex-pastors of the other two types may still be in ministry, since some have gone into specialized ministries. Our best estimate is that in our entire five-denomination sample, 30 to 40 percent are involuntary leavers; 15 to 25 percent are voluntary leavers; and 40 to 50 percent are voluntary leavers including push factors. The voluntary leavers were of two types: clergy who preferred another form of ministry, and clergy who left ministry to take care of their children or family. The involuntary leavers were mainly of three types: clergy who had conflict within their congregations, those who had conflict with denominational officials, and those who were forced to leave due to sexual misconduct or divorce.

This division into three types is more precise than the two-part division in Table 2.4, which should be seen as merely an approximation.

Men Ministers and Women Ministers

Past research has shown that women ministers tend to leave ministry more than their male counterparts do. This is the case for two main reasons. The first is that women are less likely to be chosen as senior pastors in flourishing and desirable churches; in many Protestant denominations congregations still prefer men as senior pastors, creating what is sometimes sardonically called a "stained glass ceiling" for women ministers. Women more frequently report feelings of discouragement in their search for a second, third, or fourth call. The second reason is that some women leave active ministry to care for family and children, at least for a number of years. Men seldom do this. Men ministers tend to be more career-driven than women and less likely to drop out of active ministry for any period of time.[4]

4. The greater tendency for women than men to leave local church ministry was reported in research by Wiborg and Collier and by Barbara Zikmund and her associates. See Margaret S. Wiborg and Elizabeth J. Collier, *United Methodist Clergywomen Retention Study* (Boston: Boston University School of Theology, 1997); Barbara Brown Zikmund, Adair T. Lummis, and Patricia Mei Yin Chang, *Clergy Women: An Uphill Calling* (Louisville,

Turning to our data, we can compare men and women in three de-nominations — not in the LCMS, which has no women ministers, and not in the Assemblies of God, since women comprise only 5 percent of our sample. As we have seen in Table 2.2, the rate of parish leaving is similar for men and women — except in the Presbyterian Church, where women leave church ministry more often than men. Male and female ex-pastors were different in other ways, however. Women were ordained at a later age than men, and more were never married (16 percent, com-pared with 4 percent of the men). Fewer were serving as senior or solo pastors in their last position (48 percent, compared with 73 percent of the men). During their careers they had served fewer churches than the men. Fewer women than men told us that "clergy or denominational officials here do not want me" (14 percent, compared with 25 percent of the men), and fewer were troubled by complaints from their spouses. Contrary to some reports we have read, the women in our sample did not experience worse conflicts than men with other staff or with other clergy, and they did not report more problems of loneliness.

In sum, the differences between men and women turned out to be smaller in our sample than earlier research had given us to expect. Pos-sibly the experiences of men and women ministers are converging with the passage of time, making women's experiences less distinctive.

Senior Ministers and Associates

Eighty percent of our respondents were senior or solo pastors (hereaf-ter we will refer to them together as senior pastors) and 20 percent were associates. The latter were slightly younger when they left — an average of 41, compared with 45 for the senior pastors. More of the as-sociates were female — 32 percent, compared with 15 percent of the senior pastors. Fifteen percent of the senior pastors were serving two or more congregations, compared with 3 percent of the associates. Most associates had been serving in suburban churches, not rural or small-town ones.

Ky.: Westminster John Knox Press, 1998), p. 7. Also see Edward C. Lehman Jr., *Women's Path into Ministry: Six Major Studies* (Durham, N.C.: Duke Divinity School Pulpit and Pew Project, 2002).

The principal difference between senior pastors and associates was that the associates reported more conflicts within the staff. Of all the ministers who reported conflict as one of their reasons for leaving — about 40 percent of the total — the associates reported more between staff members than did the senior pastors. Fifty-three percent of the associates reported that "pastoral leadership style" was a topic of conflict, compared with 32 percent of the senior pastors. Also, 38 percent of the associates reported "conflicts between staff and/or clergy" as an issue of conflict, compared with 12 percent of the senior pastors. On the other hand, associates reported less conflict with church members than did senior pastors; they reported fewer feelings of loneliness; and they confessed fewer self-doubts about their abilities as ministers. Fewer had experienced marital problems. As this list suggests, the differences between senior pastors and associates were greater in our sample than those between women and men.

Older Ministers and Younger Ministers

Differences between older and younger ex-pastors turned out to be small. We compared those 45 years old or younger with those 46 or older and found that the younger persons were more frequently associates than senior or solo pastors. They more often were in their first marriage and more often had children at home. They less often told us, "Clergy or denominational officials here do not want me." These differences are minor considering the amount of information we gathered in the questionnaire. Earlier, in Table 2.2, we saw that age was not a predictor of who left local church ministry or remained in service. To that we can now add that younger and older ex-pastors were not very different in their viewpoints. Age, taken alone, explains little.

Points of Intervention

What can denominations do, and at what point, to prepare effective local church ministers and to support them in their ministry? From our study we can identify four significant points of intervention: training and gatekeeping; initial placement and transition to a new church; ongoing support; and support in problem situations. To conclude this chapter we will introduce each briefly here.

The first point of intervention occurs during recruitment to ministry, seminary training, and evaluation. All denominations want seminary training to be genuinely useful for ministry. All denominational officers would like to recruit capable and committed persons, train them effectively, and maintain standards that prevent unfit persons from entering the ministry. Yet all of them can tell stories of individuals who were ordained to ministry but shouldn't have been. As the stories go, these men and women were ordained because nobody wanted to say no. Most of the denominational officials we talked with believed that their denomination's gatekeeping process was inadequate; most assumed that some ministers would eliminate themselves or would need to be eliminated. These officials do not believe it is always a failure when a minister leaves local parish ministry, since a certain percentage of ordained ministers lack the gifts to serve in that capacity and should be encouraged not to do so. Too, every judicatory officer knows a few ministers who have in the course of time earned reputations as naysayers or rebels and whose departure caused denominational officers to feel a sense of relief. How do gatekeeping systems become so ineffectual, and how can they be strengthened?

The second point of intervention is the placement process, entailing placing ministers in jobs they like, jobs that give them energy and in which they will serve effectively. The problems at this point are in part due to the limitations of placement systems in each denomination and in part due to the fact that ideal matches between candidates and jobs are not always available regardless of the efficacy of placement systems. Everyone admits that mismatches occur, and everyone hopes to minimize them. How can this be done?

The third point involves ongoing support. New ministers need help forging bonds with veteran ministers, and ministers newly arrived in a given community need to make connections with everyone there. Information sharing and feedback are crucial to the success of this kind of support; the question is how to ensure that it happens.

The fourth point of intervention occurs in problem situations. What can denominational officials do to help ministers who find themselves in trouble? When problems or conflicts erupt, ministers need support. Their denominations owe it to them to try to provide it. How can they help? When should they intervene?

In Chapter 13 we will elaborate on these four intervention points, relating them to recommendations made to us by the pastors.

Main Findings

1. Pastors who left local church ministry did so for many reasons. The seven most common were
   - Preference for another kind of ministry
   - Need to care for children or family
   - Conflict in the congregation
   - Conflict with denominational leaders
   - Feelings of burnout or frustration
   - Sexual misconduct
   - Divorce or marital problems
2. About 15 to 25 percent left voluntarily, 30 to 40 percent were forced out, and the remaining cases are the result of a combination of motives.
3. Preference for specialized ministry and frustrations from dealing with conflict were the most common reasons for leaving parish ministry.
4. Institutional and interpersonal problems were more significant factors than loss of faith, health problems, or financial difficulties.

---

3 *Pastors Who Preferred Another Kind of Ministry*

I took a call that allowed me to more fully use my skills and gifts. I am now chaplain at a life care community and love it. I would never go back to parish ministry. Far too much time was spent on meetings and administration. I was exhausted by the time I resigned — and I thank God for my chaplaincy.

A Presbyterian man, age 43

Let us now take a closer look at those who left parish ministry mainly because they preferred specialized ministry. This category of ministers comprises 27 percent of our sample. These 27 percent are the ones for whom we judged that the attraction of another kind of ministry was the *major* motivation; they do not include other persons who emphasized other motivations for leaving local church ministry while also letting us know in passing that they are now in specialized ministry. These other persons are small in number, so we can summarize that the percentage of our sample now serving in a specialized ministry is more than 27 percent, possibly 30 to 35 percent.

The majority of these 27 percent are chaplains of some sort, either in hospitals, in the military, or in retirement homes. A smaller number are campus ministers or denominational officers — a broad category that includes camp directors, seminary administrators, social ministry workers, and missionaries. In age and level of theological training they are no different from others who left parish ministry, but they are disproportionately male.

Of the seven categories of former pastors in our study, the individuals in this one are the happiest and most satisfied. They are more satisfied than all the others with the level of support they receive from denominational officials (37 percent, versus 14 percent of all others), more satisfied with relations with lay leaders (45 versus 28 percent), and more satisfied with their family lives (49 versus 26 percent). They did not report as many problems in their last parish ministry position; for example, fewer (45 versus 64 percent) said that they had experienced significant problems with lack of agreement on what the role of a pastor is, and they reported fewer problems in their relations with other clergy (25 versus 42 percent). They reported much less stress in the congregation (42 versus 70 percent), less loneliness (33 versus 66 percent), less resentment from spouses due to the amount of time their ministry consumed (15 versus 32 percent), fewer problems speaking with denominational officials (33 versus 57 percent), and fewer marital problems (12 versus 35 percent).

Put simply, these ministers reported a much lower level of stress, frustration, and non-support in their last parish jobs. This is not to say that none of them felt push factors; in our analysis of their phone interviews we estimated that approximately half felt push factors at least to a certain extent. But none of them were *forced* out of local church ministry, and the majority did not experience pressures from anyone to leave. They left on their own.

Three Examples of Ministers Who Switched to Other Ministries

Pastor Ellen: Happy as a Campus Minister

Ellen is ordained in the ELCA; she left parish ministry when she was 37 to go into campus ministry. She had long thought that she would prefer to work in a college setting rather than in a parish, and after six years of parish ministry she decided to return to graduate school for a doctorate. At that time she was married, rearing two children.

> I finished my doctoral exams, and I happened to see an ad for a chaplaincy position at [a prominent university]. And the descrip-

tion in the ad just really called out to me and I thought I would throw my hat in the ring, even though I really wasn't at a point where I was looking for another full-time position. But the ad was so attractive and alluring that I decided to send off a resume and, lo and behold, that's where I ended up. So I actually took on my first chaplaincy position while I was working on my dissertation, and I completed my dissertation during that time.

Ellen talked more about why the campus ministry job was so alluring:

Gosh, I think it was just the whole description, it was being involved so intently in the life of the mind and having the opportunity to take up questions, to create programs, to work with people whose energy was so intellectually focused. That position also had a pretty heavy emphasis on liturgy, worship, and preaching, which I also love and didn't really want to leave behind. To be perfectly honest, another thing that really appealed to me was the opportunity to let go of some of the heavy administrative tasks that I had taken on as a part of being a solo pastor for those six years, and that I did not love [*laughs*]. So it was all of that.

Ellen had not expected to end up in chaplaincy when she went back to earn her doctorate. She was unsure what she could expect.

All I knew was one thing: I wanted options. That was really the only thing I was sure of for myself. I wanted to have a number of options to choose from. And I guess that became really clear for me as a woman in ministry early on. I graduated first in my class at my seminary, but I was really one of the last ones to get a call. I mean, even in the late 80s, it was still not an easy time for women in ministry. And I just wanted to have a variety of things to choose from. I didn't have an easy time getting my first placement in a parish, and it wasn't an easy call. I was a solo pastor in a small, very struggling congregation in the inner city. I loved it; I learned a lot. I would never exchange that experience for anything. But it wasn't easy.

There [were] lots of sides to being in that congregation. On the one hand, my husband and I often talk with great affection about how . . . our first parish community was so incredibly supportive to us as a family. They loved us and they supported us. They truly did. I never felt at all as though there was something I couldn't ask for from them, and that I couldn't be honest about the demands that I experienced as a mother and a solo pastor. They were wonderful to me in that respect. And there is something about that rhythm and being a family in a parish that is just so wonderfully supportive and good. And I've always missed that since I've left the parish. I've missed that for my family as well as for myself. But it's really simply the time demands. And not only the accumulation of time, but the particularity of time, *when* the time is demanded. You're on, mostly, when everybody else is off. There is also a lot of flexibility with it, I have to be honest. There were times when I could take off to go to a school event or do something else, and that would be really wonderful. But it was the evenings and the heavy weekends [*laughs*] that just really got to be grueling. Everything in the parish really revolves around Sunday. And personally, I loved that rhythm, that my week builds up to Sunday every week, and the combination of studying the text for that week and preparing for a sermon and all of the other programs that would happen on Sunday. And then as a family, we were all there, together, for Sunday. It was very, very supportive. It was supportive of my husband in that he really found his own place within the parish and loved helping the parish. I only had one child then, and it was supportive of my child. He had wonderful Sunday school teachers, and was able to participate in and grow through his relationships with so many people in that parish. He had a dozen grandparents, because it was a parish with lots of elderly people. And they all loved him and were wonderful to him.

Ellen's current position as a campus minister is different:

I'm now in my second chaplaincy position in an academic institution. It's a dual position where I'm half-time chaplain and half-time professor in religious studies. It's a small liberal arts college, and there are small worshiping communities, I call them "cells," that provide for their own worship. My work as chaplain here largely involves my working on multi-faith opportunities, learning experiences, opportunities for appreciation across traditions. I do a few of the large Christian worship ritual moments like Ash Wednesday, and Good Friday, and lessons and carols, and things like that, but it's not a Sunday to Sunday for me. I gave that up. And I miss that. What I gained was the opportunity to take on a half-time teaching load and to develop courses. And I do a lot of other faculty-related kinds of tasks. And I'm working on my scholarship.

She misses other aspects of parish ministry as well:

I miss the community. Every parish that I've been a part of, they've been relatively small to medium-sized parishes where people really know one another well and share their lives with one another. And the communal experience of a parish, it's always been very multi-generational, and I really do miss that. I talk with my colleagues here about the unnaturalness of this 18-year-old community that we're a part of [laughs]. Actually our students, they long for and look for opportunities for encounter with older people and children and animals, and pets. They miss all of that, and families.

Ellen also talked with us about the difficulties inherent in the task of Lutheran ministry today:

I think that a huge difficulty is involved in spanning the different contexts that you really have to work at. I'll tell you what I mean by that. On the one hand, in any Lutheran parish, you are serving the die-hard Lutherans that are committed maybe to the red hymnal even, and that can only see things in this very specific way that goes back to their childhood 60 years ago in some little Lutheran church out on the prairie somewhere. I'm stereotyping it a little bit. So you've got those people, and that's their world. At the same time, I guess being in an academic setting and being surrounded all the time by so many different types of people, makes me aware of the huge world of people who have not been raised with any religious tradition, are very suspicious of traditional religious systems and traditions, call themselves spiritual but not religious, are in a kind of exploring mode, and see traditional churches as narrow and always seeing themselves as having the right answers, not open to question. And somehow, I think, a pastor worth his or her salt these days has to somehow find a way to be available to and outreach to those people. And it is incredibly difficult. It really involves having many different congregations in one locale, and I think that is really, really challenging. And I don't know how well divinity school really trains pastors for that reality.

Also, personally, I think that mainline denominations are really in a denial mode about what's happening in our culture and in our country. I think that as much as we try not to admit it, mainline denominations are not doing so well. If any denominations are growing, it seems to me it's the evangelical ones, not really the mainline denominations, even though we have so much to offer. But I think we have a very hard time admitting that, much less really looking at why that's so. And, I mean certainly Lutherans, we are an ethnic group. Lutherans with their Scandinavian, Midwestern ethos, it's a very, very hard nut to crack, incredibly, incredibly difficult. It's hard for newcomers to break in, hard for people within to grow in their openness, and their willingness to change, to try other things, to let go of some of that ethos.

I think we really need to start studying a lot more sociology and reading writers who are really analyzing what is happening on the American scene in terms of people's religious commitments. Why are people changing? What is that all about? How does the role of popular culture play into all of this? How do denominations play into this? There are so many ways in which the presence of religious voices has diminished. I found myself just thinking this morning about the way in which other aspects of popular culture, movies, I think even gyms, there are so many other things that have taken the place of sacred time for people and places where people really approach the huge meaning-of-life questions. Churches and synagogues were a primary place for that, certainly in the early part of the twentieth century. That is really, really changing. And I think somehow we have got to come to grips with that and figure out what that means for us as ecclesiastical organizations. We can't have the same kinds of expectations. I think we're so invested in hanging on to all of these old paradigms that I just don't see us doing that work. We're so involved in continuing to fight the sexuality wars, which as far as I'm concerned, they're over. It's over with. Get with the twenty-first century — but we're so invested in that, the energy and the resources that are being wasted on battling that war; it's ridiculous. So I guess that I would say, give it up! Move on.

Ellen told us that she would seriously consider returning to parish ministry later, if she wearies of academic work. But she will definitely not do so in the next few years, while her children are still at home.

Pastor Mark: From the Parish to the Navy

Mark, an LCMS pastor, left parish ministry at the age of 32 to join the military chaplaincy. He exemplifies a minister who went into special-ized ministry for two reasons — an interest in the specialized role and a desire to get out of parish ministry. Push factors are prominent in his story. While in seminary, Mark had considered the possibility of going into military chaplaincy at some point, but the stress of life as a local church minister drove him to do it as soon as he could. He was serving three congregations in Nebraska, a task he found overwhelming:

> I was called to a dual parish right out of seminary. My wife and I lived in a nice parsonage they had for us, an excellent place to live, and it was in a small town, and we got used to that. And I really en-joyed having my own congregation, actually two congregations. One congregation had 550 members, and the other congregation had 80. Being a parish pastor was very satisfying. I enjoyed preach-ing and teaching and all of the things pertaining to the ministry.
>
> But there were dissatisfying things: one was pay. We barely had enough to cover student loans. I did grow a garden to supplement our budget [laughs]. Then also, the huge stress of two churches, and two sets of meetings every month, two sets of confirmation classes, and all that kind of stuff. And then, towards the end while I was there, they added on a third congregation of 250 members. We had two preschools and a daycare at one parish, so I had a staff of about four, the three parishes just really pushed me to the brink. And so that was really tough. I tried to take a day and a half off a week, and the congregation almost made me feel guilty about that. And so, meetings every night, long work hours, and three congregations.
>
> And then there was the conflict. I waited a year before I made any

changes and then there were some changes that needed to be made. The one congregation didn't have women voters and the women wanted a say in some of what was going on at the church, and so I changed the church constitution to get women voters in, and that caused a bit of a backlash. And I changed worship styles, going from an old hymnal to a newer one, and it caused further conflict.

And then, of the 550 members, only about 300 were in the area, and having pastoral concern for those under my care, I was trying to track down these people and notify them of churches in the area where they moved, and then some backlash came from the congregation, because there were some people who didn't want to join a new congregation but wanted to remain members there. So there was a little conflict over those three topics. Also the huge workload, and then the lack of finances, those are probably the three main things making me leave.

Mark found himself in conflict with a group of leaders in the congregation.

I knew the majority of the people in the congregation wanted to have women voting. I was able to multiply by like twenty times the number of people coming to congregational meetings by getting women voters. The problem was, it was mostly just the older people that were attending. And they said, "We want to get the younger people, your age, involved." And I said, "Well, these are the two things that we need to do. One is to get a newer hymnal, because, you know, there's a new hymnal for each generation, basically, and that would address the worship needs. And also give them a say in the congregation with having the women vote."

So what happened, there was a vocal minority that [had] held power before, that were upset with losing their power. I got the circuit counselor involved, and said to him, "You know, their power [has] been threatened, and now they don't like me."

There [were] a powerful few. One of the people became the congregation president the second year I was there, so he used his power to basically get after me, by calling meetings and stuff like that. The people in this group had mentioned to me before that they didn't like my ideas, but I was looking out for the concerns of the larger congregation. These people, you know, they'd had it that way all their life, and they were older, and they had the power, and were making life difficult for me.

The circuit counselor came because some of the vocal minority called him. And he called me and asked if it would be good to have some meetings, and I said, "Yes!" So we met regularly up until the time that I left.

And then the third matter was about finances. I was making $18,000 a year from the larger congregation, and from the smaller congregation it was $3,000 a year plus mileage, and the parsonage was thrown in. But I was just right out of the seminary. I felt in an awkward position, and this was my first call. I felt like, if you succeed and do well at your first congregation, then other congregations will consider you, and so the pressure was on, you know, to do well. I wanted to stay there at least three or four years, and then maybe get a call to somewhere closer to the Northwest, where I was from. But I wanted to serve there and do well.

I was already in the military chaplain candidate program in seminary, and I had to serve two years in a parish before I could go on active duty. After two years I thought it would be a good time to move on to the Navy.

Mark came into conflict with congregational leaders when he tried to reach out to young families, a priority the church had stated when they hired him.

[T]hat's one of the things they said on their call documents: We want somebody who will reach out to the middle-aged families in the congregation and get them involved. And that's what I did, and then I got this flak over it, because, you know, I was rocking the boat. So I think there was some misleading there. And it was more between what they thought they wanted and what they really wanted. I think they really did want to involve the younger people, but they didn't want to make any changes [*laughs*].

It was quite an overwhelming thing, [being] thrown into this. I was ordained at age 29 and went right to a congregation, and so I was young, and thrown right into a dual parish of around 600 members.

Time pressures in the Navy chaplaincy now are not nearly as severe as they were in parish ministry.

In the congregation, the job was never done. I had 15 people in the nursing home to see every month, and people at home who couldn't make it to church, and [I was] just, just overwhelmed. In the Navy you have more of a 9-to-5 job, and if you can't fit everything in the day, well, it's got to go then. Where in the parish, it was like, as long as there's stuff to do, you've got to do it. And part of it is my tendency to workaholism, too. And the times that I did try to stand up for myself and say, "No, I'm at my limit," I wasn't listened to. And so the mentality that a pastor has got to put in an 80-hour workweek, that's when, you know, people burn out! At over 50 hours a week, their productivity level drops, their sermon preparation is cut short and all that, and so it winds up hurting the pastor and the congregation.

I think that that's one of the biggest complaints of pastors. They don't mind the pay, but the more hours you work, the less pay you get, when you're salaried [*laughs*]. And to build in time to take care of yourself. In the Navy I've got one Bible study that's in the evening, but other than that I have the rest of my evenings free. And in the parish it was like, four or five nights a week there was something going on.

And the finances was a difficult thing. With the Navy, I almost doubled my pay, coming on active duty as a junior officer. But the pay isn't the biggest thing. The low pay combined with high stress and long hours, I think that's the triple combination that's really lethal.

Mark told us he has had thoughts of returning to parish ministry. He has even put in his name for a call in the area of the country where he grew up, but so far there have been no nibbles.

Pastor Dan: Called to the Mission Field

Dan, a 40-year-old Assemblies of God pastor, left parish ministry to become a missionary.

The reason I left is that my wife and I felt, at a young age, both of us were called to mission. We were both called at the age of fifteen. But we knew that we were called to Europe and to missions, and we knew that God had that plan for our lives. As for me, I knew that if I was going to be a missionary, I had to be a pastor first. According to the Assemblies of God rules and regulations, there's a lot of things that you need to do beforehand in order to be a missionary. Once I hit that point, then I knew that missions was becoming a reality to us. We definitely felt like God was talking to us through our hearts and through our interests, that God wanted us in the mission field. And we've been happy ever since; we've been there for three years.

Dan and his wife were back in the United States for a short visit when we interviewed him. He emphasized that he had gone into the pastorate mainly as a step on the way to being a missionary:

Yes, that is a normal process within the Assemblies of God. I went to seminary right after Bible college. And one of the things that I kind of discovered is that I was missing out on some of the students' experiences in life. Some of them came from Bible college into a pastorate and then into seminary, and they were asking questions much different than I was, because I was still in student mode and they had life experience. So I was like, "You know what? I want to get a little more experience in life before I go in the mission field." And the other reason was, I couldn't afford to go in the mission field right away. We had to be out of debt, personally, and we had to pay up our school loans. Once that was paid off, we were allowed to apply for missions.

In these three examples the ex-pastors spoke of long-felt calls to their current professions. Other former pastors told us that they shifted ministries because they lacked certain necessary gifts for parish ministry and believed themselves better suited to other jobs — for example, they had anxiety about writing and delivering sermons or anxiety about their ability to relate to all kinds of people, both integral skills for parish ministers. They portrayed their switch as a search for a ministry better suited to their own talents and therefore better for everyone involved. For example, an ELCA man who switched from parish ministry to chaplaincy in his forties explained to us,

> I really think my calling is in chaplaincy. Early on, when I was ordained, I thought that I would like to serve in long-term care. But there was the requirement of three years of parish experience. And I went into the parish and things went well. I really enjoyed it. But I felt this tugging more toward the pastoral care end of it, of ministry. The other thing that really drew me into long-term care was the pastoral work. So now I am able to keep that pastoral care and the worship — the two favorite parts of what I like about ministry, and still be a part of that and not be so heavy in the administration end of it.

An Assemblies of God pastor who left parish ministry at 39 preferred to be a counselor:

> The counseling part of ministry was what I enjoyed the most. The preaching part wasn't my primary interest. So I checked into what I needed to do to have that kind of career, or to go more in that direction. I got a master's degree in community counseling. I'm working toward licensure in marriage and family therapy.

An ELCA minister told of tension between his ministry ideals and the realities of dealing with congregational leaders:

> I came to a place in the conflict between me and the lay ministry of the congregation [where] I realized the result that was most likely was a splitting of the congregation. I had felt like a "square peg in a round hole" for my 20 years of parish ministry. Now, as a hospital chaplain, I have found my niche!

Ambivalent Feelings about Specialized Ministries

A proportion of specialized ministers, perhaps one-fourth, expressed to us feelings of uncertainty regarding whether they are taken seriously as full-fledged ministers in their synods, conferences, and presbyteries. Some spoke of attitudes among current parish ministers that specialized ministers were not "real ministers," or that they were getting off easy. One spoke of parish ministers who seemed resentful or envious, saying in effect, "Parish ministry is tough. Why can't you stick it out like the rest of us?" According to one ELCA minister,

> One of the negative things was, in chaplaincy, it feels a little isolating. It's different now when I go to the conference meetings and the synod assemblies. I'm not sure the church knows what to do with chaplains. A lot of the programming and a lot of the conversation is parish-based. There are, in the conference I am in, three chaplains. So that does help, having three Lutheran chaplains. My support comes primarily from the chaplains' association in the community I'm in, which is an ecumenical group of about 12 chaplains. Even the parochial report forms that I get from the national church and from our local synod, are very geared to parish reporting. And the synod doesn't seem to understand when I return my report and some of the things aren't there, for example, there's no offering taken. It just takes a while to explain that this is a different kind of a setting. So in some ways that feels very isolating. I guess I've had to learn to look for support in my ministry setting from other people who are in similar settings, rather than from people who are in my faith community.

In writing to ministers who had left parish ministry and asking them to participate in our survey, we found that we had inadvertently offended some by using phrases such as "left ministry" or "changed careers." They corrected us by saying that they were still fully in ministry, they had not left, and they had certainly not changed careers! This surprised us and alerted us to sensitivities that are widespread but of which we were not fully aware. So a Presbyterian minister:

> I did not "leave" local church ministry; I "entered" a new ministry as a Navy chaplain. My reason, therefore, for leaving was a sense of calling to a *different* ministry.

And another Presbyterian, now a hospice chaplain:

I felt *called* to another type of ministry. I have always known I would be a chaplain someday. It is where my skills are best used. You seem to assume that something negative happened "to turn me away" from church ministry. Both churches I served in my 20 years had great relationships with me, and they are still healthy, viable congregations. My style, though, is one-on-one. . . . I find that being a full-time hospice chaplain suits me very well. I felt called to this ministry, and I took a cut in pay to do it. It is not easier work; it is satisfying ministry. My only source of pain is that the denomination does not acknowledge this as ministry of any significance, or I would be included on the denominational mailing list and would receive the General Assembly minutes as do church pastors. I still serve in [my] presbytery, preach in vacant pulpits, fill in doing pastoral care and triennial visits. I have not left the church — the church has left me. I no longer receive the mailings, including a Program Calendar, given to all ministers. When I called and asked the denomination about this, they said, "They are for pastors." I said, "I am a pastor." They said, "When you are a pastor of a church you'll get one."

An Assemblies of God minister:

I *knew* that God was calling me to become a chaplain in the Army. I was not dissatisfied in ministry and have not *left* the ministry. I have simply changed my ministry because of the call of God.

An LCMS minister:

I am more in the *ministry* now than ever, just not in the parish. I am in hospital chaplaincy as Director of Pastoral Care. I *preach* in many congregations on Sundays. I do resent that many people in the church considered specialized pastoral care as *leaving* the *church ministry.* One person recently said they were sorry I had left "the church!" I do resent this survey with some subtle hints at this same misconception.

We asked an ELCA minister about his transition from parish ministry to campus ministry:

In some ways, I don't even really relate to your question. It just seems like it was a new call. Every call as a parish pastor that you take, you have a radically new vision, a new mission, different expectations. You have a different parish, so it seems like a new call. And this one was different in that it was campus ministry. But even within campus ministry, there's a church, and many of the things that I would do as a parish pastor I'm still doing as a parish pastor to a student congregation and then also as university pastor. I don't see it as that I changed careers. I don't feel that way.

A United Methodist pastor changed denominations so that he could be a minister to a retirement community. He is now ordained in the United Church of Christ. He complained about the restrictions he felt as a United Methodist:

> I transferred to the United Church of Christ. I am wonderfully blessed to serve in a retirement community, which is my calling. I know that. I know I had to change because Methodists do not ordain you to a specialized ministry. That senior pastor of mine said, "You loved your unit of CPE [clinical pastoral education], but don't tell your ministry board, because they don't want to ordain ministers to a chaplaincy. They only want parish ministers." So if I wanted to be ordained and go into chaplaincy, they wouldn't be very happy. Now I'm in a ministry serving 600 people in retirement living. I've found my passion. I look at the past and say, "Okay, that's what I needed to go through to get to where I can do my passion." The United Church of Christ ordained me with the clear understanding that I wouldn't be serving a local church. I couldn't do it in the Methodist Church.

To sum up: the largest single identifiable category of ex-pastors are those who left parish ministry to take up another kind of ministry. Whether they were responding to a long-felt inner call or were scouting around for forms of ministry that better fit their skills, they are on the whole happy people. Their main frustrations seem to be that in some cases their new ministries are not as gratifying personally as parish ministry could be, and that in other cases they lack adequate recognition in their denominations.

A second group of mainly voluntary leavers, a group much smaller in size, is made up of persons who left because of a need to care for families or children. We turn to them in Chapter 4.

Main Findings

Former local church pastors who preferred another ministry

1. Are now predominantly chaplains
2. Are disproportionately male
3. Were satisfied overall with their local church experiences
4. Are satisfied now in their specialized ministry
5. In some cases felt an earlier call to specialized ministry and were waiting for an opportunity to arise
6. In some cases decided later that their own gifts were more suited to chaplaincy or campus ministry
7. Resent not being considered "real ministers" by some pastors and denominational officials

---

Pastors Who Needed to Care
for Children or Family

I'm not in ministry now because of my children. Once I have been home and out of it, it felt really good and right to be with my kiddos. I am sure I will always have my hands in ministry, but whether I'll be back in some official pastoral capacity later, I don't know.

A 40-year-old Presbyterian woman

Some of the ministers in our study left the parish for a single, clear-cut reason: they needed to spend more time with children and family. In our sample of 963 former pastors there were 41 of these, about 4 percent of the total. Twenty-eight of them were women. These ex-pastors were younger than the others; they averaged 38 years of age when they left ministry, compared with an average of 44 in our entire sample. Associate pastors made up a large portion of this group (49 percent, versus 20 percent in all the other categories). They were disproportionately Presbyterian; none were ministers of the LCMS.

While the prototypical example of this kind of ex-pastor is a mother who stopped work in response to a need to spend more time with her children, the people in this category were actually quite diverse. Some individuals left to care for ailing spouses or elderly parents. For many, the need to spend more time with family and children was not a motivation that stood alone; commonly it was accompanied by other motives — exhaustion being a major one. In more than a quarter of the cases, respondents told us they felt both overburdened by the demands of their parish and guilty over the resulting neglect of their families.

A number of these pastors left in part due to dissatisfaction with various aspects of their jobs. For some, this was the senior pastor under whom they were serving. For others, including several male Assemblies of God ministers, there was a combined need to give more time to their families and also to have an opportunity to earn more money; such individuals lamented that ministry was a day-and-night obligation that paid too little and took too much of a toll on spouses and children. Several ministers told us they left ministry because of sick or disabled spouses, children, or parents.

No one should assume that these individuals subsequently devoted themselves full-time to parenting or caretaking. On the contrary, about a third continued work in part-time jobs or in jobs with flexible schedules.

We compared the questionnaire data from this type of former parish minister with those from all the others in our sample. Ministers of this type were much happier in their ministry than average. They reported less conflict in their churches (25 percent noted major conflict, versus 40 percent of all the others), less stress from congregation members who were critical of their work (27 versus 46 percent), and less feeling of isolation or loneliness (42 versus 59 percent). They less often complained that they could not speak openly and honestly with denominational officials (22 versus 52 percent), they less often felt bored or constrained in their positions (27 versus 43 percent), and they less often reported that they felt pressure from lay leaders to leave (7 versus 22 percent). Yet they reported more dissatisfaction with their family life (49 versus 34 percent) and more feelings that their ministry work did not permit them to devote adequate time to their children (59 versus 31 percent).

Pastor Patricia: An Overburdened Mother

Patricia, ordained in the Presbyterian Church, left local church ministry at age 36, chafing at long hours that kept her from spending time with her child. After leaving seminary she got married, then served as an associate pastor in a church where her primary responsibility was for youth. Her church happened to have a partnership with another local congregation, an arrangement that, in addition to its benefits, gave Patricia extra responsibilities.

So essentially I was the youth pastor for a 1500-member church [the size of the two churches combined], and that's a lot of work. To add on top of that preaching more than once a month, most years, was a lot. It was a very supportive work environment. It was a pretty big staff, which was nice; it was not lonely at all. I would characterize the match between me and that congregation as perfect. We clicked right from the beginning. It was a very, very good fit. I was there nine years, which I think is pretty unusual for an associate. My primary duties were to the youth ministry, which was very big and active. We did trips and we did service projects and had peer support groups and fellowship activities and leading worship, and confirmation. All of the usual stuff of the youth ministry. And then I also staffed our missions or social justice committee and was directly responsible for making sure that those projects or funding decisions and things went on. That included travel to do program evaluation on their behalf. They sent me to Africa to do program evaluations as well as local stuff. That was also a pretty big piece of the job.

After about eight or nine years, Patricia's motivations began to change:

I'd been there a long time, and the nature of Presbyterian polity is that my job description really can't change all that much. Once you're called, you're called to that position. And the nature of youth ministry is very much like school teaching in that it's cyclical and you pretty much repeat the same cycle year after year after year. Having done that nine times, of course adding new things and trying different things, still it became repetitive. I felt like I had done as much as I could do for them and that, I wouldn't say I was *bored*, but I had really explored the limits of that job.

The other major factor is that we adopted a child. We adopted a child from Guatemala. I took a six-month maternity leave and came back, but it was never the same after that. Because church work in general, and youth ministry in particular, is primarily done on evenings and weekends. My husband worked downtown in [the city], and this is a suburb. It's a long commute, and he had a very demanding job in the financial world and was never home. So I was

essentially a single parent. Shortly after going back to work it began
to dawn on me that I was never seeing my child. Raquel was in
daycare in the building, so I could have lunch with her and I could
look out the window and see her playing. But my routine was when
work finished at 4 or 5 in the afternoon, I would swoop down, pick
her up, get her home, feed her, bathe her, and then sit there waiting
for my husband to come home so I could hand her off to him and go
back to work. That just was not satisfying for me at all. And then
weekends, of course, the same deal. As I mentioned, our youth ministry had a very active travel component, so I was called away for up
to a week at a time, twice a year, and then lots of weekends for re-
treats and ski trips and the usual. I felt I was being pulled away
from her far too much, and I couldn't stand that anymore. I wanted
a job that was 9 to 5.

So I took a year off and looked in the non-profit world. I went to
a local domestic violence service provider whom I had worked with
very closely. They hired me immediately, and I've been there ever
since. And it's very much a 9-to-5 job. Actually they've accommo-
dated me to leave at a quarter of five every day in order to get back
up here to pick up my child before daycare closes. It's much more
humane hours. Of course, the pay is less.

I should also mention the low pay at my former job at the
church. I was the lowest-paid associate pastor in our presbytery.
And though I wouldn't say that's why I left, it began to be an irri-
tant. I brought it to their attention, and I was vocal about my dissatisfaction. I would point out I was the lowest-paid associate in the
presbytery; they would point out we're the smallest church in the
presbytery with a full-time associate. But our town is a very wealthy
place. I am convinced, especially with what happened in the search
for my successor, that their attitude was I had a very successful husband who made a good salary, and I didn't need more money. When
they looked for my successor, two things changed. The presbytery
instituted a minimum salary requirement for associates. And the
church fought it for two years while they looked. They fought it
tooth and nail under the leadership of my former boss. He said it
just wasn't fair and it just wasn't right and they should never do
this and it's wrong, wrong, wrong. And when they finally met the
minimum, they were paying this person, right out of seminary,

twice what they had paid me when I left. Which really pisses me off. I'm sure you can hear that in my voice.

I was just so sad to leave them! They were sad. I'm even crying now. It was really hard to leave. And I didn't leave town. I'm still here in town, and I worship with them. I stayed away about two years. I'm very close to our executive presbyter and we talked a long time about what it would mean to live in the community. Because most times, clergy leave. They move away, they go far away, unless they retire. Now I worship there, but in a very back-row way. My daughter goes to church school there, but because of the divorce, she worships with her father every other weekend. So it's really a pretty minimal face-time that I have there.

A year after I left, my husband and I separated. And the presbytery has been very hands-off. They haven't pressured me at all in terms of the fact that I'm not in a validated ministry [recognized by the denomination] now. I'm not working in a church, and the work I do at the domestic violence agency is not chaplaincy. The first year and a half I was there, it was development work. I am now a community educator. I do some teaching in churches, I do some preaching as a part of my job, so there is a thread [of ministry], but it's a pretty tenuous one. The presbytery said not to worry about [continuing clergy status]. Now that I have a small child enrolled in the school system, I can't move. And there aren't a whole lot of options for me. I've certainly been willing to do supply preaching and I go to my presbytery meetings.

Patricia reflected on the effect of her long working hours on her marriage and family:

It's hard to tease out that impact, because it wasn't until the very end of my ministry that we adopted our child. Up until that point, my husband worked even worse hours than I did. So in a way, I had my work, otherwise I would have been sitting home alone. It fit a need. Now, you could also look at it as, if I had been sitting home alone all that time, I probably would have held him accountable and maybe we would have saved the marriage if we'd intervened sooner. But because I was always at work and he was always at work, we didn't really notice. I think it became much more obvious to me once we were parenting and I was single parenting in a marriage. But up until that point, it didn't really have an impact directly because he was never here anyway.

And she wondered aloud about what might have kept her in parish ministry:

Possibly if they had paid me more. Certainly now — I wasn't a single parent when I left — but if Rebecca [her replacement], who is in that church now, left that position and they came to me and said, "We'd like to hire you again. . . ." First of all, the presbytery would have a coronary if they did that, but if they did and it was okay, and they said, "We'll hire an au pair for you just like [a neighboring church] did for Mary Grace, would you come?" I probably would. I loved the work. The work I do now is teaching youth K-12, so it's littler kids than I had, as well. But junior high and high school kids are my passion and my vocation and it's what I love to do.

And if I felt like I had flexible hours, that's another thing. If they said, "Your office hours would coincide with Raquel's school hours, so you would be home to meet the bus every day. And we'd hire somebody to be at home if you had evenings or weekends," I'd do it, I would. My long-term vocational goal, though, in terms of ministry, would be to find a chaplaincy at a prep school, where I could teach and minister and Raquel could go to school, and we could live and be a part of that community. That's my goal for certainly her high school years but preferably even maybe a prep school that starts with junior high. I am limited geographically, unless something happens in my ex-husband's life, because he lives and works in the city and is a very active parent with her. So I would not be able to move away from an easy commute to him.

She talked about whether her being a woman had been important in that job:

Well, a couple of things come to mind. One is that girls that I worked with, as they grew up, went to college and even got married, say that it made a big difference to them to have a role model who was female in the church. And I was always quite aware of that and felt that as a big responsibility on my part, as a woman, to be that. And also for young boys, I think it was important for them, they wouldn't necessarily articulate it though, to see a woman in a position of authority within the church. Another way that I think it worked well for the congregation to have me was that obviously the senior pastor was a man. And I think it was a very healthy thing for the congregation to have a female and a male pastoring them. We both brought our own gifts, and it was a nice balance and a good blend. He is the kind of senior pastor who is extraordinarily collegial with his associate. There was not a hierarchy, he was not on a power trip, he was not on an ego trip. Therefore, I think the congregation saw us more as partners, almost as co-pastors in some ways, than a more traditional model. And it was good for them to have that balance.

I didn't feel limited. As I mentioned, this was a pretty progressive congregation. I might have felt it if I was more the kind of person who was preparing to launch into a solo or senior pastorate of my own someday. But because I didn't want to do pastoral stuff, and I didn't want to be preaching more, I never bumped into it. There are always a couple of jackasses in every congregation, and we had ours. This one man was oblivious to what his issues were, but obviously, from the stuff he would say and his little temper tantrums that he would throw, it was almost always around issues of my being female or on the issues that I preached about or talked about being feminist or woman-centered. But he was one person out of five hundred, and I never experienced that as a big deal.

Patricia hopes to return to parish ministry later, and she has let the presbytery know.

I've told them that. Every year you have your annual interview if you're a specialized minister. And every year in that interview I say that at a time when Raquel is old enough that if I got a call in the night that someone had had a heart attack or a car accident and needed me to come to the hospital, I would feel comfortable leaving her alone in the house. I would do it. And to me that age is probably somewhere between ten and eleven, and she's now almost six. So it will be probably another five years before I would feel like I could take a job. I know women do it.

Pastor Barbara: Two Children and Two Stepchildren

Barbara is another Presbyterian minister who left her position as associate pastor to care for her babies. She was 31 at the time. She started ministry as a single person, then got married, in the process acquiring two stepchildren.

> Once I got married, that was the point at which I tried to find a way to step back from church ministry, because I had set a standard for myself in ministry that I couldn't achieve with a family. So I thought I would take a couple of years off to reevaluate how I might work effectively with a family.

But in those two years Barbara and her husband had two more babies and became active in another church, where they expect to belong until the children are grown. She has hopes of reentering parish ministry at that time, but meanwhile she has earned a master's degree in counseling, and she may work in that field in a few years.

> My degree is in marriage and family therapy, so I could open my own practice or I could work in a clinic. There are a number of settings I could work in. In my ideal world, I would be able to find a part-time job in a church as a parish associate or pastoral staff member but also have a part-time practice on the side with therapy. I don't know if I want to work over 30 hours a week, even after two years.

Now that Barbara has a husband and children, time and money are more important to her:

> As an associate, I worked 60 or more hours per week, and I never had any self time. I never had any family to be with, so that was just fine. But now, every hour I spend away from my family really counts. And if I'm going to be doing something away from them, I want it to be both internally rewarding and I want it to be rewarding the world somehow. I want to be giving back to the world and making a difference and feeling that there's a connection. And I want to feel that I'm paid for what I'm doing so that there is some justification for that time away, in terms of contributing to the welfare of my family.

So that will be interesting when I go back, particularly having another degree which could put me in a secular profession. I don't expect to make a lot of money. I just want to be compensated for the time that I do spend, whether it be financially or psychologically.

Still, she feels a call to ministry, though it has certainly evolved since her seminary days:

I think the biggest difference I feel spiritually is since I'm not serving a congregation these last two years, my sense of call has really, not gone away, but it's shifted. My call is to be a good wife and mother and person in my community giving back, as opposed to serving a particular parish and particular group of people. The feeling that I have to be a minister or there's nothing else for me, that this is what God wants me to do, is definitely not the same as it was when I started seminary. And it's something I struggle with, because I took the ordination vows and I meant what I said and I want to continue to believe in those. But I've got to have a strong feeling that the parish is where God is specifically calling me. And I'm not sure, because I've been off for two years and I'm going to be off for another two years. Then am I going to be able to perceive what a call is? To know what it is? Because I'm a completely different person now in many, many ways. So that's really going to be hard to know. Right now I feel a strong sense of call, if you want to use that word, to bring my new baby into the world and raise these two children together with my husband and be a good stepparent to the others, and those things I have a strong passion for. And I'm very driven to spend my time and energy on that. The feeling of being responsible for my family is incredible.

Pastor Art: Stay-at-Home Dad with Two Boys

A third example is Art, an ELCA minister who left parish ministry at age 44. He told of time pressures that took away his family time:

With two boys growing up [into] teenagers, I thought they needed my place at home more and to do things like coach Little League and help with events and things like that. In parish ministry, the church

74

will let you work as much as you want to work. I just let it get me and just take over, so I worked long hours each week. And it just was tough trying to be part of the family too. In ministry, your day off during the week is when the rest of the family is at work or school, so that wasn't a good time. Being a church with lots of older people, I did have a lot of hospital work and visitation. So even Sunday afternoons, when you might be able to get some family time, a lot of those were spent going to the hospital and following up on those type of calls. . . part of my ministry was if somebody was in the hospital I needed to see them, almost every day if possible.

Art decided to leave his pastorate, take a part-time job, and spend more time with his sons. His wife is a teacher, and he found occasional work as a teacher's aide and as an assistant at a sports complex, both of which left him plenty of time with his boys. In two years both boys will be off to college, and he is now wondering if he wants to re-enter parish ministry when they go. He has doubts, thanks to all the nights spent in meetings and all the pressures from church members and from the denomination. More likely, he thinks, he will get a teaching certificate and go into teaching full-time.

As these examples show, ministers who left to care for children or a family were not on the whole unhappy with the ministry; their priorities simply shifted. Many are interested in returning to the parish after their children grow up. Temporarily, not permanently, ex-pastors, they remain potential resources for their denominations.

Main Findings

Former pastors who left to care for family or children

1. Comprise about 4 percent of those who left
2. Are disproportionately female and Presbyterian
3. Are younger than others who leave parish ministry
4. Are more often associate pastors
5. Were more satisfied overall than others with their local church experience
6. Are often interested in returning to local church ministry when their children are grown

---

5 *Pastors Who Had Conflict in the Congregation*

I would say conflict is essential. If there's no conflict in a church, I would point to a church that's probably doing nothing. I think conflict is traumatizing for people, and most of us are frightened. And most of the people that are attracted to seminary are really horrible at handling conflict.

Frank, former ELCA pastor

One of two main reasons why ministers left parish ministry was the stress of dealing with conflict. (The other was preference for specialized ministry, which we explored in Chapter 3.) Our research agrees with all earlier studies in finding that conflict distresses many Protestant ministers and ultimately drives some of them away. We divided the conflicts facing ministers into two categories: conflicts in the congregation, either with laity or staff, and conflicts with denominational officials. In this chapter we will explore conflicts and difficulties encountered within the congregation; in the next we will address conflicts with denominational officials.

Conflict is part of life; psychologists consistently remind us that it should not be seen as something inherently bad. It is an inevitable part of any close relationship, especially relationships in which people have a strong personal investment. Marriage, the quintessential example, brings together two people with different, often unvoiced, expectations regarding living life together. Church members and their pastors make a similar emotional commitment to their church, bringing sometimes radically different, unacknowledged ideas of just how the church should function and what its goals should be. In both cases, conflict is a strong indicator that people are invested — that they really care about their marriage or their church. Where conflict is present, apathy is not a problem.

But conflict is always uncomfortable, and people expend a good deal of energy trying to avoid the persons and settings that call up disquieting feelings. Marriage counselors and other conflict experts, however, encourage their clients to voice their feelings rather than stifle them, pointing out that working through conflict successfully is what creates growth in relationships.

An estimated 27 percent of our sample of ex-pastors left parish ministry mainly because of troublesome conflicts, but many more than that had been through serious conflict. Many former pastors whom we ultimately placed in other categories told us about conflict they had been through — even though that conflict did not seem to be their main motivation for leaving. Here we will look at pastors who left parish ministry primarily because of conflict with their congregation. These persons differed from other ex-pastors in several ways. In their final years of ministry they experienced more dissatisfaction with their effectiveness as leaders, with their ministry positions, with denominational support, and with their relationships with lay leaders. Figure 5.1 on page 78 summarizes the principal ways in which this 27 percent of the sample was unique. When comparing the five denominations in our study, we found that Presbyterian pastors had higher rates of conflict with their congregations than did those in our other four denominations and, of the seven main reasons for leaving, this type of conflict was number one in frequency among Presbyterians. We are uncertain why, but possibly the denomination's democratic approach to decision-making brings more internal conflicts.

Major Types of Conflicts

In our questionnaire we asked former pastors if they had experienced conflict in their church during their last two years of service and if so, what the conflict was about. In all, 39 percent of the respondents reported having had major conflicts in the last two years of their parish

Figure 5.1
Pastors Who Left Due to Conflicts in the Congregation
versus Those Who Stayed

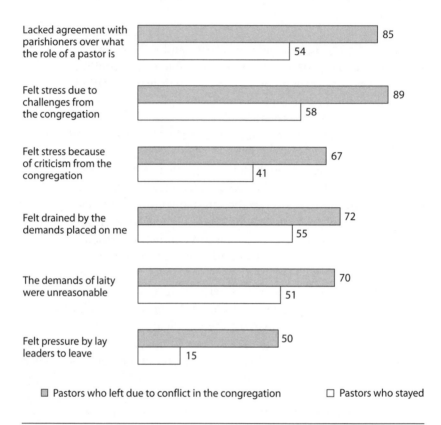

Lacked agreement with parishioners over what the role of a pastor is — 85 / 54

Felt stress due to challenges from the congregation — 89 / 58

Felt stress because of criticism from the congregation — 67 / 41

Felt drained by the demands placed on me — 72 / 55

The demands of laity were unreasonable — 70 / 51

Felt pressure by lay leaders to leave — 50 / 15

☒ Pastors who left due to conflict in the congregation   ☐ Pastors who stayed

ministry. The top five issues in the conflicts were pastoral leadership style, finances, changes in worship style, conflicts among staff or clergy, and new building or renovation issues. Table 5.1 on page 79 shows the responses to both questions, including the top five areas of conflict. (The complete list of fourteen areas is found in Table C.10 in Appendix C.) The percentage who had had major conflicts in their churches was similar in the five denominations. Presbyterian and Assemblies of God pastors reported slightly more conflict related to pas-

Table 5.1

Conflicts in Last Church

	UMC (%)	PCUSA (%)	ELCA (%)	LCMS (%)	A/G (%)
In your last local church ministry position, during the *last two years* of your service, was there any conflict in the congregation?					
Yes, major conflict	37	38	42	42	37
(If a conflict:) What was the conflict about? (check as many as apply)					
Pastoral leadership style	29	41	36	29	42
Finances	30	19	31	25	19
Changes in worship style	24	27	20	29	24
Conflicts between staff and/or clergy	16	21	17	18	18
Issues about new building or renovation	25	15	18	18	18

toral leadership style, while the United Methodist and ELCA clergy had slightly more concern with financial issues.

The same question about conflict was included in the survey of the control group of current senior pastors. Compared with ministers who left parish ministry, fewer reported major conflicts during their last two years (17 versus 40 percent). This information is presented in Table 5.2 on page 80 (only senior and solo pastors are included in this comparison, so the percentages are different than in Table 5.1). Although current pastors experienced much less conflict, the issues causing conflict when it did happen were similar to those for the ministers who left. Pastoral leadership style, finances, changes in worship style, and issues about a new building or renovation were the top four problem areas for both. The relative importance of the areas of con-

Table 5.2

Conflicts in Last Church
(Senior or Solo Pastors Only)

In your last local church ministry position, during the *last two years* of your
service, was there any conflict in the congregation?

		UMC (%)	PCUSA (%)	ELCA (%)
Yes, major conflict	Former	36	40	43
	Current	14	25	12
(If a conflict:) What was the conflict about? (check as many as apply)				
Pastoral leadership style	Former	26	32	34
	Current	20	28	20
Finances	Former	31	35	29
	Current	17	16	18
Changes in worship style	Former	25	27	21
	Current	17	16	20
Issues about new building or renovation	Former	26	20	16
	Current	17	18	16

flict was the same for both groups; the current pastors simply reported fewer instances of them.

Conflicts Experienced by Associate Ministers

As we saw in Chapter 2, former associate pastors experienced more
troublesome conflicts with staff or clergy than former senior pastors
did (37 versus 12 percent). Also more of the associates reported conflict in the church over pastoral leadership style (53 versus 32 percent)
while fewer said they were satisfied in their relations with other clergy
(22 versus 36 percent).

These differences tell us that the experiences of conflict by associate pastors are unique. Associate pastors have less autonomy and authority than senior pastors. When dealing with other clergy or staff they must negotiate with other staff for power, whereas senior pastors wield power by virtue of their position. Associates are disproportionately women (32 versus only 15 percent of senior or solo pastors).

In our interviews, many associate pastors reported difficulties with their senior pastors. Some of them told us that their senior pastors were controlling or micromanaging; others said the senior pastors were unaccustomed to having an associate and did not welcome them; still others told of staff members whose personal issues affected all their colleagues. Associates told us they often felt unable to control their lives because they were too much subject to the whims of the senior pastor. One LCMS associate pastor who left at age 33, for example, discovered that the senior pastor did not want an associate:

In my very first call I was an associate. And I found out, even on paper, that the senior pastor didn't want me there. He told the elders, "I don't want an associate." So I got into that situation where there was no communication, and they wanted to give him an associate because he was getting older and tired and they wanted to help him out. That was right out of seminary. I was there 13 months.

He found that one's first call really can set the tone for later ministry.

It does, yeah, and I've talked to friends about it. Some have even said, "It's a shame you didn't get placed in a bigger church where maybe all those expectations aren't there." I don't know. In a smaller church, some look at you, "Oh, you're going to be the savior from the status quo. We're a dying church!" Or "Come on, change this and this, because the senior pastor has been here a long time." I just didn't know how to handle it, not at all. Nothing could prepare me for that. I didn't have any experience to lean on.

A Presbyterian woman who left local church ministry at age 48 similarly found herself unwanted by the senior pastor.

It was really frustrating, because I think he was ambivalent about me being there. Because he was not that excited about this idea of getting a full-time associate. It was interesting because what had happened was they had one half-time associate who lasted a very short period of time, but who he really, really liked because she was a woman from the congregation. She was somebody who had been a member of the church and then gone back to seminary. That seemed to work for him pretty well. She didn't really start anything new. She ended up just doing whatever he didn't want to do, so that worked out perfectly. I think he knew, at some level, if they took on a full-time associate, new stuff was going to start. Because otherwise, it would absolutely not make any sense to get a full-time associate. And that would maybe require him to be involved in new stuff, or at the least, to put his work in a new light, kind of like, "Well, why can't you do *this* if she's doing all *this*?" So when I would go to talk to him, I think he would try to be supportive of my pain, hear my sadness, but I think maybe, he wasn't completely disappointed in my leaving. He could go back to the more comfortable thing. And it's interesting, because what the church has done since I left, they've had a series of half-time associate pastors who have been really relegated to youth work.

Many associate pastors enter ministry as youth pastors, charged with developing a youth ministry, but find themselves slowly being burdened with responsibilities unrelated to their call. One Assemblies of God associate, who left at age 39, struggled in his position because he lacked financial support for himself and for the youth group.

My first youth ministry experience was in 1985. I went to a church of about 200. We grew, in that church, over the next two years to over 800 people. The youth group started from nothing and we had, I believe, 130 kids in the youth group and 85 or 90 in the junior high. My job description was also to take care of the five acres of lawn that surrounded the church, which included not one blade of grass out of shade. So that consumed a lot of my time and I constantly was frustrated because I wanted to devote myself to the youth group and feeling divided having to take care of the lawn. And with the size of the church and the size and progress and growth of the youth group, I was becoming discontent because I was making about $1200 a month when I first came to the church and after two years I was making $900 a month without any medical insurance.

But the primary reason I left the church is, we were ready to go to Six Flags, like a Disneyland-type trip with 50 or 60 kids. And I went to send my check down to the park and I was told by the senior pastor that the money wasn't available. He explained to me that once I get more "mature" in the ministry, I'll realize that all the money goes into one big pot and everybody kind of takes and gives to this big account. I said to him, "So if I give to missions, what expectation do I have that my check is not going to the church fund, that it's going to be given to missions?" And he didn't answer me. Anyway, there were thousands of dollars that we needed to go to Six Flags, and it wasn't available. I ended up quitting the church over that. I told him that he could explain to the parents the reasons why we couldn't go to Six Flags at that point, and why there wasn't any money available, because I had the kids pay for this trip. We had done fundraisers, all the expenses for the trips had been paid, I'd already rented vans and a bus. It was all paid for, I thought, but the money, when we needed it, wasn't available.

A Presbyterian man who left at age 34 recommended a wholesale reevaluation of the position of youth pastor:

It would be helpful to meet some people that were doing youth ministry whose lives seemed enjoyable and normal. I didn't really meet too many people like that. Even now, it seems like the youth pastor job maybe just is a beast. It's hard to find people that thrive in it, even in our church now. My wife and I just pray for youth pastors. We see them come and go, year after year. Since I left that job, they've had four people in there, and they just got another guy who is commuting a long way.

And, particularly the fact that youth pastor is an entry-level job for so many pastors. I think it really is something that maybe needs to be looked at. Because if you start someone out and they're excited and then you put them in a job that just overwhelms them, like in my case, it's hard to want to go back or to feel like it's going to be manageable again.

Everyday Issues

Most notable about the main conflicts experienced by ministers who left parish ministry is their "everyday," prosaic nature. They were not doctrinal differences or inflammatory issues such as the ordination of gay and lesbian ministers, but rather the day-to-day functioning of the congregation: the style of the pastor and of worship, the relationships among staff, and the handling of finances and building space. Congregations clash over small things. Pastors and lay leaders clash when there is a difference in styles of leadership. They clash when worship traditions are challenged or modified. They quarrel over money and how it is spent. We reflected on this and came to believe that the conflicts most often experienced by our participants are ones that could probably be resolved and in the process offer growth experiences for both pastor and congregation. Instead, they become catapults out of parish ministry. Let us look at three examples.

Pastor Frank: Needed Changes Brought Conflict

Frank, ordained in the ELCA, served three different churches over eighteen years before leaving parish ministry at age 44. In all three he was troubled by conflicts, which finally led him to quit. His story is not unusual.

> In each of those parish settings I experienced conflict. They were different, but one thing I noticed that they had in common was, how conflict gets handled in the church is usually pretty poor. And that's one of the real dilemmas. In the first church that I served in, the pastor had been there for 28 years. He had really been "retired" but was on the job for a while. He gave me an enormous amount of freedom and responsibility. And when he retired, I was smart enough to know at that point, that whoever came in and took that role was going to experience a lot of conflict, because the congregation hadn't had any change in that role for 28 years. It was kind of a classic case.
>
> Things got tense when the senior pastor retired and the congregation overrode the call committee by voting to elevate Frank to the po-

sition of senior pastor rather than hire the committee-recommended candidate. Frank accepted the call, but conflicts cropped up in the congregation on issue after issue.

> We called in a consultant. It was a *great* thing. He said, "I've never been in a congregation that has so little sense of common mission." He did interviews with groups of people. And everybody had a sense of mission, but there was no *common mission*. Everybody was operating with their own little agenda and being critical of what was going on or not going on. And he said, "This is not possible. No pastor can do what you're asking, because there is no agreement here. And the congregation is not going to be able to move forward." By that time I got the sense that I had done my job, and it was time for them to have a new senior pastor.

Frank then moved to another church to be associate to a pastor who had served alone for 30 years.

> He'd never worked with anybody. It was hard for him. He had a really tough time adjusting to working with somebody. The first few months he was livid! We had disagreements. Because I just didn't think it was worth my time to go and pick up paper and paper clips . . . to drive thirty miles downtown just for that. What I would notice there was the process that happened — they didn't tell me this going in — but after about three years, people began telling me that they were calling the senior pastor to do something, but then the senior pastor would say he couldn't do it. He wasn't comfortable with it. And the feeling was kind of like the congregation was compensating for him, but they couldn't really let him know that, because it would be too upsetting for him. The people saw that he had weaknesses, but they couldn't really say that. So the procedure was that they would call an associate to do some of the things that would be most threatening to him. And I walked into that [*laughs*].
>
> And my perception of part of what happens is that the whole ability to be honest is one of the biggest problems for the church. I think, had these folks been able to really say to the senior pastor, "Here's what we see. Here are your strengths. . . ." To sort that

through, it would have started from a different place. Frankly, he was a solo pastor, and that's what he should have been doing. It was a stressful time. After I had served on a staff and had been leader of a staff for a few years, I can remember, we went to one of the leadership seminars on "breaking the 400 barrier," about the role of the senior pastor in a large church, and we were sitting together and he just looked at me and said, "I can't do that!" And he knew it. He saw what needed to be done, and that wasn't him. There was no way!

After five years in that church, Frank moved to another. But the discord there grew so overwhelming that it led to Frank's resignation from parish ministry altogether.

The last congregation I served in had once been an 1800-member congregation and had dwindled down to having 54 people at worship. And helping congregations grow was my passion — really my passion. And they knew that, and they asked me to come. They recognized that they had to do something different, either close the doors or do something radically different. And they were kinda open to a whole bunch of different things. So I accepted that call. We spent about 18 months praying and visioning and planning, and then we took a *very* different direction in terms of how things had been going. Their prayer had been, help us reach people that were unchurched, as opposed to grabbing people from other churches. And that's what happened. About 85 percent of the people who came either hadn't been in church for five years or more. A lot of them, for many, many years. We tripled in attendance, and things were really moving along. The budget stuff — we set a goal and got mission partners, and I am kind of an entrepreneurial type. There was a lot of that. I helped connect with people all over the country to be mission partners, and wrote a grant to the denomination for a special staff person for three years.

Not everybody liked it. It was sort of a classic old-school, new-school situation. As the power changed, and this group of people who had been in there for years and years and were ready to take a break, now when a new Sunday school superintendent started, it just got ugly! And that was the pattern. It kept getting worse!

A number of families who'd been in the church for many years resisted the changes:

> "We want our old church back!" Well, it took three years for them to say that out loud. And that was a group of probably ten families. This group of families who were mad because things weren't the way they used to be, they stopped giving and kind of just organized to resist and attack what was going on. We had a congregational meeting, when we had mostly new officers in the church. The president, secretary, treasurer were fairly new. But this group of four guys who had been officers themselves many, many years, just kept picking at what the president was saying. He couldn't even say anything without them interrupting and saying something. So I spoke up and said, "Dennis is leading the meeting here. You need to let him do his job, and let's keep the process going." And it just got uglier and uglier. We started the meeting with about 75 people there, which was a great attendance for this size of congregation, and within 20 minutes, because of how ugly it was, we were down to 19. They just bailed!

A year later Frank left the ministry. It was not the conflict itself but the lack of support in the midst of conflict that pushed him out of parish ministry. He thought back:

> When I came [to the last church] I had only served in relatively healthy congregations. So this was a new thing, to see how you *restart* a congregation. I went to a number of events to kind of get some help with that, because this is really a volatile kind of stuff. And what was clear to me, in a setting like that, was that to do a turn-around involves a lot of conflict, because a lot of the habits that help a church die need to be changed. And you also have people who have given so *much* of themselves just to keep some place surviving. They're *so* deeply invested, and often it's difficult for them to let go enough for these new people to take power. So *some* conflict is going to happen. It's just going to happen, that's just how it is. So, frankly, I think it is exactly those disagreements, and sorting it through and hashing it through to get to the place where you really can agree on a mission, that is the energy and the juice that really

makes it flow. But what I noticed was that regionally, and our bishop's staff, and nationally, our staff really didn't have a clue about that. They really didn't. For example, when this conflict developed and this group of people stopped giving, the national church stopped our grant. They said, if there's a fight going on here, you need to solve that problem.

Frank summarized:

I think my leaving had two or three parts. One, I was really worn down by the years of conflict there. It had been three years of steady, steady conflict, of people lying about me. I felt beat up, and it took a while to just get over that. I think, second, there were other congregations that would have called me. The bishop wanted to give my name to some others, and several approached me, and there were interim places. He wanted me to stay. But I felt that the structure doesn't work. It isn't working. I think that the synod structure at this point in time is much more about what is politically correct, and kind of "idea stuff" than it is about doing well. And it's more about pretending to be in the game than it is *being* in the game.

In Frank's view, avoiding conflict is a sure way to keep a church from growing.

I would say, conflict is essential. If there's no conflict in a church, I would point to a church that's probably doing nothing. I think conflict is traumatizing for people, and most of us are frightened. And most of the people that are attracted to seminary are really horrible at handling conflict. I went and got training. I went to a number of Alban Institute training events, to learn how to deal with it. But I would say I was the exception, in the Lutheran structure, in going to events like that. It's scary for people. I don't think they even saw that they needed it. Their whole way of proceeding was of keeping conflict down. Smoothing. Pastors are great smoothers, I think. You can kind of keep it looking like it's smooth, but when you do that, then things slowly die, I think, in a spiritual sense.

Pastor Bill: Coping with a Powerful Family

Like Frank, Bill was confronted with infighting among congregation members; it was his burden to deal with a family who tried to assert their dominance in the congregation. Bill, an Assemblies of God pastor, left the ministry when he was 48.

> In the church we had one large family that many people were related to. There was one lady that was kind of the mother hen that was there when they founded the church. I think she had a lot more control, and was able to control them. And there were a lot of problems created from that. After she died, there were several relatives, daughters and stuff like that, seemed like it got to be real competitiveness for control, and that created a lot of problems. Sometimes, if anyone else tried to do anything, any ministry within the church, it was like they would cause problems or complain or at times it even felt like they were trying to run some [other church members] off.

In spite of these conflicts, the church grew under Pastor Bill's leadership. Attendance increased from about 20 to 100 on some Sunday mornings. But tensions escalated and Bill, while talking to his district superintendent about other church issues, discovered that the same family had made complaints about decisions he had made. Bill received little support from his superintendent:

> I just asked him about it. To be honest, I really hadn't considered leaving. I would have just stayed there. It had gotten to a place, it would have been pretty hard to starve me out or run me off. I had been there long enough it didn't bother me a whole lot. I mean, I was a little tougher-skinned than what I was a few years ago [*laughs*]. But I didn't get a whole lot of support from him and I just asked him, "What do you think?" He said, "Well, you've got it to a place where you've got money in the bank, you've got a lot of people coming there, and there's a lot of good things going on. To be real honest, I'm afraid if you stay there, with that family upset, if they leave, you're going to lose half your congregation, with those they take with them. It's not going to be good for the church." He didn't ask me to leave, but he was saying that he *was* concerned about it.

But I really felt like there wasn't a whole lot of support there. Because before, when I first went there and some problems came up there, where I had really had to stand my ground, and we had 20 people there and no money in the bank, and working outside the church and everything, his answer was a lot different. It was, "You do what's right and stick by your guns. You just do what's right and if everybody leaves, it's not important. If the church is supposed to be there, there'll be somebody come." And so I kind of felt just not really supported there, and it was kind of a shocking deal for me.

Bill reflected on what he might have done differently to resolve the many conflicts:

I probably would have done more stuff openly, and let them know what I was doing a little more openly probably than what I did. Because I had just gotten to talk to a couple of them, and there were some of the others I wanted to talk to, I just hadn't gotten around to talking to them. And we had changed some of the ministry stuff we were doing around there of just going a *little* different direction. We were looking at doing some home cell groups at night, and not taking anything away, but just trying to add to what we were doing, kind of an outreach type deal. And they felt like we were bypassing them on doing some stuff. There were some of them that were already doing more than what they could effectively do in the way of ministry or had time to do, and when we would try to start the new ministry and I hadn't asked them to do something, I think they probably felt rejected. I probably didn't do a real good job of trying to explain to them until they were already upset. So I'm sure there were a lot of things that I could have done differently.

So Bill left the church and the ministry. Although he now sees things he could have done differently, he also wishes he'd had more support from his district superintendent:

To be real honest, I *really* felt like a lot of it came down to a money issue. Because when we didn't have anything, he said, "The main thing is you do what's right. And if everybody leaves, that's all right. The main thing is you do what's right." We'd had an issue before of some people not married and living together in a situation there, and a bunch of them had threatened to leave. And we had a very large Hispanic population in the community and in the church, probably half Hispanic. But at the beginning, the first problems, he said, "You do what's right." And we did, and our church grew from it. And I think ultimately there were a lot of them that had a lot of respect for a decision that I had to make; they saw that I had to make it. So it worked out. But later on, I think he was a lot more concerned about the numbers of people coming there and the church was doing well and don't rock the boat with them now. We'd grown it up and built a lot. We'd gone through some building programs and built everything debt-free and had a good deal of money in the bank for that little church.

Now Bill feels an ardent desire to reach out to the unchurched, yet he has not returned to pastoring a local church.

Pastor Phil: No Support from the Bishop

Pastor Phil, a United Methodist, left pastoral ministry at age 46 after 17 years of service. He and his wife were both pastors at the time, serving different churches. Troubles in his congregation were worsened by a lack of support from the bishop. Phil's story illustrates how congregational conflicts can become problems with denominational officials and how a pastor needs support in a conflict situation.

I had been serving churches for 17 years. I turned 40 a couple of years before all this, and started doing a little inventory. This is a tiny little church, I think I ought to be in something bigger by now. I'm still at minimum salary after all these years. What's going on? I asked the district superintendent. You know, you learn you might not want to ask certain questions; you might not like the answers! But I got so frustrated I wanted to ask. "What's going on? Am I incompetent? Why am I still at this level?" He said, "Because you're half a clergy couple. Because you're harder to place." I said, "Okay." And then he said, "But you know, maybe this would be a good year to try to move and see what happens." Well, they moved me to this strange little church [*laughs*], very ingrown little place, bigoted little place. I was frustrated and tired and didn't want to put up with it, got very depressed. I was there two years. Things were actually going very well, I thought. The last year I was there, we had a 10 percent net membership increase. We had a great year financially, paid all the bills and had $7,000 left over in the bank. Great for a little bitty country church. I gave them the biggest vacation Bible school they'd ever had, the biggest Sunday school class they'd ever had. But what I forgot is, when you're the big fish in a small pond, and the water starts to rise, you got to do something. Well, one member of the church got on the phone and started telling everybody I was sleeping around and invading the funds. And I found out about that and thought, "I don't need to put up with this, I want to go somewhere."

We have a new bishop, and he doesn't like moving people. My district superintendent understood; "Okay, let me put you up for this place." Recommended me for a couple *good* appointments, much bigger than anything I'd ever served! But this bishop said, "He doesn't deserve this." And he appointed me to a church that would have been like a two-hour commute from where my wife was serving (we had an eight-year-old daughter), and a 20 percent pay cut. I said, "I can't do this."

Phil resigned his ministry and took courses in computing; he now works as a technician.

And just before we left, the district superintendent told me, "I was sorry you got this church. I know how mean they are. I wish I could have done better for you." They had crucified my predecessor. You know, some animals, once they get the taste for human blood, that's all they need.

Phil feels as if he was betrayed by both the congregation and by his denomination. He thinks he might have been able to continue had he been supported by his denomination.

I expected the betrayal from the parish, I expected there to be people who wouldn't like me. It was a matter of "I'm going to come into your church, I'm going to do my very best to help it become what I think God wants it to be. That means I'm going to make changes. People are not going to like that." That's okay, that's what my job is. But if I had the backing of the hierarchy, if they're sending me in there to try and help this church become what God wants them to be, if they're going to back me up, then we can work with that. But if they're going to kick me out because I cannot keep people happy when the only way to keep people happy is to get up every Sunday morning and pat them on the head and tell them, "You're wonderful and everything you're doing is wonderful. Your bigotry is wonderful, your exclusivism is wonderful," which is what I would have had to do to be a success in this place. Yeah, I feel I could have handled it from the people but I needed the backing from the denomination. I didn't get it.

Two Recurrent Themes in Conflicts

In the accounts of pastors faced with congregational conflicts, two themes came up again and again. One was that churches, even those that say they want to grow, are unwilling to make the changes necessary to do it. For example, Pastor Bill, who told about problems with a controlling family, also observed that too many people had little interest in reaching out to others:

> It seemed like people were a lot more concerned with kind of a self-centered attitude of what we're going to do for *them*. I guess the biggest thing was just an absence of trying to reach the lost. We were at a smaller church, made lots of sacrifices over the years. And you just get tired of making sacrifices and sacrifices and everybody else wanting to give out of their excess or whatever, a lot more concern with what you had to offer them instead of what they had to offer other people. *And* very little change in them. I'm not saying that I didn't feel they were saved or anything, but of just, "Well, we've got our ticket punched to heaven, and this is fine."

Here is another case. Pastor Susan, a Presbyterian, accepted a call to a congregation that said it wanted more local, hands-on missions work, a more active youth group, and new members who would bring more diversity. She found them unwilling to expend the effort such changes required.

> I think they wanted what they said they wanted, in a sort of like, "Gee, it would be great," kind of thing. But I don't think they understood that to really get what they said they wanted, they needed to be really involved in it, and really committed. So a congregation can't say, "We *really* want to do mission," and then not want to show up to do it or not want to participate in figuring out what that is. It was almost like they wanted to feel good about what their church was doing, but they weren't doing it. And they had to understand that *they're* the church.
>
> They hired me to be their social conscience. None of this was conscious on their part, of course. And certainly there were things that happened that were great and that people really rose to the occasion, especially stuff with the youth. In fact, through the youth group, I found people who really wanted to do mission. The kids had energy for it, and we did great things. And the congregation as a whole took pride in that. But it stopped short of them also joining in. So I could take 12 youth to a week-away mission program working with homeless people in rural Virginia, but I would be lucky if I could get three adults to do Habitat for Humanity once a month. It was that kind of thing.

Pastor Phil's congregation resisted growth especially if it meant reaching out to people of color. He related his frustrations:

> The question that keeps coming to me is: How do you restart a little church that stays little? If you're offering the love of Christ to your community, somebody's going to respond. Well the answer is, you don't offer the love of Christ to your community. You have what I call a "two-family chapel" and that's what so many of these little churches are. The first meeting we had with them, everybody explained, legitimized their being there, by saying, "I'm related to the Smith family this way," "I'm related to the Jones family that way." This is where the Smiths sit, this is where the Joneses sit. They don't want strangers, they don't want new people. They advertise

themselves as the friendly church on the hill, and they think they are, because they're real friendly *to each other.* When I was offered the church, I called my mother and I said, "Well, the district superintendent says they want to grow." And my mother said, "That's good." I said, "It doesn't mean a thing." She said, "It doesn't?" I said, "Mom, I tell everybody I want to be skinny. Big deal. I don't want to diet and exercise, but I'd love to be skinny." Well, that's the way so many of these little churches are. And I made the mistake of causing some growth. I had a meeting with my trustees one night and the chair of the trustees and I were talking after the meeting. And I was so impressed with how many people are moving into the community. And he said, "That's right, we've got a lot of people moving in, but we can't get the right *kind* of people to move here." Meaning the right color. My first board meeting they were talking about the possibility of black people coming to church. And in United Methodism, if you want to join the church, the pastor says "yea" or "nay." The pastor has the authority. And like I said, I've been in this for a while. I was tired of putting up with all the garbage. And I just told him, I probably signed my death warrant right there. I said, "As far as I'm concerned, anybody Jesus died for is welcome in my church." I was probably done for from that moment on.

The conflicts these pastors faced came over the difficulties involved in making changes, reaching out to the community, and growing. Small congregations, research suggests, often want to grow but are unwilling to step out of their "comfort zone." In many cases, an "old guard" that has controlled the church for years no longer has the energy or interest necessary for new programs, but is unwilling to turn the reins over to newer members. For pastors hoping to revitalize the congregations, the lay leaders' verbal assent yet practical resistance often breeds the tension that drives pastors out.

A second recurrent theme is an assumption that if there's a conflict in the church, the pastor must be somehow at fault. Pastor Frank talked about the impressions pastors coping with conflict get from their denominational leaders:

There is a sense I had, and I think it's common to pastors, that if there is a conflict, then you [the pastor] did something wrong. It's very subtle. It's like, "If you were really good at this, this wouldn't happen." And there are enough guys around where in their congregations there isn't a big conflict, that it *works* to some degree to view it that way. And in certain settings, that's how it is. If you've worked through some stuff, and you've been there for a while, you can have some pretty productive years when there isn't a lot of big-time conflict. You know, there is always little stuff.

Pastor Phil has wondered about the possibility that United Methodist bishops have had the good fortune to serve only healthy congregations and can't relate to the devastation of pastors in destructive churches.

One problem is people who end up serving these clergy-killer churches, they never become bishops. The people who become bishops, the people who become district superintendents, somehow they have lucked into the nice, friendly, easy appointments. One of the fine members of our conference, when he became a district superintendent and had to deal with all the churches in the district, and he saw all the ugliness that some of these little churches can perpetrate, he told his friends, "I am *never* going back to the local church. I might get one of these churches." He'd never served one before. He had kind of lucked his way through the nicer ones. So maybe the bishops don't know, they haven't been there. The people who serve these churches become branded as losers and they never get to be superintendents and bishops.

Reflections

As these interviews attest, conflict in the congregation can have devastating effects on pastors. We identified the five topics on which it is most destructive — both to former and current pastors: pastoral leadership style, finances, changes in worship style, interpersonal conflicts, and issues about new building or renovation.

Conflicts arise in the lives of all pastors, and they will not be going away. Possibly what is unique in the lives of pastors who resigned due to conflict is that these persons lacked the support and understanding from denominational leaders that might have sustained them. All of the former pastors regardless of denomination — from relatively autonomous Assemblies of God pastors to carefully regulated United Methodist ones — *all of them* need help and encouragement in handling conflicts in their congregations.

Main Findings

Pastors who left the pastorate because of conflict
in the congregation

1. Comprised 27 percent of the total
2. Felt high levels of stress and pressure
3. Were less satisfied with their local church experience
4. Were more likely to have staff conflicts if they were associate pastors
5. Experienced more conflict than current pastors, but in the same areas: pastoral leadership style, finances, changes in worship style, staff conflicts, and building or renovation issues
6. Were not unique in experiencing conflict, since 39 percent of all ex-pastors reported major church conflict

---

6 Pastors Who Had Conflict with Denominational Leaders

Instead of getting paranoid and angry, the denominational elders need to wake up and say, "Here's a person in trouble. What can we do?" We have to put the same effort into saving our clergy that we put into saving our lay people.

A 49-year-old United Methodist man

Unresolved conflict, as we have seen, is ministers' most prevalent motivation for leaving local church ministry. Having reviewed in the last chapter the issues producing conflict with congregations, we turn our attention now to a second major locus of conflict: interactions with denominational leaders. Ex-pastors who left primarily because of conflicts with denominational officials or disillusionment with their denomination comprise an estimated 10 percent of our sample.

Looking at denominational variations, we found that United Methodist clergy were more likely than others to leave because of denominational conflicts. About 20 percent of the United Methodists in our sample left parish ministry because of issues with their denomination. The Assemblies of God pastors were next highest at 10 percent, followed by ELCA ones at 9 percent and Presbyterian and LCMS clergy at 3 percent each. These percentages represent pastors who were motivated to leave *primarily* because of denominational conflict. Others had conflicts with denominational officials, but those conflicts were not their primary motivation for leaving parish ministry. The numbers are not precise, yet the comparisons suggest that denominational issues are relatively more important to United Methodist pastors leaving the local church.

In quite a few cases congregational and denominational conflicts were intertwined. A problem in a local church can easily expand to include bad feelings toward and distrust of denominational officials like district superintendents or presbytery executives. Conflicts may also spill over in the other direction, that is, from denominational officials to local churches, but we saw few cases of that. In this chapter we give our primary attention to the experiences of the ministers for whom denominational conflict appeared to be the *main* motivation for leaving.

Conflicts have two sides, and it is important to hear the voices of judicatory officials as well as of pastors. Through focus groups and interviews we listened to judicatory officials in all five denominations. They did not have the opportunity to respond case-by-case to the ministers' stories recounted here; they could only give their general insights and tell of various experiences. Nevertheless, their comments provide an important perspective, which we will show in Chapter 10.

Responses to Survey Questions

In our survey we asked three questions directly related to attitudes toward the denomination. Table 6.1 on page 100 shows responses to two of them. (Detailed responses are in Tables C.4 and C.5 in Appendix C.)

Not being supported by denominational officials was given as a factor for leaving parish ministry by 42 percent of the respondents. It was presented as part of a series of twelve questions about motivations for leaving; it came out third highest, surpassed only by feeling drained by demands (56 percent) and feeling lonely and isolated (51 percent). For United Methodists it was the number one reason for leaving, named in 54 percent of the cases. Former pastors of the ELCA were next highest at 45 percent.

The second statement in Table 6.1 tells us that half of our respondents said they could not speak openly with their denominational officials. United Methodists again had the highest level, at 63 percent. The next highest was from Assemblies of God pastors with 58 percent, followed by ELCA pastors with 47 percent. We were surprised that a higher percentage of Assemblies of God ministers had problems speak-

Table 6.1

Responses Regarding Denominational Officials

How important was each of the following possible reasons why you left your position in local church ministry? (Percent "Great importance" or "Somewhat important")

	All	UMC	PCUSA	ELCA	LCMS	A/G
I was not supported by denominational officials.	42	54	35	45	37	38

Do you agree or disagree with these statements? (Percent "Strongly agree" or "Somewhat agree")

	All	UMC	PCUSA	ELCA	LCMS	A/G
In my last pastoral ministry position, I felt I could not speak openly and honestly with denominational officials.	50	63	41	47	40	58

ing with their denominational officials than did Presbyterian and Lutheran ministers, and we inquired about it in our personal interviews.

We also asked people to tell us the motivations or feelings that led them to make the decision to leave church ministry. Conflict with denominational officials or lack of denominational support was the second most frequent response out of 16, surpassed only by leaving because of seeing a new ministry opportunity. All five denominations were similar, but for United Methodists it was the number one motivation reported. (For a list of all responses by denomination see Table C.3 in Appendix C.)

We wondered if feeling a lack of denominational support was something limited to those who had left parish ministry, or if current ministers feel it as well. Table 6.2 on page 101 compares current and former ministers in their levels of satisfaction with denominational support. Thirty-nine percent of current pastors said they were very satisfied with the support they received from denominational officials, compared with 18 percent of former pastors. Clearly current ministers feel much more support from their denominations than do the resigned, but fewer than 40 percent were very satisfied — a relatively low level (see Table C.6 in Appendix C for more data on former pastors' levels of satisfaction). The need for more support from denomi-

Table 6.2

Levels of Satisfaction in Ministry Reported by Former and Current Pastors

At present (in the final years of your last local church ministry position), what is (was) your level of satisfaction with the following? (percent "Very satisfied")

		All	UMC	PCUSA	ELCA
Support from your	Former	18	9	21	24
denominational officials.	Current	39	39	38	40

national officials is something both active pastors and ex-pastors feel. Table 6.2 shows that resigned United Methodist pastors expressed the least satisfaction with denominational support. Only 9 percent said they were very satisfied or somewhat satisfied with the support they received from denominational officials, compared with 21 percent of resigned Presbyterians and 24 percent of resigned ELCA ministers.

A possible gauge of the level of dissatisfaction with any denomination is the percentage of ex-pastors who left it after leaving the pastorate. That is, some of our respondents not only left local church ministry but left their denomination as well. Table 6.3 below shows the percentages. In all, 24 percent of respondents were no longer affiliated with the denomination they had served as pastors. Eight percent said they now had no church affiliation, and 16 percent were affiliated with another denomination or church (including nondenominational churches). United Methodists were most likely to have left their de-

Table 6.3

Current Affiliation of Ex-Pastors Who Left Their Denomination

	All (%)	UMC (%)	PCUSA (%)	ELCA (%)	LCMS (%)	A/G (%)
Ex-pastors who are now affiliated with another denomination	16	19	7	16	13	24
Ex-pastors who said they have no denominational affiliation	8	14	1	8	13	6

nomination (33 percent) and Presbyterians least (8 percent). We do not know exactly what drove so many United Methodists to leave their church or what keeps so many Presbyterians loyal to theirs.

If they joined another denomination, which one? Pastors who left the Assemblies of God generally left for Pentecostal or independent churches. That is, they moved to churches similar to the Assemblies in theology and organization. LCMS pastors who left most often affiliated with the ELCA, while ELCA ex-pastors were most likely to move to the PCUSA or to the more liturgical Episcopal and Roman Catholic Churches. A few ELCA ex-pastors moved in a more theologically liberal direction, joining the United Church of Christ or the Unitarian Universalist Association. Presbyterians rarely changed denominations.

By comparison, United Methodist ministers moved to denominations covering a broad doctrinal range — including Roman Catholic and Episcopal churches, Baptist and independent churches, the United Church of Christ, even the Bahā'ī Faith. Why so many United Methodists changed and why they disproportionately moved in different directions is unclear, but it may be a result of the diverse theological perspectives present in United Methodism. Comments from two United Methodist ministers illustrate this diversity. First, a woman who left parish ministry at the age of 44:

> I felt the denomination was unable to stand for their doctrine and polity. They were too interested in not offending the membership rather than kindly and lovingly supporting the clergy as they call their members to be a changed people, to live in spiritual holiness. I really doubt, after studying [John] Wesley [the founder of Methodism], that he would recognize or associate with the UM church today.

A man who left at age 33 had a markedly different opinion:

> I was frustrated with "mainline Protestant" pastoral ministry. My personal faith, theology, and life philosophies differed from denominational goals, statements of faith, and the assumption of what Protestant ministry and belief entails. In all honesty I had become more Unitarian in my thinking than Methodist. Reconciling this with my given affiliation was becoming more and more difficult. I have also been quite disgusted with the narrowness of church

stances on what I believe to be normal, healthy human sexual orientations and practices.

To sum up, although concerns about lack of denominational support were expressed in all five denominations, they were most frequent among United Methodists. We conclude that the more a pastor's career is determined by his or her denomination, the more conflict that pastor will potentially feel with denominational leaders. In addition, the more a pastor's life is largely independent of denominational leaders (as in the Assemblies of God), the less support he or she can expect. Theological pluralism may also be a contributing factor. Our interviews with former pastors of all five denominations gave us insights into their experiences.

Pastor Scott: A Call for Help Ignored

Scott, a 41-year-old ELCA pastor, described his frustration and disappointment with his denomination's support when a staff conflict arose. While serving a growing church with many employees, Scott and his colleagues became worried about repeated inappropriate behavior by the senior pastor. This happened while the church was in the midst of a building campaign. Staff members approached the bishop but were rebuffed.

> The bishop has a real reputation of being a wonderful, caring person, but an avoider of conflict. And his staff was very loyal and did what they were supposed to do and protected him. I think what disturbed me was, in my opinion, this was a clear case of a lack of accountability, a leadership crisis in the congregation. And the synod and the bishop and the lay leadership saw that there were other priorities that were higher than those. And for me, those are the highest priorities in leadership and in ministry. And if bricks and mortar, building programs, new ministry ventures, whatever they may be, take precedence over that, then I don't really need to be a part of that.

Scott felt a pastoral obligation to try to resolve the church's leadership problems regardless of the price he might pay personally:

While I was going through that, I had my own support network, I had people whom I had known for years in ministry and gone to seminary with. They said, "You're probably doomed there; you will not survive this call. You need to think about the repercussions for what you're doing and understand that going in." And I sort of knew then that I would move on, that I probably would not survive where I was. But I thought that this was what we should be about. There was also a history in this congregation of dysfunction. They'd had a previous pastor just disappear for about two weeks; they couldn't find him. So I thought, this is one of these classic examples of some kind of cycle of leadership and congregational dynamics going on that needs to be broken. And I, along with other staff members, felt it was necessary to do that. The bishop didn't want to hear it. I lay most of the responsibility not on the senior pastor for his behavior, but on the synod and its inability to respond appropriately. It took a long time to get to that point.

As the church staff struggled, neither the bishop nor anyone at the synod expressed concern or offered any help.

I think the synod understood very clearly what was going on. Nobody ever came forward to me and said, "How are things going?" This is what I finally realized after a period of time: there were no staff people at the synod saying, "We understand what's going on. How are you doing with this? What are your plans for the future?" There was none of that, no conversations like that. And I would go golfing occasionally with the bishop with some friends. He would never discuss it. It was like just a nice day on the golf course, never discuss anything with me. He didn't ask me to come in or ask how I'm doing. And at that point, after a while I thought, "Hmmm, okay, I'm done here. Time to move on."

Scott recognized the importance of a support network comprised of both officials in the hierarchy and peers.

I think you have to build your own network of support within the church. But that can only go so far unless that network includes people who are in positions of leadership that can either find you a new call, find a new position, or help change the situation that you're in. My support networks were basically peers that weren't in positions of authority over me. And that can only go so far. It's wonderful to have friends saying, "Oh, you're being courageous, I really admire what you're doing. I'm here for you. When can we have lunch? When can we get together?" But it's another thing to have the congregational president or the council or the bishop or his staff say, "This is what we're going to do about this. This is where we can go. How are you doing?" That is a whole other network. And that group, that kind of level, was not supportive of me. You need both. You really need both. It's not that they weren't polite and cordial and kind when we were in public. But the phone never rang, either at my home or at my office, from the bishop or his office in the whole time. It never rang.

Frustrated, Scott decided to remove himself from the roster so he could step back and consider whether he wanted to continue in parish ministry. Later he decided to return to the roster, only to be rebuffed.

I made a decision to leave. I called the bishop and I said, "I just want you to remove me from the roster. I need to separate myself completely from the church to make some decisions about whether I really want to be a part of it. I don't want any ties to it at this point that would shape my decision." He said, "That's fine, you have my endorsement if you ever want to come back." I said, "I appreciate that." And I didn't think much of it at that point. So I left kind of not quite knowing whether I permanently wanted to leave or not. And then, after a period of time, kind of deciding, "Okay, what do I want to do now?" I decided that I wanted to go back on the roster and probably do interim ministry. And I met with the candidate committee here in the synod. I went over for a meeting and I had to go discuss with them getting back on the roster. That meeting did not go well, in the sense that I basically told them everything that I've told you. And their decision was to not say no to me, that I couldn't get back on the roster, but that I had significant anger issues with the church that I needed to deal with before they would put me back on the roster. And I said, "Yeah. Don't you think that's reasonable?" At that point, I guess maybe that was the critical moment. They didn't say no. They said, "Yes, you have wonderful skills and wonderful gifts and you have wonderful ideas about the church. And you've served these other congregations in our synod and people have really enjoyed your time there. But this issue you need to deal with." And I thought, okay.

They're also not really willing to kind of deal with me and everything that comes with me as a leader in the church. I had met with a couple of counselors just to kind of sort some things out, met with some colleagues. And I kind of got comfortable with the idea that it was okay to not be involved in full-time ordained ministry any more. And since then, I've been enjoying it. I'm going back to school to get a credential in teaching high school. My family still worships at an ELCA church.

Though he is involved in his current parish, Scott limits his commitments.

I teach an occasional class. Actually, their pastor went on sabbatical two summers ago and he asked me to do the interim. So I did a three-month sabbatical interim for them two summers ago — which was really hilarious because the pastor sits on the candidacy committee and I said to him, "I'm a little confused here. You trust me with your congregation for three months while you're gone. The bishop doesn't seem to have a problem with this, yet both of you sat on a candidacy committee meeting and decided that it wasn't appropriate for me to be put back on the roster. He said, "Well, the bishop doesn't have a problem with that." And I said, "Fine, that's for you to decide." I needed the money at that point, and I thought, "Your money is as good as anybody else's. If you don't have a problem with this, if you don't see some incongruity here, then so be it." And so I served for the summer.

Scott imagines that more open communication and a different hierarchy of values might have kept him from leaving parish ministry.

Looking back, I think what probably could have kept me in ministry is if we'd gone to the bishop, and he had said, "We need to meet with the senior pastor. We'll sit down together, we'll bring all parties together in a room and find out what's going on." And then at least my voice would have been heard and other staff members' voices would have been heard. He could have heard the pastor's story. The bishop could have been there as an authority figure, because the senior pastor was my boss. The bishop could have played mediator or heard the concerns and the council leadership could have all been there and heard, "This is what we have. What's going on here? How can we fix this?" And that path was not taken. And I'm not going to crawl inside the bishop's mind and wonder why he chose not to do that. He just chose not to do that. And there were consequences.

The loss was tremendous. And what was accomplished? A 6.5 million dollar sanctuary got built; the bishop got to stay bishop for the rest of his term, and [was] well liked and loved; the senior pastor got a new call making more money and [serving] a bigger congregation. So the church spoke volumes about what it valued. And it destroyed relationships: mine with the church; mine with other people in the congregation; close friends for 25 years who no longer speak to each other because of this. What's going on here? That's sick! It gives me the willies just thinking about it.

Based on his experiences, Scott is critical about how the church hierarchy interacts with the local church, but he doubts that there is much motivation for change.

I don't know what the vested interests of the synodical leadership are. I mean, I kind of have a hunch of what they are, from my own experience. But I don't know that there is enough motivation for leadership to change. What's the carrot out there for a bishop to deal with a situation like I had, or to be supportive of my story? I don't know what the incentive is for him or her. What causes one to change one's behavior? Severe pain or the possibility of something new in the future that is better than what you have. I don't know that what they're experiencing isn't enjoyable for them. The synod leadership has a tremendous amount of power. They've surrounded themselves with support groups that say what they need to hear. And so I don't know when an outside voice comes in and kind of says, "I'm asking you to be accountable for behavior that I see happening." If that doesn't fit, if that's seen as a challenge and a threat, what's the incentive? They'd rather silence that and keep the status quo.

I know they get a lot of pastors who want to see radical change in the church on issues of sexuality and you-name-it. And they probably get bombarded with crisis in those areas and they just kind of become numb. And they don't know what to do. They're stifled by the fear, and I don't even know if this is a legitimate fear of some kind of lawsuit.

The bishop said, "The senior pastor is very smart. He knows how the system works. He may just get himself a good attorney and think that we've slandered him in some way and the church would have to defend itself." And that was in the first meeting. In the second meeting, I can remember the staff saying, "A year ago, we would have done something about this. But we've become wise now." Meaning what? You're not willing to take on serious issues in the church any more for fear of what? Well, for fear that a flagship church in the synod has a major crisis. And what does that say? What does that speak about the synod and about the church in general? There's money involved, there's finances involved, there's political positions involved, there's reputations involved. Everything that some of these folks have built their lives on. Why would anybody want to touch that? Well, I did, I poked around too much.

Scott's story illustrates a range of often overlapping frustrations experienced by many pastors: the lack of interest on the part of church officials in hearing from pastors or supporting them, the inability of pastors to garner support or advice when in a quandary, and the subsequent removal from the roster of clergy because of this system.

Pastor Evelyn: A Losing Encounter with an Unanticipated Foe

A second example is Evelyn, a 54-year-old United Methodist pastor who faced different dilemmas, some unique to the United Methodist Church. As a licensed local pastor she followed her denomination's prescribed pathway to become an associate member, which is a permanent status for local church pastors who are not ordained. But a national committee decided not to award Evelyn associate member status.

I was called a *local pastor* and I was serving in a local church. I don't have a master's of divinity and I wasn't fully ordained. But in the Methodist church you can become a local church pastor by doing some other things. You go to licensing school, after which you are licensed but not ordained. Then you're asked to go to a "Course of Study," which is a seminary course of study that does not lead to a master's degree. You go for five years for four weeks a year. So you're actually going to school while you're serving, and you learn practical things. And you learn intellectual things. It's not on a graduate level. It's made a little bit easier so that older second-career people can do it. The purpose is to get people into small churches, to serve small churches and to get them somewhat educated and somewhat Methodist educated.

I did that and I did very well at it. I got what they call seminary credit, which means that if you decide to go to seminary you can use that for credit and get a master's degree. Well, anyway, I did that and then the next step for local pastors on a national level is, you can become what's called an associate member. An associate member is somebody who is not fully ordained. That's sort of the next step after you've completed the Course of Study school. You are also required to take some seminary courses to do that. So I completed that and started taking seminary courses.

Meanwhile, I went before a routine committee for ministry. There was a person that came on to that committee who for some reason was extremely hostile. He attacked me and was rude to me and accused me of a lot of things. And it didn't amount to anything. He made fun of what I do for my leisure time. It was nothing about my ministry in the local church. It was attacking my leisure time, that I didn't spend enough time with people. Well I'm an introvert. I deal with people all day long in the local church. When I [have] time off, I like to spend time with my family and I like to cook. I have to spend time cleaning my house and stuff, so that's what I said instead of hanging out with friends.

I tried to follow the recommendations he made that I didn't really agree with. Looking back now, I should have stuck up for myself more. But I didn't. I just toed the line. The next year I came back and I got a committee that he wasn't on. They approved me. No problem. The next year he was back on the committee, and he was attacking me again. I went back and he asked the question, "Is there any reason why we should approve you?" I just told them about some people that I really connected with. And so they approved me, very provisionally with reservations. I don't know what was going on. This one guy has been attacking me but anyway it was pretty strange.

The following year, before Evelyn went back to the committee, a crisis arose in Evelyn's church. An older member, a woman who had been in control of much of the church's work, refused to yield to new members.

She just did things her way and she didn't want to do it anymore but she still wanted it done her way. She sort of wanted to get rid of the new people because they wanted to have a say in things, because they were doing all of the work now. You know, it was a hard time for her. She had conflicting desires. She wanted to quit, but she still wanted to keep control. It's hard when she had done so much for the church and been so involved; it was hard for her to just walk away. So she was causing some problems because of that, and instinctively unhappy with me. I really don't think it had too much to do with me, but that kind of led to a crisis. I think that was used against me the last year I went before the committee.

They decided not to approve me, and it was kind of like out of the blue. I had been doing this for ten years. I got my bachelor's in religious studies. I had taken seminary classes. I have completed the five years Course of Study school. Most of this was at my own expense. I did get a little assistance for Course of Study school, but I had done all the rest at my own expense. I had figured that I would be a pastor till I was 70 and I really didn't have any other career track. They just said, "You're done." And it was. They said, "There is no appeal," which there isn't in the Methodist Church. It was pretty bad. I wished I had handled it different; I wish that I had spoken up for myself more, looking back. I should have, you know. I just kind of let them do it to me more than I should have. But there wasn't a whole lot that I could do. I thought it was just outrageous.

Most of the leaders in my congregation were just like hit in the gut. At least three families said, "This is it. We will never darken the door of the United Methodist Church again." No, it was at least four families, and this was a small church. That was a lot. So it almost killed the church because of that. It was just awful.

Evelyn believes that at least part of the reason she was not approved by the committee was an unspoken disapproval of the denomination's use of non-ordained local pastors.

In this annual conference there was a history of not using the local pastors at all. And I think it is very definitely a factor, but it's sort of under the covers. I think this may be why this guy really attacked me. He wouldn't give any reasons. What he said really didn't make any sense. They didn't have any substance. Why did he really attack me? One thing that I think, after hearing stories from other people, is that he just likes the power trip of getting at people. But another thing may be that he has the sort of underlying idea that if you don't have a master's of divinity, you shouldn't be doing this. As a matter of fact, he actually had said that many times. He is openly hostile to the fact that local pastors even exist. He makes no bones about it.

Evelyn continued to serve as pastor in her parish for more than two months after her associate member approval had been denied. The district superintendent wanted to meet with the congregation to explain what had happened. He arranged the visit on a day when Evelyn could not be present.

Well, I shouldn't have trusted him, but I did. So I really publicized it and I asked everybody in the congregation to come, and they came and they were angry. They were very, very angry. They were just, you know, "What are you doing to us?" The district superintendent had always been a really nice guy and who had voted to retain me. When he sat on that committee, he did vote to keep me. He did not vote against me. He came and I don't think this was necessarily his intention at first, but when everybody was angry, he said, "Well, for five years there were issues raised and she did not address them." Nothing could have been farther from the truth! I did everything they asked. The guy on the committee even said, "You did everything we asked." And so he told my congregation this and did it when I wasn't there to defend myself. When I got back to an administrative council meeting and this came up, one guy said, "Well, he said it like there was something every year and every year you didn't do it." And I was just — I went home that night and just cried. I just felt so betrayed. And the district superintendent had always been this really nice guy. I don't think he went there necessarily with the idea of "Well, I will let them know, I will make her the bad guy." But that's what he was doing. It was like everybody was angry, and instead of dealing with that or saying I don't agree with it but this is the way it is, he said that. And that was so wrong. It was not only a lie. It was like telling my congregation I didn't care enough to do what was required or acting like I blew it off. I mean I am the one who had no college and went and got my bachelor's in religious studies. I am the one who went to Course of Study. I am the one who had already taken seminary classes. And I had learned Spanish, so I could do Spanish masses. We had a lot of Spanish-speaking people, and here I was in my mid-40s. I took Spanish. I did everything they asked. I did everything I could.

For him to say *that* was, I think, the ultimate betrayal. Then I said, "That's it. I am walking away from the United Methodist Church." So I went to the Lutheran church and basically have lived happily ever after with that. I still would like to be a pastor. That is where my training is. That's where my passion is.

Though Evelyn's experience is unusual in that she was a non-ordained local pastor, her story raises broader issues. Unchallenged power in the denominational hierarchy, difficulty with confrontation and conflict, and hazy communication all help explain why Evelyn left both local church ministry and the denomination.

Issues Unique to the Assemblies of God

Resigned Assemblies of God pastors, like United Methodists, often said that they could not speak openly and honestly with denominational officials (58 and 63 percent respectively; see Table 6.1). Two characteristics of the Assemblies of God may shed some light on their feelings. First, Assemblies of God pastors work in a culture of independence from higher church structures that is a part of their felt call to ministry. If God has called you to a ministry, they feel, then God will supply all your needs. This includes financial as well as spiritual needs. In other words, nobody should count on a denomination to help them. One pastor described it this way:

> In the Assemblies of God, in my experience, there is such an intense peer pressure to exhibit being this model Christian, that to even share how you felt with another pastor, say about leadership, was interpreted as gossip. Therefore you shouldn't be talking about that kind of thing.

Second, Assemblies of God churches are more autonomous than churches in the other denominations. They own their buildings, for example, and the land on which they are built. They can make many decisions without consulting district officials, and the flipside is that pastors can sometimes be left with little if any support from the denomination. One resigned pastor described the relationship between individual churches and the district:

> Each church is pretty much sovereign. But through the denomination you have a basically what they call council and districts. In the districts, there are leaders that basically are there to support churches, but they don't call the shots at the local church. The only time that the district would step in is if there was gross misconduct or total outright doctrinal issues with the church that were contrary to what the denomination believes in. That's where they would step in. But basically the actual churches voluntarily cooperate in the denomination. They have a choice in selecting pastors and basically choosing what they want to do.

Each denomination has unique practices, traditions, and doctrinal approaches that affect denominational interaction with pastors and congregations. In our study, the United Methodist Church and the Assemblies of God stand out as different from the others, but we should not overemphasize their uniqueness. We found many commonalities among the churches. Former pastors in all the denominations felt the need for support in times of congregational crisis and often feared asking for help lest they be seen as the problem rather than as part of the solution. They experienced an absence of open and honest communication and an inability to give their viewpoints without fearing repercussions. Some believed that pastors are viewed as expendable, that it is easier to replace them than to deal with congregational conflicts that are byzantine in their complexity. Many said that an avoidance of conflict had become a part of their denomination's culture.

Summary

In this chapter we have examined one of two main types of conflict driving ministers out of the pastorate: conflict with denominational leaders. We learned that denominational conflicts are more prevalent among resigned United Methodist pastors than in the other denominations. Our conclusion is a general one: the more a pastor's career is dependent on denominational officials, the more conflict he or she will potentially encounter with those officials.

We also found that 24 percent of our sample had left the denomination in which they served as local church ministers. More United Methodists left for other denominations or no denomination at all.

The problem of how to provide helpful denominational support is complex, and there are no easy solutions. Pastors may find support from family and friends or from other clergy, but these are not a substitute for the support denominational officers can provide. Everyone involved seems to agree that more denominational support is needed, and that institutional innovations are in order.

Main Findings

Pastors who left local church ministry because of conflict with the denomination

1. Comprised 10 percent of the total
2. Were disproportionately United Methodists
3. Were not unique in feeling a lack of denominational support; 42 percent of all who left cited a lack of support from their denomination
4. Felt that their denominational officials were invested in avoidance of conflict

---

Pastors Who Were Burned Out or Discouraged

It seemed like we were fighting the city, we were struggling with the district, and we had enough of our own struggles with different people in the church and different families having problems. . . . And it came to the point where a decision had to be made, and it was to leave.

Andrew, former Assemblies of God pastor

In our research we encountered numerous ministers who told us they left because of strain, weariness, burnout, and frustration. They did not attribute the problem to specific conflicts within the congregation or with denominational officers; their complaints were more general, more colored by self-doubt, and more typical of individuals who are depressed. We lumped these ministers together under the heading of "burned out; disillusioned; felt constrained; sense of inadequacy." Admittedly this is a broad category, but it felt to us like a distinct enough motivation to study separately. The borderline between this category and the one we examined in Chapter 5, pastors who left due to conflict in the congregation, is indistinct; indeed, the two often overlap.

These persons usually felt blocked in some way, either by external conditions (apart from specific conflicts, as in Chapters 5 and 6) or by personal inadequacy. Therefore they were frustrated and saw no solution to their malaise except to leave parish ministry. They expressed feelings of hopelessness and isolation, stating that other people did not help them or even want them in the ministry. Many felt lonely and unsupported. Their distinguishing characteristic is not the kinds of feelings they expressed — which we heard from others as well — but rather the absence of any outward location to place the blame. They expressed less anger than others about the laity, the other staff, or denominational officers.

Twelve percent of the former pastors we studied fell into this category. We compared these persons with all the others and found that they were not unique in gender, age, denomination, or position. They *were* much less satisfied than average in their past ministry position (19 percent, versus 37 percent of others in the sample). They were different than all others in the sample in several key respects, shown in Figure 7.1 on page 117. In sum, they felt more stress due to challenges from the congregation; they felt more lonely and isolated; they felt more bored and constrained in their positions; and they felt more doubts about their abilities as parish ministers. The complaints of these ministers were not directed at denominational officials; in fact, they agreed *less* than average with the statement that "clergy or denominational officials here do not want me." They saw their problems as within their churches — or within themselves.

Excursus: Ideal versus Real Ministry

This is a good point at which to relate an experiment we made with our sample of ex-pastors — the whole sample, not just those who left due to burnout or discouragement. It had to do with the gap between the ideal ministry position as these persons envisioned it and the real ones they were forced to live out. Ever since the earliest research on how Protestant ministers spend their time, done in the 1950s,[1] it has been found repeatedly that ministers hope to devote themselves to preaching, teaching, and pastoral ministry but instead find that they

1. The classic article was Samuel W. Blizzard, "The Minister's Dilemma," *Christian Century* 73 (April 25, 1956): 508-10. It demonstrated that Protestant ministers hoped to devote themselves to preaching, study, and pastoral work, but instead they found they needed to spend the bulk of their time on administration and organizational tasks. For later research in this tradition see Samuel W. Blizzard, *The Protestant Parish Minister: A Behavioral Science Interpretation* (Storrs, Conn.: Society for the Scientific Study of Religion, 1985).

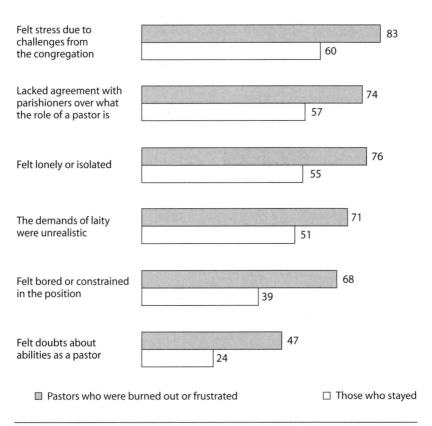

Figure 7.1
Pastors Who Left Due to Conflicts in the Congregation
versus Those Who Stayed

Felt stress due to challenges from the congregation: 83 / 60

Lacked agreement with parishioners over what the role of a pastor is: 74 / 57

Felt lonely or isolated: 76 / 55

The demands of laity were unrealistic: 71 / 51

Felt bored or constrained in the position: 68 / 39

Felt doubts about abilities as a pastor: 47 / 24

■ Pastors who were burned out or frustrated   □ Those who stayed

need to spend the majority of their time on institutional tasks, administration, and program planning. Cherniss found that this problem of being forced to do unwanted tasks, especially tasks outside one's specific professional skill, bedevils all professionals and depletes morale in many fields (as we saw in Chapter 1).

We were able, with our sample, to make a direct test of the hypothesis that a gap between ideal and real time allocation depresses morale. We asked the ex-pastors to tell us how much time they spent in each of four task areas in their last ministry position: (1) preaching

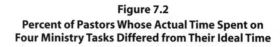

Figure 7.2
Percent of Pastors Whose Actual Time Spent on
Four Ministry Tasks Differed from Their Ideal Time

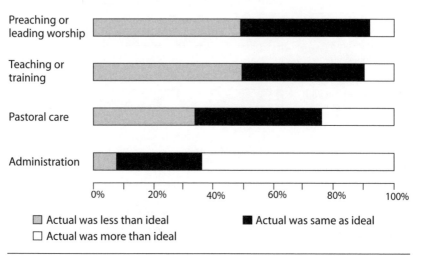

or leading worship, including sermon preparation and special services; (2) teaching or training adults and youth; (3) pastoral care, including visiting; and (4) administration, including planning, paperwork, and meetings. We also asked them how much time they ideally would like to spend on each. By subtracting the one from the other we created four measures of imbalance between ideal and real.

It turned out to be true in our sample, as it has been in past research, that the ministers commonly experienced a gap between ideal and real expenditure of their time. In the areas of preaching and teaching, the actual time they spent was much less than their ideal: on preaching, 8 percent said that the actual time they spent was more than the ideal, while 49 percent said it was less. In the area of teaching, 10 percent said the actual time was more than the ideal and 50 percent said it was less. In the area of pastoral care the gap was smaller: 24 percent said the time spent was more than the ideal, and 34 percent said it was less.

The fourth area, administration, was just the opposite. Sixty-four percent said the actual time spent was more than the ideal, versus 8 percent who said it was less. See Figure 7.2 above.

The five denominations were surprisingly similar in these gaps, with the small exception that the LCMS pastors reported *less* of a gap than did the others between actual and ideal time spent on preaching. The explanation for this is unclear.

Was it true that the greater the gap, the lower the ministers' morale and satisfaction? Yes. But it turned out, to our surprise, that a significant gap *in either direction* predicted a lower level of satisfaction felt by the ex-pastors in their last ministry position. That is, the greater the difference between actual and ideal time devoted to all four tasks — preaching, teaching, pastoral care, and administration — whether actual positions demanded more or less time — the lower the ministers' satisfaction and the more stress they felt in their last job. This finding has seldom been demonstrated empirically in research.

The gap between what ministers would ideally like to do in their work and what they are actually required to do is a problem for seminary educators and denominational officials. It is a structural problem contributing significantly to burnout. We suggest that the first step in alleviating the problem would be to bring the situation to the conscious attention of seminarians and ministers of all ages, so they can search out concrete steps that could be taken.

New Church Developers

Returning to our ex-pastors who left due to burnout and discouragement, one subset of this type was ministers doing new church development. This is a job known to be difficult, stressful, and risky, and the chance of success is never high. It is a job for the bold and the brave, and when a new church does not grow, despite the efforts of everyone involved, the minister who led it feels downcast and defeated. We spoke with a number of Assemblies of God ministers who had been through this experience, of whom Pastor Andrew is one.

Pastor Andrew: Struggling against All Odds

Andrew left the ministry at 37. He started the task of planting a new church with high hopes, but when it went poorly he felt he had to give it up.

I became a Christian at about 22, and I was full-blast into it. My wife was similar. But from the get-go of our ministry, we had come into some really rough churches.

The first church was a church that's been around a long time, in a smaller rural town. I served as an associate there. The people were very controlling; it was *their* church. The leadership of the church was very weak. And I probably came in somewhat green and naïve and thought we need to really follow God and get on the train with God, and I guess it doesn't work that easy [*laughs*]. And so that caused some problems, and I guess I could have handled it better. I was there six years.

And then the district asked us to start a new church, and we agreed to go. This is a pretty monumental task. We were basically told, "Okay, this is where you're going to go. You're going to get one year's worth of insurance, and you're going to get $400 a month. And that's it. You have to get this thing going, you have to raise your own support." Of course, I had to have an extra job. It was a real struggle; we were working ourselves to death! But amazingly, we did get a church going of about 50 after about two years. It was fairly stable, but we had trouble with the city we were in. We wanted to acquire some property and a building and we were just beaten back on every angle every time we changed. The Assemblies of God district, [which] we were hoping to have support from, not monetarily but just some real support, ending up saying, "No, you can't do this, can't do that, can't do this." I said, "Why do you put people in positions and then stop their every move? You put someone in this position, you're trusting them to start this church, then why do you not let them go with it? They're there every day, and you don't even know what's going on, because you're 200 miles away." Getting the report every two months is all they really got. So it became very frustrating.

Andrew was discouraged at the limits the district officers put on him.

My honest opinion is, the person in charge of home missions was a bit on the controlling side. He had some unrealistic expectations. The city we were in was a suburb in western Michigan. It was a fairly affluent area, the land was very expensive, property was expensive, housing, rent was very expensive. And our goal as a church was to acquire property. No, it's not going to be perfect, it's not everything we want, but to get something to get established and then use it as a stepping stone. In five years we could sell it and move on or rebuild or whatever. And the district would say, "No, you should be on Highway 80," which is a major highway, but the land was *so* astronomically high! "We want you up front, we want you to have five acres of land," when we couldn't even afford *one* acre of land. It seemed like their expectations were unreal. That's when I really began thinking: "Why is it you put somebody in here and you trust somebody to mold and shape the lives of these people, but you do not let them have any power or decision as far as how to build this church, what property to take on?" It was a very big question, it became very frustrating. My wife and I had started developing friendships with other pastors that had pioneered a church, because we needed to develop a support group. And we were seeing that the same thing was happening a lot to them, they were really not getting the support and the help they could use from the district. We all began to feel like we were just left out. It was, "Here, you guys do this job" and if, for whatever reason, you become very successful, they were there. But if you were battling, well. . . . And the majority of the pioneering churches at that time were really struggling. The odds were *very* bad.

It seemed like we were fighting the city, we were struggling with the district, and we had enough of our own struggles with different people in the church and different families having problems and whatnot. And then my wife became very ill, so I had that, and I was working two jobs plus the church. And she was working one outside job. And we weren't super people; we weren't supermen. Sooner or later there was going to be a collapse. And it came to a point where there had to be a decision to be made, and it was to leave. And it was a hard decision, but something had to go.

The district said almost nothing. That was very disappointing [*laughs*]. "Sorry to hear that you decided to go." And that was it. They've not done any kind of real follow-up. They haven't said, "Boy, this minister has really been beat. We need to get together with him and show some support. Send a couple cards, make some phone calls, do some follow-up. Get the pastors in the area where he's living to communicate some support and fellowship." None of that happened. I certainly don't expect that they're going to come down here every day and hold my hand or anything like that. But it was pretty traumatic, and they knew it, because I expressed it.

If anybody in my church was going through a trauma, I would have been there and not living in their house but there and checking in at least. But, I don't know, maybe they felt they were doing it. Maybe they think they had done it well enough. I don't know what their real thoughts were, how they felt. It might be totally different than what I think.

We asked Andrew if he thought the job expectation was unrealistic to start with.

Well, I think they began to see that the way they were going about getting these churches started was very unrealistic, because they changed their whole format two years after we left. Instead of sending one pastor in they were sending two. Instead of giving you $400 a month and one year's insurance, they had changed that whole thing and you had to raise X amount of support. You had to go for training. So they realized it was a big failure, to be honest. I think they realized that there had to be some changes. Unfortunately those changes came after probably a lot of people had gotten hurt. The one family that we were really close to that was pioneering a church, they're out of ministry too.

They lost some people. The ones we knew we liked, and we thought they were good people. It's not that the people going to these places were dummies. They were smart people. It was just that the odds were really against them. But it was the way it was being done and handled.

I don't think we were misled. We knew we were going into a situation that was going to be very hard. And the success rate was going to be hard. The biggest disappointment was how, when it all came to an end, the district just wasn't there. And again, I didn't expect them to hold my hand for a year, but we were crushed! That month afterwards, when we had left the ministry, we had nowhere to go, we had no church, it just seemed everything had failed. All our efforts, our time, everything we had put into this was just for naught. And we were just kind of left on the side. It's been probably three years or four years since we left, and my wife will have nothing to do with the church.

Andrew regrets the pain his wife felt during this time.

They wanted her to do too much. She felt the pressure to do more and to be more than *God* wanted her to [*laughs*]. That was a real imposition on who she was to be. I mean, I was filling the pastorate role, and everybody seemed satisfied about that. But they expected her to be as big a pastor as me, and be a preacher and everything. And that's not my wife. My wife is a very quiet person and will be glad to work in the background, but they wanted a female pastor.

We had two girls. It was tough. Considering we were working three different jobs and having kids and trying to keep the house together. I look back, I don't know how I did it. I really don't know how I did it!

Andrew told about a turning point that made him decide to quit:

It was called Black Monday. We had been struggling with the city, we'd been struggling with the district. There came a divisiveness in the church. Our church was pioneered, but there was one family that started from the very beginning. The woman was kind of the impetus that called on the district to get a church in her town. Apparently she felt like it was *her* church and not God's church. She wanted to control, and she had expectations. And I wasn't giving her those controls. It became very divisive to the point where I had to, after counseling with the superintendent, ask her to leave the church. And then came the attack!

She fought back, yeah! [*laughs*] From early on, she was realizing her attack wasn't fazing me very much, and then they attacked my wife and my kids. And that was kind of where the real turning point came. That was where I said, "No, my kids and my wife don't need to be attacked." We took enough guff from a few people there, and it was hard enough. And nobody could appreciate that, and then to throw an attack on top of it.

This woman and the few people that followed her wanted certain things and they thought they knew how to do it. One woman came up to me and said, "I've been in revival, I know revival." And I thought, "Oh, that's so dangerous! You've experienced something with God in the past and I don't deny that and I don't doubt that." But to say, because you've been in the past, you know how to run the future, when God could be doing a whole different thing, I thought was dangerous. But it was that kind of mentality, "I know and you don't know." So that little group did get quite divisive.

Andrew felt that the district official to whom he was responsible provided no help when it was needed, and that as a result some good pastors were lost.

Yeah, he did lose some. I have no idea about his attitude. I really can't answer, because there was no follow-up. When we left, it was just, "Okay, you're done. That's fine." So they just never followed up. Even when we left, I don't think he ever called or anything. It was just, "Okay, you've resigned. Now we've got to find someone else."

A year before we left I called and said, "I'm just about ready to leave. This is starting to kill us." So they were aware of it, but after that initial phone call, I never got a reply or follow-up from it. They should have said, "Oh, there's an alarm going off; we better pay attention to it."

Andrew reflected on his experience:

If we're going to put people in ministry and trust them with touching lives and souls for Christ, they need to have full confidence in them to do everything in regard to the church. And not say that we at the local level cannot make decisions on the direction of the church. The district is so far removed.

Another thing is if we're going to stick someone out in an area, in a ministry that has a really high stress level and a very high failure rate, we need to be there ready to catch them if they fall. And that was not done. It's a tough job, high stress. And there are men and women who will go through years of pain dealing with what happened. My wife is a case of that. She is bitter about ministry in general, yeah. Upset with the district, bitter about ministry. I've talked with her and said, "At some point we have to move on and get over it." But it's been three plus years now, and it doesn't leave too easily.

I love the ministry, as hard as it was. You know, with all the pain and stuff, for me, time has washed some of that away. I don't hurt a lot about it. I wouldn't do the ministry the same way I did back then. I'd be glad to go back into it. But with my wife in the state of mind she's in, I don't think it would be right to bring her back into that. It was a shame that it all went the way it did. But God has a bigger plan and a bigger picture. And we patiently wait and see what God is doing. Because I feel like my life now is not what God has called me to do. Well, we'll see what God's going to do. Just patiently wait. Maybe I'm in my 40-year desert, I don't know. Hanging with Moses for a while.

Andrew left the ministry to work as a salesman for a grocery company, a job he has now held for three years. But the stresses felt by him and by other new church developers were visible, to a lesser extent, in many others. Here is an example of a youth minister.

Pastor Brad: Drained from Overwork

Brad, a Presbyterian youth minister, resigned at age 30 to go back to university for an advanced degree. In his last church he was responsible for a large youth program, a task that overwhelmed both him and his wife. He talked about the burnout youth ministers often feel:

I don't think it's unusual. I think it happens for a lot of people. All the conferences I would attend, they'd always talk about burnout rates of youth ministers. That seemed to be the theme all the time. This is a big issue.

Brad told of his last church position:

The congregation was wonderful, I had no problems with that. They were nice and basically supportive. It was a thousand-member congregation in Texas. I really appreciated the people. But the job description was quite overwhelming. We (my wife and I) did junior high, high school, and college ministries in this large church. And the expectation was not so much that the groups would grow, that was actually very verbally put forth to both my wife and me: that we're not into the groups growing — we just want them to be *maintained*, which was nice. So this was in many ways an ideal situation, and I was very eager for the job. But then, I think after about a year and a half, the programs that they were hoping that we would do would be a separate program every night of the week, one for junior high, one for high school, and one for college. And I tried to combine those, because we were out then three nights a week and I often had session meetings or another meeting. On the average I was not home five evenings a week, and then planning for those meetings was just an incredible amount of work. And then there were weekend trips and each group wanted about one weekend trip a month or so. On the average then, I was gone five evenings a week and then two weekends a month. And then I worked from 7 in the morning until as long as I could, just to keep on planning for all these events. So it really was a lot. And I was trying to pare things down. And there were people saying to me, "You're working so hard, why don't you cut things down?" But then in the same breath, they would say, "I have a great idea for youth ministry!" But they didn't want to help — but they had this idea, which I could never follow up on.

I worked there for a total of four years, but after a year and a half, we thought, "We really need to set our boundaries." And even so, just working that kind of a schedule, and then trying to cut back programs, it wasn't very fun. It got tiring rather quickly. And as I looked at other job offerings in the Presbyterian Church, I kind of appreciated my situation because a lot of entry-level jobs are broader than mine, they'll be for kindergarten through college. I remember feeling so discouraged just looking at those job offerings and feeling like actually I've got it pretty good. I felt like my life was hell, H-E-double-hockey-sticks. But I thought it could be worse. Of course, those might have been smaller congregations, but it was a hard call for us because we really did love the congregation, but we didn't like our lifestyle. And then, when you do that, for every age group we had a roll of say 200 students. And so every night we come home after doing all this work and there would be twelve messages on the machine. It just got to be a lot pretty quick. We really did hang in there, working for two and a half years after we felt like wow, this is really too much. We continued for two and a half years and we were really dedicated to cutting it back, making it manageable, trying to enjoy ourselves. But then it didn't seem like it was working. There were times in there when I thought, "Gee, I could do this for ten years and like it." But I had other interests. I was interested in going back for a Ph.D. program as well. And just that lifestyle — there were times that I really hated my life and I thought "This isn't good."

Through the whole time, Brad's wife helped him constantly almost as an assistant.

She wasn't employed there but she was heavily involved. She was in every evening program that I was involved in, and there were times when she was running one program and I was running another. So when the church hired me they really got two employees, and we really very much did work as a team. We did everything together. She loved junior highers and really felt like this was how she wanted to spend her time anyway. So the church was just really lucky in that when they got me they got a full-time, top-notch volunteer as well. She enjoyed it.

The reason we left was because both of us, we just felt like it's really too much, it wasn't worth it. It wasn't worth the drain it put on our lives.

Brad tried to warn the senior pastor that he was burning out and couldn't go on this way.

The senior pastor and I had good relations. I would openly talk with him and I told him about my concerns. It never really seemed to get anywhere. We did some major restructuring, but my job was more than a one-person job. They helped try to get me an assistant, but there wasn't a lot of money for that, so I only had someone very part-time and it didn't seem to make much of a difference.

Brad's wife had made a decision some time earlier that their situation could not go on indefinitely.

She said we had to quit, quite early on. And so we said, "Okay, we'll just set a limit on this." And then for three years after, I mean even as recently as last year, we would just breathe a sigh of relief that we're out. "Oh, we would now be in Mexico with 50 people for a week, living in the desert in a tent. Isn't it wonderful we don't have to plan for that and do that!" Taking 50 people across the border and we're responsible for everything — tents and everything. This was a big tradition in the church, everybody loved it, so the expectation was really high but nobody had time to help. So they'd sign up to go but then I'd say, "I need to get tents together for 50 people, can you help?" They're like, "Oh, we don't have the budget for it, we don't have time to help you out." That was a massive project, and that was just one. There was a ski trip and summer camp and it just goes on and on.

We really felt like we couldn't have children [while we were in that job]. That wasn't even an option, really. I mean, people do, of course, but we didn't feel like it was possible.

Are other youth ministers in the same predicament? We asked Brad about this, and he said yes.

Yeah. I could find more than five or ten. It's a very common thing, over and over again. I think it's epidemic, I think it's part of the job. There is something wrong in the church, and not just the Presbyterian church. These youth conferences I would go to were not specifically Presbyterian, although there were lots of Presbyterians there. But everybody had the same kinds of issues — work all the time, don't feel the support.

Brad did not find much help from presbytery leadership. The presbytery seemed preoccupied with other things.

They introduce themselves in meetings every year and they say, "Here we have a curriculum center." But our presbytery in particular is overwhelmed with, well, sexual misconduct is a really big issue. Seems like a lot of the people and the resources that they have are dealing with that. So there wasn't a lot of addressing other concerns. "Maybe you're really unhappy in your job and you need to find someone" — that kind of thing never came up. It was always:

"We've got 27 sexual misconduct cases that we're working on dealing with, and we're keeping really busy." That kind of thing.

Brad is now studying for a doctorate in New Testament studies. He is hoping for a career combining academic and pastoral work.

Now I'm in a Ph.D. program. I haven't left the church, I'm still a member of the presbytery, I'm involved in the financing and property committee, and I go to the presbytery meetings. I'm teaching Bible at a junior college. Maybe someday I could be a pastor and a professor, a chaplain and a professor. That's my goal, to teach part-time at a university and then to serve as a chaplain.

Summary

As these cases prove, ministers are at risk for emotional burnout due to the multiple roles they must fulfill and the pressures they feel from all sides. We might go so far as to say that ministry is a high-risk occupation in this respect. All church organizations need to recognize this problem and institute safeguards — which, as we saw in the cases of Andrew and Brad, were sorely lacking.

Main Findings

Ex-pastors who left due to burnout or discouragement

1. Comprised 12 percent of the total
2. Experienced more problems, more stress, more loneliness, and more self-doubt in their last ministry position than other ex-pastors
3. Resembled ex-pastors who left because of conflicts, except that they tended to blame themselves, not others
4. Felt unable to manage work pressures and demands
5. Had often been engaged in a new church development which failed
6. Felt less satisfaction when the time they needed to spend on required tasks differed significantly from their ideal of ministry

---

8 Pastors Who Left Due to Sexual Misconduct

I have often wondered if having an affair isn't a sick way of reliev-ing the stress, that to shoot yourself in the foot is the only way to get out of a terribly stressful pastoral situation you're in. It's "I can't handle this, but I can't say, let me out."

A Presbyterian executive

We encountered 55 ministers who left local church ministry due to sexual misconduct, real or alleged — 6 percent of our entire sample. Perhaps understandably, many ex-pastors gave us vague or sketchy re-sponses when questioned on this topic, so we consider 6 percent a low estimate. (Sexual misconduct was not the only kind we expected to encounter; throughout our research we were also on the lookout for ministers involved in *financial* misconduct, due to the numerous re-ports we have heard of financial irregularities in parishes. Yet we found none in our sample. Financial misdeeds were recounted in sev-eral interviews, but invariably our interviewees were whistle-blowers, not perpetrators.)

All but one of the pastors who left due to sexual misconduct con-fessed to being guilty of the charges against them, and all had been forced to leave parish ministry. All but two of them were men, and all but one of the individuals with whom they were involved were women. (The exception was a teenage boy.) Teenagers were involved in two cases; all the rest involved adults. The most common pattern by far was that of a sexual relationship occurring between a male minister and an adult woman, and in half of the cases the woman was a parishioner, staff member, or church secretary.

The persons in this category were slightly older than average when they left ministry (an average of 46 years, versus 44 years in the overall sample). But they were not different from others with regard to the denomination they belonged to or in their ministry position.

Most of these ministers had histories of marital problems greatly affecting their lives (74 versus 26 percent). More said that they had been dissatisfied with their family life (59 versus 33 percent). These ministers also reported more dissatisfaction with their social life with persons outside of the church, although they did not report greater dissatisfaction with the lay leaders or other staff in their church.

They expressed dissatisfaction with the low levels of support they reported receiving from denominational officials and with their own loneliness and isolation. Nearly half said that a very important reason for their leaving was that "clergy or denominational officials here do not want me" (47 versus 11 percent). The majority reported frequently feeling lonely and isolated (75 versus 57 percent). Marital problems took a toll on them; many said that their spouses had voiced resentment over the amount of time they spent in their ministry (48 versus 26 percent), and many said that they had had too little time to devote to their children (43 versus 31 percent).

Persons in this category felt unsettled and ambivalent about their experiences leaving the ministry. Many showed signs of continued unresolved feelings about the events that led to their departure; many had feelings that seemed ready to burst out. A few of the interviewees were overcome by emotion when they talked with us — a clue to the emotional burdens they bear. Here are two examples.

Pastor Edward: A Past Affair Came to Light

Edward served in parish ministry for 25 years in the LCMS; he was forced to leave at age 50 when a past affair became public knowledge. At the time he was divorced.

> After my divorce I continued there in that church for a couple years. In the process of the divorce, I began to date again, and it was a

woman from out of state. I confided with that woman some personal issues and a past relationship that I had had. So she was hurt by it, and she went to her own pastor, I think, to counsel. I know that she was not wanting to do harm. Well, he took it the next step and he said, "You're telling me a story of sexual impropriety, and I have to report this." He promptly reported it to my district president. It was all past history. However, because he reported it, it brought it to the forefront. So I was surprised when I was asked for an appointment with the president's assistant.

The three of them were there — the woman, her pastor, and the district president's assistant. I think it was the next Monday that I had a meeting with the district president. He insisted that I, first of all, write a letter to the new congregation to which I had just been called, and tell them that I would have to refuse that call. That was fine, I understood that. But then he said he was going to have to make a full disclosure statement to my congregation that, as I said, I had lovingly served and I think had very lovingly embraced me, even going through a divorce. The farewell dinner and the laughter, it was just a festive, delightful occasion! Of course, it was bittersweet for me because I knew what was going on, that I was going to have to step aside in my ministry here, I think he said for at least five years. But I think I was accepting that.

But then he said he had to make this disclosure statement. When you make a statement like that, [it] didn't give any specifics, it just said that there was some sort of sexual impropriety. I said, "That could be interpreted as that I'm gay. Of course in today's world right now with the whole Catholic thing with children, it could be presumed pedophilia." He said, "Well, if we don't say something, they can assume all kinds of things." I said, "I would rather they assume I'm going through severe depression, that I'm alcoholic, or who knows what. But you make a statement like that and you start tongues wagging." I said, "Don't I have any appeal in this process?" And he said, "No." And I said, "Well, we've got this committee for appeals." And he said, "Well, that's only if you're being removed from the clergy roster, and we're not doing that at this point. We're simply telling you that you cannot serve for five years, but you're not being removed from the clergy roster." So that's when I said, "If I were convicted of murder, wouldn't I have the opportunity for appeal?" And he said, "Yes."

I guess [it] felt almost like a public flogging without any kind of an appeal process. I was somewhat accepting of my career being totally diverted, but my reputation, without any opportunity for that appeal process. My income, my family, all of those things were losses then. And it was a hard pill to swallow. Now, I don't deny that there were some behaviors on my part that brought this about. Had I not shared that with this woman that I was dating, we probably would have been married and this would have all been in the past. But that's not the case.

Edward reflected on why the district president felt the need for a full disclosure.

I feel that the Lutheran leadership was probably more aware of the legal ramifications and the lawsuits that were potentially there that the Catholic Church is just now realizing. Our district president had had us all gather at a variety of local meetings to explain their no-tolerance position, which referred to any kind of sexual problems. And they said up front, "We are going to take the word of the person making the allegations before we will that of the clergy." It basically was zero tolerance. So I guess I was aware of that, and I guess the reason for it was to protect the church from lawsuits that could have been damaging. But what I have a problem with is that I had no appeal process.

He didn't give them the specifics. I think it's like in business: you can't reveal why somebody is fired to the next employer because then there might be lawsuits from the other end, because you've broken confidentiality. So they can divulge a generality, but you can't divulge the specifics. That would be my guess as to why. Oh, that's what was devastating to me! I thought, oh, golly, I'd rather stand before them and tell them. And in fact I said [to the president], "I'm willing to go before that council. If you're insisting that this disclosure statement has to be made, why can't I make it? You can be there." Nope, *they* have to do it. But yet I know I brought this upon myself.

Edward talked more about the affair. It was with a member of another church outside the immediate area whom he met in denominational meetings, and it lasted eight or ten years.

The person that I was dating asked, "Well, did you love her?" Yep, I did, or it wouldn't have lasted ten years. Dr. Laura — I listen to her now — would say there's no need. It's past, keep it past, keep your mouth shut. And that's what I should have done. My wife was not aware of it.

Then [after the disclosure] I was granted some psychological profiling and some counseling. It was helpful, but I think it needed to be longer and there was only a limited amount of time. That was after the insistence upon my refusing the call and my being told that I could not serve in any form of pastoral ministry for five years. What happened then, I actually resigned from the clergy roster. I was then offered a job within the same denomination in one of the social service portions of it, where they have nursing homes and other programs, and it's been good.

I certainly don't go out and talk about this. But because of what I guess I'm sensing [is] the nature of your study, I maybe can help. And it's been far enough down the road that I really enjoy where I am in my life right now. I still feel I'm doing ministry in the youth opportunity program which I am now managing. And I love it, I absolutely love it. In fact, I wouldn't go back. People say, "Would you like to go back if you could?" I would be willing to consider what, I guess, way back in seminary they called a worker-priest approach. That always had the greatest appeal to me and I think that I would probably, with more and more congregations that are vacant, I wouldn't mind doing that at all. Now [in this job] I am more free. Now I would not have to feel like my job and my career is at risk if I say what I feel is the gospel or the truth or something that needs to be said. So I would consider that kind of ministry. But I have no desire to go back to full-time pastoral ministry, none whatsoever.

I was talking to my ex-wife this evening. We talk on a regular basis, we see each other. We're friendly. We deal amiably with regard to our three daughters. But I wouldn't go back to that relationship. It was not a healthy marriage for twenty years. And do I regret the affair? No, I felt like it was a very beautiful thing. And this will be hard, I think, for a woman to understand, but this person very much loved her husband and her family and had no intentions of ever leaving. And I never expressed that expectation. She basically loved two men and I loved her, and I really don't have a regret over that love. It was something very significant and I think it kind of kept me going. So the regret that I have is the allegation made, this full-disclosure statement to the congregation, just really made me feel, maybe I deserved it, made me feel like a real slimeball. Without them knowing the facts, they just knew some generality. And that's a regret that I still continue to feel.

There is a need for acceptance and love and intimacy, I think most human beings have, and I needed it then. And my wife just seemed incapable of it, at least in the realm of our relationship. I looked for it elsewhere. I didn't look for it, it happened. I mean, I wasn't out grasping for it.

When I was asked to leave the ministry, at that point I was really devastated. I, for a while, moved away from the area. I was really concerned that this woman not be revealed or identified, that she be protected.

Edward emphasized that the Lutheran district is not nearly supportive enough of pastors. He is not the only one who has needed help.

No. There are others. I don't think there is anywhere near enough support from the district. We talk about forgiveness and restoration in God's healing and I brought this up to the president and he said, "Well, you've got it from God, but that's about as far as it goes. You can be assured of God's grace. But as far as the church is concerned, you've been bad." And so the church as an institution or its leadership, I felt, other than what I got — ten counseling sessions — they basically said, "You're done, you're bad, you're out."

I think the counseling [they offered] is one thing, but that's almost like washing your hands, because there is confidentiality there. And I frankly feel that that, in and of itself, is a way of sort of absolving themselves legally of any liability. I think this all revolves around the church not wanting to expose itself financially to the consequences of lawsuits. And frankly, I don't blame the church for doing that, because they can't afford it, it would be the death of many denominations that don't have nearly some of the assets that, let's say, the Catholic Church has.

I didn't get calls from them to say, "How are you? What can we do? What can the church do to be of support for you?" It was like, well, we've rid ourselves of a bad egg and we've done it in somewhat of a responsible way by sending him off to ten counseling sessions and please don't bother us any more because we really don't want you to taint what's here. And, frankly, I say that somewhat facetiously, but it's probably not a bad thing for the church to be doing. But I do think, because we are individuals, and sinful individuals, that we also deserve, when we've given years of service, some sort of spiritual and emotional support. And I really feel sort of cast aside. I still feel a real sense of this scarlet letter on me when I run into people from there.

Pastor Marvin: Stress Led to an Affair

Another pastor who left due to sexual misconduct is Marvin, an ELCA minister who was forced to resign at the age of 50 after an affair with another staff member. Several stressors had taken a toll on him. We asked about the events leading to his resignation.

> Well, there were really two parts to it. One was my physical and emotional breakdown, and the other was the affair that resulted from that. I had probably been running on about two hours' sleep for the last year before the breakdown. So my decision-making wasn't very good, and a lot of it had to do with me not dealing with past issues of anger toward my father. So I was looking for any kind of encouragement or support, and turned to the one who seemed to be at least listening. The woman happened to be the DCE — Director of Christian Education — at the parish where I was pastor. As I look back on it, I really needed to resign about two years before that, which was before I even knew her, before she ever came to work at the church or anything. But at the time I wasn't aware of that. I see now that I was in trouble emotionally and spiritually, probably about two years prior.
>
> There wasn't a good relationship among the local pastors of our denomination, and when I'd asked for some support from the synod level, the response was that I was uncooperative, and that it would be put in my permanent record that I was being uncooperative. So

there really wasn't any understanding with them, and there wasn't any attempt to try to provide any kind of support.

There was a combination of factors. I look back and realize that within a period of about eight months there were seven major trauma events, any one of which would be considered a lot within one year just by itself, and there were about seven within about a seven- or eight-month time period. And that all kind of culminated all at the same time. One was the death of the best friend of my younger brother — suicide — then there was the death of a teen-ager in the congregation.

My uncle had died when he was 49, and he was the only uncle I had on either side of the family, and that year I was turning 49, and his oldest daughter had had severe heart attacks, and in fact she died just a couple of years ago, and I was very much like my uncle, so I was thinking, "Am I even going to make it to my 49th birthday?" So that was preying on my mind a lot. And then my father had died about six years before that, but I had never really dealt with the anger or with his death or anything.

I started going to a Christian counselor, and I did that for about a year. But I didn't have any option of continuing that, financially. And when I resigned, the congregation was going to decide how to handle my termination and so on, and the bishop's statement was, "We need to be as hard as possible on him, to make him an example for many others." So there was no severance or any kind of support. The day I stopped was the last day I got a check. And it's been al-most four years, and there's been not once that the circuit pastors and not once that the bishop has ever even called to find out how I'm doing and how my wife is doing. I understand that I sinned greatly, and it was wrong and I accept full responsibility for that, but there was never once even an asking of how my wife was doing. Both of us needed support. I think I've kind of moved beyond it, but it hurts that they didn't have any concern for my wife.

Marvin talked about stresses in his congregation.

In our church there was a fair amount of conflict. When I took the call, I wasn't aware of how deep the conflicts went, but some of the conflicts, at that point, were about 20 years old. And I would say there were about five major antagonists who kind of had their own following or whatever. And two of them were elders, so that made it very difficult. So in addition to everything else, there was tension there. After about four years I finally got all the elders to be involved in Bible study, which ultimately made quite a difference and there was significant improvement.

Stress built up, and Marvin had difficulty sleeping.

I would usually work until midnight or 1 o'clock, and I'd usually be awake by 3 or 4 in the morning. And then everything else goes bad. I was drinking a lot of Coca-Cola and eating a lot of chocolate [*laughs*], which compounds the problems.

We lost some members, but we had seven major building programs during that time, and we never borrowed money or anything, and our attendance grew by about 100 on Sunday, and Bible study went from 15 to about 90 in a four-year period. So the church was doing okay. And we were averaging about 12 to 15 new adult members a year.

Marvin raised some issues in the circuit (about which he did not elaborate with us), and this caused tensions with other pastors. This made him think about leaving the area.

Basically I had approached the bishop, asking whether there was an alternative, could I go to another circuit, saying that it was difficult in the circuit. And the only response at that point was, "Then we'll have to put you down as being a troublemaker and non-cooperative." Well, one of the other pastors in the circuit was of a similar mind-set as I was, and so I talked to him about my frustration among the circuit pastors; I didn't talk about my personal issues. And he would always encourage me and say, you know, "You can speak up and I'll be with you" and so on, and what I found over a period of a year, a year and a half, is that he never once said a word to back me up publicly.

And it was about that time that we hired the Director of Christian Education. And we got along. In the process, I found it harder and harder to talk to my wife. A lot of the things that my wife was saying, I was taking and hearing the same things that my father had said to me, 30 years earlier. So in my mind, I wasn't receiving support from my wife; I was being reminded of an area where things weren't right, so I kind of withdrew from her as well. The more I worked at the church, then, the more I was kind of open to finding somebody who would listen to me. In the process, the DCE was having trouble in her marriage. And the first mistake is, that I shouldn't have been the one to do any counseling with her. That was a very poor decision, but like I've said, at this point I wasn't making good decisions.

I think, as I look at it now, if I were a pastor and had a staff member who needed help, I would probably *not* be the one to do it. And I don't think it's necessarily healthy for any staff member to get counseling in that way from the pastor. So that was kind of a major mistake on my part. And I think from that point on it was just a matter of crossing very small borders over a gradual period of months; if you cross one, it's not a big deal; if you cross two, that's still not a big deal; you cross three — individually it's not a big deal, but put them together and now you've crossed too many. And that's what happened. Our relationship lasted several weeks. We actually had a sexual relationship just five times. Then she said that we needed to stop. I realized it, but I was fighting against it. But we did stop. And then, of course, trying to work together, when we had been down that road, it got to be a very strained relationship. The affair happened in the summer, and then I didn't say anything and she didn't say anything, and finally in March of the next year she told her brother, and that's when I knew that there was nothing more to hide now. So we met with the elders, and that Sunday we publicly confessed at both worship services. I think it was fear on my part, because I knew that I would have to resign, but fear that I wouldn't be able to get another job. I was 50 years old.

The public confession was very difficult to do, but it was necessary. There were many in the congregation who were supportive of us, especially of me, because I had been there seven years. The DCE had only been there about a year and a half. In fact there were four or five families, that if it hadn't been for them, I don't know how we would have made it through. I should have sought help, informally, maybe even outside the circuit, from other pastors. I think that admitting that I was in bad shape — like I've said, prior to her even coming on board I was already in bad shape — and having the courage to admit that I was not doing well. I was raised, and I lived, by the motto that you don't ever show your weaknesses. So I think *that*, for me, that would be the biggest thing. And the other is to recognize my limits, and the lines that I can draw, that are healthy lines. Not only in terms of relationships with people, but lines that I can draw personally, where I feel comfortable saying "No," and not having to defend or explain myself. Which I never did, and couldn't.

At the synod level, after I resigned, I met once with the bishop, and he indicated that maybe there would be a possibility that I could work as a layman for facilitating ministry, helping congregations. I called him a month and a half later and he said, "Absolutely not, don't even think about it." His words to me were, "Just go out and get a job in the real world, in the secular world." That's the last thing that he's ever said to me. He's never had anybody call or follow up or anything. There have been two pastors here in the area who have reached out to me and to my wife. They're not in that circuit, but they've at least given us a church home. They've allowed me to do a little bit of preaching and some teaching. And then there was a large charismatic church in the area that welcomed me before either of these two pastors did. And the senior pastor there, I told him all of what happened there, and he just gave me time and space, and I didn't join the church or anything, but I went there for a few months and as a result of that, the executive pastor hired me to teach in their Bible college. I've been teaching at that for the last two years.

So I guess, even if the synod had called *once*, it would have made a big difference after the fact. It would have helped before: it would have been beneficial to have somebody to talk to ahead of time, and to wrestle through some of the issues prior to anything bad happening. But even afterward, if there had been at least one phone call. I mean, it's like we *died*.

In my circumstance, when a pastor resigns, you don't just lose your job. You lose the *entire support network*. And so you're asking someone to go through something that the church has been commissioned for two thousand years not to do: to isolate. Yes, I sinned, but I confessed, and now what do we do with a confessed sinner? And it seems like the very thing that the church has been called to do, it doesn't. It's given me a new appreciation for people who are hurting in churches, who really are neglected by the traditional approach to church.

Now Marvin is teaching part-time at the Bible college and enjoying it. He would like to teach full-time, and he is considering switching to a different denomination.

Our interview with Marvin was not the only one that elicited strong emotions. We discovered intense feelings in many pastors who had been forced to resign or who felt they had been mistreated, and they all mourned that they had been cast aside. Several interviews were interrupted when the ministers cried. Denominational officials and parishioners need to be reminded of the existence of these forceful, unresolved feelings among pastors who were forced to leave.

Let us look at two other brief examples. A United Methodist pastor who left at age 55 illustrates the complexity of some situations of misconduct:

My work hours were 24/7, literally. I didn't take a day off. I should have. I tried to. And the family suffered because I never was home. My wife and I kind of separated ten years before we divorced. In retrospect, and from a lot I've learned in AA and counseling, being raised in an abusive, alcoholic family, there [were] a whole bunch of wounds inside of me that I didn't know about, therefore I couldn't share. I couldn't talk to my wife about, like, "I've got some real problems, and I just don't want you to get beat up. I can't handle it." And every time we'd get in a battle or a fight, I'd just withdraw more.

One lady that I counseled, because her husband left her, was just the most gentle. And that's when it happened. And I don't know why I couldn't leave her and why I would go down with the *Titanic*, which was stupid. But it made no difference. At the time, I just couldn't. I knew it was wrong in every aspect of what we talk about. It was wrong. But I couldn't let go. So probably the pressures of work, the 24/7, I could never take time for me, didn't care for me, my family situation was not good, you need somebody who touches exactly what needs to be touched [inside you]. But I didn't know what needed to be touched, not until now. And that's why I just couldn't let go and I just went down. And you get bounced out of the church if you do stuff like that, and I understand that, too.

An ELCA pastor who left at 41 told us that he was falsely accused of sexual misconduct, but he felt he could not fight the charges:

After being falsely accused of misconduct during a time in the church when sexual McCarthyism was rampant, I decided to resign rather than deal with the synod's unconstitutional policy. I felt thoroughly betrayed, isolated, and shunned by synod and local pastors, due to directives from the former. The only saving graces are that the parish was good to me.

As we conclude this chapter we should point out that, in studying cases like this, researchers work with incomplete and one-sided information. We heard only one side of every story, and thus we are in no position to comment on the justice or injustice in the handling of any case. Our contribution is to present a generalized picture of the size and contours of the sexual misconduct problems of ministers based on our sample, and to convey their subsequent feelings. And as the examples of Edward and Marvin attest, most of them feel that they were treated too brusquely — in some cases almost cruelly — by denominational leaders. This is a topic demanding constructive dialogue from all sides.

Main Findings

Ex-pastors who were forced to leave ministry
due to sexual misconduct

1. Comprised 6 percent of the total
2. Were mostly men, and their most common misdeed was an affair with an adult woman
3. Usually had histories of marital problems and stress
4. Often expressed strong, unresolved emotions of anger, shame, and remorse in their interviews with us

---

9 Pastors Who Left Due to Divorce or Marital Problems

Working 70 to 80 hours a week and having only one evening to my family a week is wrong. Obviously my wife became the bearer of my workload. And I'm sorry, to this day, that I burdened her down without the wisdom and maturity to see the difference.

An Assemblies of God pastor

We discovered 44 ex-pastors who left due to divorce or to other serious family problems that made it impossible for them to continue in parish ministry. They comprise 5 percent of our sample. The vast majority — 42 of 44 — were men. They were slightly younger than others, averaging 41½ years old when they left ministry, compared to an average of 44 overall. They were not distinctive in their denomination or in their type of ministry position, except that they had served disproportionately in small-town and rural churches.

In about 90 percent of these cases, the ministers were divorced or permanently separated from their spouses; in the remaining 10 percent, a crisis had disrupted the person's ministry, but the marriage was saved later. Most of these 44 ministers had been forced out of their pastorates either by denominational officers or by local leaders, but some left voluntarily, believing they could no longer minister effectively.

We need to remember here something that we discussed in Chapter 1: that in three of our five denominations, divorce is not grounds for dismissal from parish ministry. In the United Methodist Church, the Presbyterian Church, and the ELCA, the divorce of a minister has no automatic effect and often has little or no effect at all. In the other two denominations, however, matters are different. In the LCMS, the district decides what action, if any, needs to be taken after a divorce. If the clergyperson has engaged in adultery, he is usually dismissed summarily. But in cases where the minister seems to have done everything possible to save the marriage, district presidents may give only mild penalties.

In the Assemblies of God, penalties for divorce are decided by the local lay committee. If the pastor is perceived as not having been at fault in the divorce, typically nothing is done; if, on the other hand, his or her behavior is perceived as questionable, dismissal is not unusual. Local lay committees also consider any scandal surrounding the divorce and its impact on the congregation in rendering their judgments.

In the questionnaire survey these 44 parish leavers voiced very few dissatisfactions with their ministry positions, but all of them reported troubles with their family life. They said that they had had problems creating a private life apart from their ministerial role (79 versus 63 percent of all others) and many often felt that their work did not give them enough time for their children (52 versus 31 percent). More of their spouses had expressed strong resentment against the amount of time their ministry took up (68 versus 26 percent) and against their financial situation (48 versus 17 percent). The ministers also reported that more of their spouses or families disliked the congregation they were serving (39 versus 19 percent).

Pastor Lester: Wife Asked for a Divorce

Lester, a 36-year-old LCMS pastor, left the parish after a divorce. He was not forced to leave the parish, but after consulting with others he elected to go into military chaplaincy, with hopes of returning to parish ministry later. He explained the situation:

> Sadly, a couple of years before I made the decision, I was divorced. That was a very, very difficult time. And even before that, when I was still in seminary, I'd been involved in military chaplaincy. After

my first parish in Colorado, I had an offer to go into the military chaplaincy, but my wife and I agreed that it was not quite the right time. After the divorce, I was a parish minister in a very small town, and the parish was still very supportive of me, as was my district president. We talked about the possibility of going into chaplaincy to get a new start. Not that I was unhappy with the parish, nor was the parish unhappy with me, but after the painful event of the divorce, I felt there might have been a better chance to start over in a different place.

The district president and I agreed on this. He would not force anybody, saying you should go or you should not. He simply said, "This is an option you may very well wish to consider." He was saddened by the divorce, but the situation was such that he and the congregation could be very, very supportive of me. What occurred was that my wife had an affair with another individual and wished to end the marriage. The congregation may have known some things but was not told. We just said that we were having some difficulties, and that was the high road to take. During that time I did leave the parish, probably for about two to three weeks, just to get away. But again, afterwards, yeah, there were some highs and lows, and very low lows, but the congregation ministered more to me than I did to them.

They just took care of me, they loved me, you know. It was "Hey pastor, we'll get through this." There were no recriminations, there was nobody that said, "Hey, you're a terrible guy" or "This is horrible." They may very well have known the circumstances, but I don't know that they did. But they just took care of me. I was adopted by several grandmothers who cooked for me and brought things over, cookies, et cetera. In a small parish, especially in my denomination, if you get a divorce, usually the elders take you out back and say, "Hey pastor, thank you, but it's time for you to go." But that was definitely not the case with my situation.

The reason I did not resign was that the district president said, "No, you're still effective." He was not one to force anybody. And the congregation, the elders, and the leadership, said, "We don't think you ought to resign. We think you can still serve us, and we think that's what God would want." That was not something I was ready to hear but after the year and a half, I finally decided to resign.

I'd gone back to seminary and asked people that I admired what they suggested I ought to do. I happened to find four that I really found helpful. Two of them said I should resign and two of them said I should stay. What it finally came down to was if I resigned, I would have regrets. If I stayed, I would have regrets. But the direction that I believe God was leading me by having these people in my life whom I respected and I knew were people of God, I guess the district superintendent and the congregation, they asked me and encouraged me to stay. So I thought, I could probably live with myself with less regrets that way than the other. But there was no clear answer, so I had to make a decision. I left the next year.

At that time, financially I was struggling. I had to declare bankruptcy. During the separation, I provided my ex-wife money for another household, so I was supporting two households. And I couldn't do that. That was also a pretty dire thing. I finally took my finances to an official of my denomination in that area, who was a banker. And he looked at the situation and he said, "Man, you're in a world of hurt and you need to declare bankruptcy." And I said, "I can't do that." And he said, "Listen, God uses the government and they have these laws for the protection of folks, so you need to do this." And so kicking and screaming, I went that way. But still financially in a great deal of pain and hurt.

So I thought about the possibility of chaplaincy for financial reasons, but also it had been a longing that I had for many years. The most difficult thing is, though, I have two children and they are still back in Missouri. That was the hardest thing. Not a day goes by that I don't think about them. I get back once every three months.

Lester pondered whether being a minister had contributed to the divorce.

In and of itself, it didn't. See, I came from an alcoholic background and there were some things that probably contributed to the communication aspect. The issue of ministry, I think, had only a tangential impact, not a direct impact. Maybe the hours being away, the demands, the almost sense of taking care of everybody and family being second or third on that list.

But we're working with the assumptions and the paradigm that the pastor is a 24/7 kind of guy. And in some situations, that very much needs to be the case. But there also needs to be some free time. And I think there's also the assumption that pastors are our servants, which they are. But it's kind of like, if you live in the Hilton all your life, you kind of get used to the folks coming in and bringing you towels and such. I don't think there is a conscious effort to abuse that, but I think it does happen at times. As much as it comes from the congregation and the parishioners, I also think though that oftentimes in the parish ministry, there are ministers (and I think I'm one of those) that as I walked into the situation, kind of thought that I was Superman, that I would go ahead and be able to do a great number of things.

A good analogy is a fireman. Pastors are firemen: a situation comes up, you have to put it out. Luckily though, a fireman has shifts, you're 24 hours on, 24 hours off. So there are times when you're not on call. For a pastor, you're always on call. But the priorities, while important, need to be adjusted in such a way that a congregation has clear and set expectations, as do the pastor and his wife.

The other pastors we interviewed who left the parish because of divorce talked, in most cases, about more than one factor in their decision to leave parish ministry. Marital crises were central, but they were not the only thing. Usually they were connected to other problems such as emotional burnout, time pressures, depression, financial problems, or conflict in the congregation.

An ELCA man who left at age 50 is typical of these persons, who now regret what they view as their overcommitment to the pastorate:

Technically I resigned as a result of sexual misconduct. But that occurred two years after my divorce and much of what led up to that has relevance to your study. My first wife and I were married 27 years. We were married while I was in college. She was with me through seminary and most of my ministry. When she filed for divorce she told me that a major reason was that she was tired of my "mistress" — which was the church. In truth she played second fiddle to the ministry, as did my children, much of the time. And I deeply regret that. Our relationship suffered because I was trying to prove myself as a good pastor. Which is how my advisor described me when I told him of the divorce. "You are a good pastor," he said. To which I thought, and still think, "I should have been a better husband." I regret the time lost with my first wife and children.

A year ago we were together at one of our grandchildren's soccer games. It was a Saturday. I told her how much I enjoyed seeing them play and that if I was still a pastor the likelihood of my being there that Saturday afternoon would be extremely remote. I said, "I missed so much while I was a pastor." She said, "Tell me about it." I now have three years before I can request reinstatement to the clergy roster. It'll give me a good bit of time to reflect on whether such a request would be a good thing relative to my current wife and to those grandchildren.

An LCMS man who left at age 36 told of his anger at mistreatment from his district president:

I decided to resign the call to the congregation because my marriage ended. My ex-wife informed the elders of the congregation that she was leaving me and filing for divorce on account of my relationship with a single woman who was also employed by the congregation. My wife had spread rumors that it was a sexual affair. It was not a sexual affair, not physical at all, but it was an inappropriate relationship just the same. Despite the wishes of the congregation's elders to the contrary, I felt it best to resign the pastorate. The district president insisted I resign from the synodical roster at the same time, which I did. I think his desire was to be rid of me and wash his hands of the matter as soon as he could. Apart from a few days of psychiatric evaluation, there has been no effort by the district president or anyone else from the synod to follow up.

An Assemblies of God man who left at age 36 expressed similar anger about his district:

My ex-wife ran off with the guitarist of the church and there was little or no support given to help me. I was kicked out of my house, and the denomination said they would pray for me. They gave me time off with no counseling, and then when she went through with the divorce, there was silence on the district's part. Divorce is the unforgivable sin. Because I was emotionally unstable, I resigned after a year. I struggled to get back on my own, which I finally did.

Another Assemblies of God man, who left at age 45, spoke of his tendencies to be a workaholic:

> What really hurt was when my wife called me on the phone. I was at my other job, and my wife called me and told she was leaving and taking the kids. That really caused stress for both of us. It was terrible. Terrible. *[cries]* I want to pastor so bad! But right now my wife and I are going through a divorce. And the Assemblies of God *do* allow you to pastor, but right now, I'm still kind of recovering from being burned out. The divorce, I feel it would be hard for me. How would I counsel somebody, tell them about their marriage, if mine had ended? That is something that I place high regard on, and I don't feel that I could do it.
>
> The marriage problem started towards the end. I think my wife saw that I was getting burned out. I didn't recognize it, because I'm like a workaholic, almost. The church had just been going on and on, even the last pastor, I'd seen it with him too. I worked with the same things, same people, and I didn't have any more success than he did. I wound up doing more and more and more. I was doing everything. I was working 80, 90, sometimes more hours a week.
>
> I've always worked two jobs. I've always seen the church grow. My wife was always involved in the church. I think a lot of it was, my wife was just dissatisfied because I wasn't making a lot of money. Her sisters, they had houses, they were making good money, they could live comfortably. We were living in a parsonage and we weren't making a lot of money. We had five kids, all the kids were provided well with everything. But I think she just got tired of it. I think maybe she just kind of felt nobody was paying attention to her. That could have been an error on my part.

A third Assemblies of God pastor who left at 33 spoke of his long work hours and his wife's unhappiness:

> Just this last year, my wife had an affair and we just divorced. But I know, there was a tremendous amount of difficult circumstances that she was exposed to, that shut her down in her own way. And I

wasn't sensitive enough as a husband to really take care of her at that point. I was more consumed with how things were affecting me. I've seen a number of friends in ministry that have gone through divorces, I've seen friends separate, and it's heart-wrenching. There seems to be a lack of pastoral care for ministers. I think that here we are in the limelight, being exposed to so much, and yet there's not enough nurture for us. So I became a statistic, and I am now sitting on the sidelines with no hope to ever go back into the ministry.

My work distanced us. Working 70 to 80 hours a week and having only one evening to my family a week is wrong. Obviously my wife became the bearer of my workload. And I'm sorry, to this day, that I burdened her down without the wisdom and maturity to see the difference.

An ELCA pastor who left at age 44 told about his work life leading to divorce:

I think it's quite possible to refer to the parish as "the other woman." Many of us who are called to ministry, and I think I'll just speak for myself, push ourselves hard, have high expectations of ourselves, and probably in less positive ways are afraid of rejection. And if there is an extraordinary fear of rejection, which I think lurks in the soul of many if not most pastors, and I would certainly own it, I'm going to work so hard that they couldn't possibly reject me. And that takes a toll, particularly in the early years of a marriage when children are young and resources are scarce. What have you got? The only thing you've got is your time and your love for one another. And if you're not giving that time and attention and energy, I mean, even if the time is there but you're exhausted, what good are you? So I certainly own some significant responsibility in that regard. I've been doing this 25 years now and I haven't made peace with the fact that when you go home at night, there's one more call you could have made, there's one more thing you could have done, there's one more student you could have counseled. Maybe by the time I die.

Another ELCA pastor whose wife divorced him and who left the pastorate at age 56 told how the divorce affected his relationships in the synod:

I think in some ways I got stereotyped and labeled. And therefore who I was, my feelings, my person, my family, was simply seen as expendable. In other words, it was not important for the synod to reach out and to nurture me in any way. I think I was perceived as, "Hey, you've been to seminary, you should be able to stand on your own two feet. You should be strong enough to know all, do all, whatnot." When I went through a divorce, the synod didn't know how to deal with it. The bishop said to me, "Okay, what caused the divorce? Were you drinking? Were you running around? On drugs? Did you beat her?" And I said, "None of those issues. She just saw the grass greener on the other side of the fence and she was tired of the fishbowl. And she just couldn't cope with it, so she wanted out." And then all the bishop said was, "Well, if you haven't done anything wrong, then I'll support you."

Once I was divorced, with the other pastors I really wasn't welcome. And their wives were very cautious about me. It was almost like, if he gets together with my husband, then maybe it'll rub off and then he'll want a divorce. I was really the black sheep. And it's not just fellow pastors, it's also in the church. There are people that would say that. However, once they get to know me, they realize that I'm probably *more* qualified to be a pastor because of that experience.

The accounts in this chapter tell us that divorce is devastating for ministers, even in denominations that do not consider it sufficient cause for removal from the ministry. It is traumatic for everybody. Unfortunately, the ministry as a vocation seems to contain within itself some risk factors for divorce, among them emotionally demanding work, the obligation to be constantly "on call," and unspoken expectations from laity about the role of clergy spouses. These are not easy to avoid. It seems to us that seminary students, beginning ministers, and judicatory officers need to be aware of the conditions leading to divorce and the effects it has so that preventative measures can be taken.

Main Findings

Ex-pastors who left due to divorce or marital problems

1. Made up 5 percent of the total
2. Were almost entirely men, and younger than average
3. Almost always left following a divorce
4. Noted that their spouses complained about the amount of time that ministry required, their financial situation, or lay expectations regarding the role of a clergy spouse

10 Perspectives from Judicatory Leaders

The first thing I say when I go to a conflicted situation, I tell the pastor and congregation that I am there because my job says that I am to defend the members of the Synod, and the pastor is a member of Synod and the congregation is a member. So I am caught in the middle, and I try to be as objective as possible.

An LCMS district president

If we are to offer a balanced view of ministers who leave the pastorate, we need to hear viewpoints from judicatories. Pastors, as we have seen, sometimes criticize judicatory officials, but the opposite is true also — judicatory officials talk about pastors who are a problem to work with and even describe a few, in the words of one person, as "real losers." Inevitably pastors and officials come into occasional conflict, as we have seen. In these cases, whom should we believe? We need to hear all sides.

We asked officers of the five denominations to talk about pastors leaving local church ministry. In three denominations we used focus groups, and in the other two, personal interviews. Our discussions covered all aspects of the topic. We found that denominational officials seldom saw themselves as being in an adversarial position over against pastors, though sometimes that occurs; most of them took a broader view of the history of cooperation, conflicts, negotiations, successes, and failures they have experienced. We heard less criticism from the officials about pastors than vice versa.

The judicatory officials reported the same array of motivations for leaving that we found in our survey of ex-pastors. We heard only one difference: the judicatory leaders talked more about financial problems than the ex-pastors, especially about the debts incurred during seminary training and the cuts in pay that second-career ministers were faced with when they entered the ministry. For whatever reason, these topics surfaced less often among the ex-pastors themselves.

The officials also talked about some clergy who were simply incompetent. They said they sometimes had to "weed out" incapable pastors or problem pastors, insofar as they had the power to do so, for the sake of the denomination. All of them said that there are some active pastors who are simply unfit for the job, and the church would be better off if those individuals could be persuaded to leave. The United Methodist district superintendents named incompetence as one of two main reasons for involuntary departures from the ministry (the other was sexual misconduct). Yet no ex-pastors avowed being incompetent in our surveys or interviews (though they did note incompetence in other pastors!). We conclude that what looks like incompetence to judicatory officials often looks like congregational conflict or denominational conflict to pastors in the midst of problems. We believe it is safe to say that a portion of the many conflicts described in Chapters 5 and 6 arose at least in part due to incompetence on the parts of the ministers involved, but we cannot know how much.

This chapter conveys the main points of view voiced by judicatory officials in the five denominations. In the pages below we will summarize their opinions, grouping them into the following five categories: (1) today's new pastors; (2) pastors who left; (3) problem pastors; (4) higher expectations from laity today; and (5) the need to provide more support to pastors.

1. Today's New Pastors

Judicatory officials spoke again and again about how pastors today seem to have a feeling of independence and entitlement that their predecessors lacked. A United Methodist district superintendent talked about the independence desired by the young:

What I see in clergy, and of course these are changes that are in younger clergy, is that "I'm not going to sell my soul to the church. I'm not going to spend 60 to 70 hours a week. I'm not going to neglect my family." Some of it's positive, but there's a conscious desire not to be always the company person, not to always be there.

The United Methodist district superintendents reflected on how the new pastors look at the United Methodist itinerancy system, under which all ordained ministers are appointed and deployed by bishops. They said that many new pastors resist the demands of the system. For example:

One of the things that has changed in the last ten or twenty years in our area has been in the whole concept of itinerancy. More and more pastors are saying, "I can't go there to that church because of my spouse's job" — or such and such considerations. It has affected morale, in that some other pastors are saying, "Look, I go every time I'm asked, and this person doesn't move." And there are some persons who just say, "I won't move." Making appointments is much harder than it was ten years ago. We have a system which is based on the readiness of the ministers to move easily and when needed. So now we really struggle, because you're dealing with someone's spouse who makes twice as much as the person makes, or "I can't move thirty miles from my therapist," or whatever reason they have.

A United Methodist district superintendent voiced related concerns:

The observations I've made have to do with itinerancy. People who come into the system with an expectation that it is a profession, rather than a calling, have the expectation that they will move up as they would in the corporate world. If they do a good job, they get a promotion. And we've had pastors in our conference who have been in the itinerant process fifteen or sixteen years, and when the opportunity for a move comes and it's not up to their satisfaction or doesn't meet their expectation, . . . I even had one pastor say to me "When do I get the plum appointment?" At which time I couldn't identify any "plum" appointments in our conference.

So did another United Methodist:

> I think especially in the last five years or so I've known people who, whether they stated this was so or not, left for what I would regard to be cultural issues. For many Baby Boomers in particular, it seems strange not to ever own a home or to have any choice as to what schools your children go to. It's not so much that they're materialistic, but those attitudes are very much ingrained in some cultural and maybe even generational things, where first and foremost, people feel like they should have some determination.
>
> After calling a pastor one day and asking him to move to a church, he was very gruff with me. I called him back the next day. His way of apologizing was to say, "Do you think we'll ever get used to having somebody call you up and tell you where you're going to live, what you're going to do, where your kids are going to go to school?"

Indeed, all the United Methodists in our focus groups agreed that both clergy and laity today are becoming more and more willing to question the system.

A Presbyterian official went so far as to describe pastors' attitudes as "arrogance":

> In today's market for pastors there is a certain amount of arrogance, especially among younger pastors. I believe the seminaries are saying to pastors, "You can write your call. There's a shortage out there. You can do whatever you want." We have churches that are extending themselves way beyond what they set as an upper limit in a call because somebody they fall in love with says, "It's going to cost you $20,000 more a year for me to come, but you're not going to find anyone else, because there aren't any pastors out there." This one church has been looking at no referrals for a long time, so they kind of write the beginning of their end, then and there. You get a small church that goes $20,000 higher for a salary compensation, and you're going to be in trouble financially.

A large number of pastors, these denominational officers feel, view their ministry not as a calling but as a profession, and themselves as employees more than as persons committed to a call from

God. They lack what one LCMS officer described as a "servant attitude." Young pastors seem to feel that they deserve what have become norms in North American society: owning a home, having freedom to make choices, and giving primary attention to personal needs. So one Presbyterian executive:

> We see more and more younger ministers who come out of seminary with the notion that ministry is a 40-hour-a-week job. I'll put in my 40 hours, but don't call me after hours, don't call me on weekends, don't interfere with my family life. And I think that when they're confronted with the reality that pastoral ministry is a 24/7 kind of thing, and sometimes you have your vacation interrupted, and sometimes you make sacrifices that involve your family, it begins to bind.

An ELCA bishop expressed similar concern:

> The sense of call to ministry is different today. Many pastors want specific types of places to serve that will provide them with good resources for their lives and ministry. We have many places where people need someone to serve as pastors that are not attractive or able to provide financial rewards. We need more pastors who are motivated to serve in different settings and places where there are struggles. This deals more with a pastor's sense of call than anything else.

Another ELCA bishop agreed:

> Increasingly, younger pastors are looking to work a 40-hour week instead of serving when and where service is needed or requested. Some are coming out of seminary thinking that the church owes them a call. Some are not open to going to small, rural congregations or multiple-point congregations.

So did an Assemblies of God district supervisor:

> There is a cultural climate today that is different from the climate that I grew up in. I call the culture today the "culture of the uncom-

mitted," because people shun commitment today. They want to be free, they want to keep all options open, they want to pick and choose, whereas, you know, Tom Brokaw wrote about the "greatest generation" — about a generation of people who early on in their life made a commitment. My father pastored people in west Texas who worked for Gulf Oil Company or for Texaco *all of their lives,* and they would never think of leaving Texaco to go work for Gulf. If a man got a job with J. C. Penney, he would never think about leaving that company and take a job with a competitor. Whereas today it's totally different. I wonder if the culture has created a lot of the movement among pastors today, that we did not have a generation ago.

We heard much talk, like that from this Presbyterian official, about how seminaries need to provide more practical training in church leadership:

I'm not sure that our seminaries are helping people be prepared for the realities of ministry today and the issues they have to face in the ministry. Various seminaries do different things wrong, I think, but I don't know *one* that in fact is saying, "When you get there, you're going to be dealing with a lot of bald-headed, blue-haired people who live in a different world than the one you know, and here's how you deal with that."

Another presbytery executive:

I think either the seminary does it, or the presbytery has got to do it, to say, "Okay, here's the real life now. You've gotten *this,* but *this* is what you're going to run into!" Maybe the presbytery has got to do it. There are wonderful studies of ecclesiology in seminary, but unfortunately they don't have a lot to do with the reality of Tuesday night's session [lay governing committee] meeting. And there is no bridge point across there that the church provides for them. And I think that a sense of burnout arises very quickly for those who are newly out and have no way to figure out what that's about, because then they feel they're hitting a hopelessly rigid brick wall, and in some cases they are. In some cases they're *creating* the brick wall.

An ELCA bishop:

> Seminaries need to show them how to bring about congregational change among older people who don't want to change and who are in control. We need to teach more about change in institutions and give folks skill and practice in doing it.

2. Pastors Who Left

Denominational officials also talked with us about pastors who left. They generally agreed that those pastors tended to be loners in the district or presbytery, for whatever reason not part of ministerial friendship groups or action groups. They surmised that such individuals felt isolated.

The Assemblies of God officials, like Assemblies of God pastors, held some unique assumptions. They emphasized church growth as the mark of ministerial success. They believed much more strongly than those in other denominations that success in a pastorate depends on the pastor and that a good pastor can grow a church in any circumstance. So one Assemblies of God supervisor:

> The Assemblies of God, we really are kind of Darwinian, if that's a word. It's sort of survival of the fittest. But that's not all bad! And our young people coming out of our schools need to be taught, "Look, there's no freebie in this whole thing. All you're going to have is an opportunity, and you're going to have to be very entrepreneurial. When you're racking up this debt [from college and seminary], you better be thinking of how you're going to pay it off, because it's probably not going to be paid off with ministerial dollars."

Another district supervisor agreed:

> Any pastor who succeeds, I believe, must have an entrepreneurial approach to his life and ministry. Some come into the ministry because they think it's going to be easy to find a place to minister, and they fail to realize that every minister is a freelance operator. He's got to find his own place, in our constituency. Nobody appoints him

to a pastorate. To some, lacking the entrepreneurial aspect of life, they weary in their attempt to find a fulfilling pastorate.

The Presbyterian pastorate is a bit different. Here is a summary statement by a presbytery executive about pastors who leave:

> There are four things that I think somehow connect with why ministers leave, whether it's three years out, five years out, 25 years out. One is a changing context that they're ill prepared to address, whether by seminary or continuing education. The second is what I call disappointment with God. Somehow their personal relationship with God has suffered in the process of becoming a visible servant leader. Then I think there's two other things: unrealized expectations, that is, I wanted to make a contribution, I wanted to help the world, I wanted to do something good, and I find myself running session meetings that argue about whether I go to one or two services in the fall. The fourth one is unrewarded vocation. I believe we live in a culture that has such low valuing of ministry, and you really do sacrifice financially, and in esteem, and in lots of ways now that wasn't true before. Well, maybe the financial part has always been true. I think some are ill prepared for that. Two other things are lack of patience and an inability to disassociate from the congregation's anxieties. That's what ultimately will drive pastors away.
>
> People are impatient. They want to see change. They get frustrated and they get hooked by the culture's expectations of immediate results. So, if I'm two or three years out and things aren't changing, well, shoot! Or they get hooked by the congregation's anxiety and they don't know how to live separately from that, because the congregation wants change to happen. Like, "We've got to turn things around. We've got six months, Pastor." I see a lot of churches who call somebody and their anxiety is so high that they really are saying, at the one-year mark we want to see change. And then some people will start to surface this and to recycle their garbage into the system.

Another presbytery executive also notes churches' roles in ministers leaving:

We have some churches, when we talk with their PNC [search committee for a pastor], it wants the church to grow, and wants to change, and wants to be attached to the community, and the pastor wants to help a church change and grow and be attached to the community and do mission, and then gets there into the institutional church with people that want to worry about what color the carpet will be, whether to have kids in worship, and don't you dare take out that old green hymnal, because that was the best stuff ever written, and all that kind of *crap* about daily life in the church. And that's in the context of communications and expectations going in opposite directions, where expressed needs are not the real needs. Those churches are going to die, and the pastors don't want to be on a ship that's about to sink and doesn't want to do the hard work of changing. They leave.

A United Methodist official focused on ministers' expectations:

I find that some mid-career people, who in mid-life decided to go into the ordained ministry, sometimes confuse "conversion" with "call," if you will. They have some kind of revelatory experience, or they go on some faith or spiritual journey where they have a closer walk with God, they encounter the Holy Spirit in some new way that they never had before, and they then see that as a calling to ordained ministry. Then they get into the ministry and find that they're not prepared, that the skills they bring and the expectation of their congregation are very, very different. And here are ministers who in many cases were successful in other fields. And probably the worst part of that is, not only do they leave the ministry, but they also leave the church. They become so disillusioned by ordained ministry that they can't stay related to the church.

An Assemblies of God district supervisor put it even more strongly:

I have seen some leave the ministry, particularly during the first five years of ministry, whom I believe never came to grips with the call of God. I believe some of these have gone into the ministry as a vocation and not as a call. They've chosen the ministry because they have a particular perception of a lifestyle. Upon discovering that the lifestyle was not equal to their expectations, they became disillusioned and left the ministry. Sometimes the disillusionment comes from broken relationships with members of a church staff or difficulty in relationships with people in the congregation. So the fallout I would attribute to not fully understanding what the call of God means. Most of the pastors I relate to who've been in the pastorate for a long time have no options. That's *my own* testimony. When I dedicated my life to preaching the gospel there was no other option. So for me over the years, leaving the ministry has never been a consideration. I do what God called me to do.

Another Assemblies of God district supervisor echoed these feelings:

Since I was about fifteen or sixteen, I knew that God had called me. It was a lifelong assignment from God himself that was non-amendable, non-negotiable. It was a mandate kind of thing with me. When the going gets tough, I say, "Man, this is some kind of a job I got," but I never question the call. I just know there is nothing else I'm supposed to do. Without a clear call to the pastorate, you don't have a chance of survival.

The Assemblies of God officers discussed why some pastors are voted out of their jobs within a few years. They attributed many cases to overeager pastors who made changes and thus lost their followers. One officer added:

Pastors who are voted out, it's seldom because of their preaching. It's because of how they handle people. It's the way he handles finances, the way he handles his own life. If there's real character there, and a sense of call, people are pretty tolerant about the preaching.

A final note: The United Methodist officials noted that, in their experience, African Americans and other pastors who are ethnic minorities leave parish ministry less often than others. They reflected that one reason for this could be that the United Methodist Church wants more minorities in the pastorate and therefore affords many opportunities to such individuals.

3. Problem Pastors

The judicatory leaders recognized their responsibility to support their pastors, yet they pointed out that some pastors are problematic. Most of the "problem pastors" they talked about were persons in their first decade of ordination, whose problems were partly incompetence and partly misconduct — especially sexual misconduct. Several officials lamented all the sexual misconduct charges they had to deal with.

A group of Presbyterian executives compared notes on how frequently sexual misconduct had occurred in their areas. One said that there are problems in 10 percent of the churches at any one time, and another said that in his presbytery there had been problems in one-fourth of the churches in recent years. A third guessed that 20 or 25 percent of Presbyterian churches nationwide have faced this problem. Everyone agreed that a case of sexual misconduct takes a toll on all involved. Indeed, even subsequent pastors in these churches had terrible problems dealing with the turmoil, in one person's words, "because those congregations are going to get their pound of flesh for that, and they do."

These same Presbyterian executives agreed that committees supervising candidates are not doing a good job of weeding out persons with psychological problems. They talked about pastors who were unable to control anger, pastors who acted out inner feelings in destructive ways, and pastors who could not maintain sexual boundaries. They wished that somehow the committees would have eliminated the problem pastors before they came into ministry, and they also wished that they had more power of supervision over the pastors in the presbytery — a view not shared by pastors, who by and large wanted more autonomy.

In a United Methodist focus group, denominational officials discussed problem clergy and the gatekeeping process:

First Speaker: I think a very significant change is when we changed the percentage that it takes to get a person into ministry, from a majority vote to a two-thirds vote. That helps with the incompetence issue. In the old process you had 100 ministers there and 51 felt that this guy or this woman was good enough, and 49 had serious doubts. That was a setup for what we've got, which is, a fair amount of people who should never have gotten into ministry who are now a part of our system.

Second Speaker: So you're saying that the people who should leave, who are not competent, that their non-competency was there all along. They should have been screened at the beginning rather than saying that the drop in competence was due to the dynamics of their lives in the church after they got in.

First Speaker: Absolutely. I agree with the fact that the incompetent pastors made it in under the wire through the system we had, and that we've been paying that price for years. Their incompetence didn't grow because of the pressures of the job, it was there right from the beginning. And most of the people in the room knew it when they were first interviewed, but didn't have the intestinal fortitude to say "I'm sorry. I know you've worked hard. I know you've spent a lot of money on seminary, but you really need to find another way to make a living in your life."

Third Speaker: Our experience on the Board of Ordained Ministry has been that the board is much better at interviewing than when I first came on ten years ago. Previous to that there had been very little involved in the interview. It would have been, "Okay. We know who you are. Thank you very much for coming and seeing us." That's a little bit of an exaggeration, but I agree with you that we in some cases have been paying for the incompetence year after year after year. I think of one particular case where we don't know what to do. We've known of and carried this person for 15 years, and we can't do it any more. And now it's difficult, but we need to take action.

Another United Methodist agreed:

We have found that a significant number of people have been going into seminary as a result of some crisis in their life, and they were on some kind of spiritual quest. They go to seminary and get to the end of their three or four years and are ordained. And they carry that crisis — which is unresolved yet, because seminaries aren't good at resolving crises [*laughs*] and then they get into the ministry and of course all of that baggage is still with them. And it was borne out in an article in the *Atlantic Monthly*. That impacts how some people come in. They come in "wounded," and they continue to somehow expect that life in the church is going to help them heal those wounds. And sometimes then they project to their congregation the expectation that they are going to be taken care of by the congregation, while the congregation on the other hand wants to be taken care of by them.

A Presbyterian in a focus group described a personality problem addressed too late:

> Some pastors go through the Committee on Preparation for Ministry process, they go through career counseling, they go through seminary, and when they get out they're just not suited to serve a local parish. We had one person in her first call out of seminary, before too long she had very inappropriately expressed anger, both physically touching some elderly women as well as explosive verbal inappropriate behavior. It was clear that this didn't surface the minute she came into our presbytery. We looked back and before she became a pastor, we checked where she'd worked. The point is, we were just scared to death of her. We'd been intimidated, so the same behavior carried on. It was a problem within the individual. This is a person with great energy, great natural gifts, a good communicator. Everything on the surface looks like here's a born pastor, but, in this case, internal issues were never resolved well enough, so they didn't stop controlling her.

Another Presbyterian described another case:

> One young man came out of seminary with a great deal of zeal. It didn't take him long to discover that the pastoral issues he was confronting in helping people cope with problems began to hook a lot of stuff from his past. It came out that he had been raised in a very abusive alcoholic family, and his behavior came out in some counterproductive ways. We ended up with a judicial case as a result of some of his behavior, and we suspended him from the practice of

ministry for two years. We required some counseling, some CPE, and career guidance. That stretched to a third year, but in the process he got the help he needed and is now in a chaplaincy. I had hoped the Committee on Preparation would have caught the issue and dealt with it before he was ever ordained. Our presbytery has communicated with his home presbytery about that, I hope in a constructive way, saying that you really need to be more circumspect in dealing with these folk, and don't just pass them through because they come out of an influential church in the presbytery that bankrolls your benevolence budget [*chuckles*]. Essentially that's what happened. The Committee on Ministry moderator said, "We couldn't turn him down because of the church he came from. We knew there were some problems."

In one Presbyterian focus group the leader asked presbytery executives if there is a system in place through which information about the problem person can be passed on if he or she wants to take a call elsewhere. The others said there is a formal process but that it seems to be breaking down because of litigation problems. This problem complicates the ability of denominations to address problems with pastors. One executive:

There is something going on between executive presbyters. When I call an EP [executive presbyter] and say, "One of our churches is interested in talking with this person," I want to know where they are on the continuum of theology, talk about the matches, and so on. My assumption, which may be really dangerous, is that EPs are going to tell each other the truth. But, if I'm going to get sued for that, then that's scary to me, because I don't say to the pastoral search committee, "Well, this EP says thus and so." I say things like, "You may want to ask this person about this. Have they ever been in a conflict situation, and what did they learn from it?" Because you know they've been in a conflict situation and the other EP is not entirely sure they learned anything from it. If we EPs think we don't have the privilege of being truthful in a confidential way, then we're in trouble.

4. Higher Expectations from Laity

Judicatory officers agree that today laypeople have higher expectations for their pastors. They talked about what some call a "consumerist culture" among churchgoers, in which a high priority is placed on getting family and personal needs met. So an LCMS district president:

> This has to be one of the hardest times to be a pastor. Along with all the changes in the laity, I think the respect for the pastoral office has declined. A generation or two ago the pastor was generally the most educated man in the congregation, sometimes, depending on what immigrant group he was a part of, he was one of the few around who could read and write the English real well. That's all gone. The education level of the average parish is light-years beyond what it used to be. The expectations, therefore, of pastors, everything from perfect grammar in his sermons to business acumen, and all of that, that has risen very much. The "me generation" and the self-centeredness, the "I need to be pleased," and pastors are pushed and pulled eighteen ways till Sunday. That stresses them.

An ELCA bishop echoed these concerns:

> Today laity are more knowledgeable and more willing to be vocal about concerns and issues. Also there is less reverence for the pastoral office than there was twenty or thirty years ago.

So did an Assemblies of God district supervisor:

> I think the expectations for proficiency in ministry have increased among the laity in the last thirty years, because there is much broader exposure to a variety of ministries through Christian radio, Christian television, cassette tape ministry. When I was a kid growing up, the only person to compare my father to was the pastor across town or the pastor down the road. But now every pastor is compared to Robert Schuller, T. D. Jakes, and prominent names on television. So people in the local church have increased their expectations.

A by-product of this consumer-oriented culture is a decrease in denominational loyalty. A United Methodist official understood this:

> In our conference we have a lot of shifts in population, and I think those shifts also affect the denominational identification, because those people are used to going into a community, find a church that kind of meets your and your family's needs, and "I don't care if it's United Methodist, I need something that meets my *needs*." And you can understand that; it's not a judgmental statement. And a church has to work pretty fast and furious to maintain any percentage of growth, because people are in and out. And likewise I think there's a lot less tolerance to hang in there with your church, even by people who've been a member of the church a long time. There's less tolerance to hang in there when things aren't going well. When there's not a match or there's a problem, things fall apart much more quickly.

An Assemblies of God focus group of district supervisors seemed to agree:

> First speaker: Denominational loyalty is not very strong out there. People simply do not have denominational loyalty; it's a thing of the past.

> Second speaker: Like free agency among athletic teams, that attitude has come into the church. When Mickey Mantle played for the New York Yankees, he never thought about playing for another team. But, today, free agency means you're playing on the team that makes the best offer. And so today people are going to the church that has the most to offer.

> Third speaker: Today we see premier church pastors, teachers, and evangelists who are able to have broad television time and national prominence, a lot of them are not denominationally anchored. So therefore a lot of their comments and statements are saying, you don't need denominations. God didn't call a denomination. So now this is being fed into the people, and so their concept is, I don't want to be part of a denomination. There's too many restrictions, too many guidelines.

A presbytery executive considered how a consumerist culture and a lack of denominational loyalty interact:

> There is no consensus about what the church is, what a Presbyterian is, what a Presbyterian ought to be, what's it okay for Presbyterians to do or not do. And in the midst of that chaos, here comes Joe Family, who wouldn't know Presbyterianism if they fell on it, now walking in the door of your church and wanting all these things for their kids. And over here in the session is a raging conflict over whether you're going to have children in worship or not. And here's this young pastor saying, "What the heck am I doing here?" I think that the consumer piece and that internal chaos of what is a Presbyterian anyway, and who gets to define that, from what I'm hearing from young pastors, this is a part of the conflicts they face.

5. The Need to Provide More Support to Pastors

Denominational leaders are concerned that pastors, who have high expectations of themselves, can often be discouraged by the realities of pastoral life. Pastors need support, but often they do not take advantage of opportunities for support that are available. A United Methodist district superintendent:

> For too many years, too long, superintendents and bishops just *expected* pastors to do a good job. There was very little affirmation for a pastor who did a good job, was not a superstar but just did a sound, sound, job of pastoring a local church. And I think one of our roles, a key role in the supervising aspect of this, is to affirm that "You're doing a great job. I want you to know that. I know it and I'm going to let your people know that."

One LCMS district president told of his personal effort to provide support:

> One of my main projects has been rebuilding a relationship and trust, that the pastors have a support system among themselves. And knowing that they have a support system within the district, a

relationship with me, where we can trust and counsel one another and deal with one another as brothers. So they will share with me and seek my counsel and advice, and I will help them choose battles to fight. By doing that we can also raise the view of the clergy, to get rid of some of the distrust, to help them deal with some of the conflicts in the congregations, to heal, reconcile, and go on in ministry. It comes down to working and building trust and relationships.

Another LCMS district president agreed but was frustrated by the pastors' lack of involvement:

I think to get them to stay, we need to provide them the kind of support and encouragement from a variety of sources, whether that's the judicatory or the congregation. A lot of the guys that end up in the seminary are kind of "lone rangers," and when they get out there they don't intentionally find support groups. That can be troublesome, so finding a way to keep them connected and supported, and finding the resources to help them grow and continue to develop as leaders, to be able to share their frustrations with people, and just those kinds of wholesome things, that's a key to keep people in the ministry. And whether that's through coaching or mentoring or whatever it is, it provides a kind of support and helps them see that what they're doing makes a difference.

A third LCMS district president described why denominational efforts to provide support are sometimes ignored by clergy:

I am responsible for the churches, at the same time I'm responsible for whether or not each person stays on the roster. So if a pastor has a real burden, they would be reluctant to talk to me for fear that it would put them in trouble in terms of their roster standing. So I can hardly be a father confessor to anybody.

The first thing I say when I go to a conflicted situation, I tell the pastor and congregation that I am there because my job says that I am to defend the members of Synod, and the pastor is a member of Synod and the congregation is a member. So I am caught in the middle, and I try to be as objective as possible. So whatever happens, we get criticism. We get it from both sides.

Based on what we heard from both pastors and officials, support is clearly a major issue. But there are other pitfalls that undermine a successful pastorate. A presbytery executive described another reason why new ministers feel disappointment in ministry — unwarranted expectations:

> As a culture we seem to put tons and tons of weight on preparation for graduation. And we have this "happily-ever-after" fantasy that if we do the preparation right, we'll live happily ever after, and that's baloney. A full colonel in the army told me that the single most helpful thing that was said to him in seminary was that seminary is like basic training in the infantry, the purpose of which is to teach you enough to keep you alive long enough so that you can really learn something. He also said when you go to a new ministry, you should plant a peach tree, and do not expect your ministry to bear fruit before that peach tree does. Well, it takes three years before you get a peach off that tree.

Another presbytery executive concurred:

> I remember, centuries ago when I graduated from seminary, I came out with that same idealism and all of those good ideas. And I couldn't see at 26 why the 63-year-old I worked with didn't get it. But there was a bond of community with other ministers that could help me get over my naïveté without a war, and I'm not sure we've got that for young pastors today. They feel themselves torn between two or three groups everywhere they turn, and so they can't figure out where home is.

Some executives have encountered a particular dilemma with second-career ministers. Everyone recognized that a percentage of the second-career persons, having had an epiphany experience in their spiritual lives, enter the ministry filled with zeal but ignorant of denominational life, while others fixate rigidly on doctrine. Still others bring a wealth of experiences matched by a wealth of unrealistic expectations. The judicatory leaders discussed the pros and cons of second-career ministers and seemed to conclude that they bring much-needed wisdom and experience to the ministry, yet many are set in their ways and not as educable as their younger colleagues. They need the same level of evaluation during seminary as first-career seminarians do, because, like them, second-career ministers are here to stay.

Summary

We listened to judicatory officials as they described the difficulties they have experienced and the changes they have seen both in new clergy and in the laity. These men and women were very thoughtful about problems pastors face today and what denominational officials could do to help the situation. They recommended more careful screening of candidates; more realistic seminary training for the pastorate; better remuneration of pastors; and more support from laity, other pastors, and denominations.

In the next three chapters we return to the ex-pastors themselves to listen to their feelings on specific issues in their lives.

Main Findings

Judicatory officials voiced their views of pastors today, concurring that

1. Pastors today have a stronger feeling of entitlement and independence than in the past. Young pastors are not as willing to go unquestioningly where the denomination needs them.
2. Pastors' commitment to their denomination is weaker today.
3. Pastors are not prepared for the practical, mundane, slow-to-change parts of ministry.
4. Laity have higher expectations of pastors.
5. Sexual misconduct is a problem in many places.
6. Denominational leaders need to provide pastors with more and better support than they do now.

---

11 The Impact of Gender and Sexuality

I guess what I would say is, of course we need to encourage women, but I'm not so sure it's an easy terrain out there for women, for lots of different reasons.

A 43-year-old ELCA woman

I continue to believe that it's not fair for sexual minorities that we have to choose between the call to serve God in the church and having a fulfilling personal life.

A 43-year-old United Methodist woman

Gender, sexuality, and marriage are important in ministers' lives, and issues relating to them often force ministers out of the pastorate. Already we have seen, in Chapters 8 and 9, plentiful instances of sexual misconduct, marriage conflict, and divorce. Here we look at three other kinds of experiences: those of women ministers in general, those of clergy couples, and those of gay and lesbian pastors.

Women Ministers

As we noted in Chapter 2, past research indicates that women ministers leave the pastorate more often than do men (also see Appendix A). This is partly because of the traditional preference of many laity to have men as ministers in their churches. The preference for men seems to be strongest in large and affluent churches, thus creating what is sometimes referred to as a "stained glass ceiling" for women ministers aspiring to those desirable positions.

In our questionnaire survey the rate of leaving the pastorate was about the same for men and for women, except in the Presbyterian Church, where women seem to have left church ministry disproportionately more than men; this overall similarity in men's and women's rates of leaving surprised us. In our sample the women were different from the men in several ways. The women had less commonly been senior or solo pastors (48 percent, compared with 73 percent of the men). They had been ordained at a later age than men, on average, and more women than men were unmarried when they left the pastorate (16 versus 4 percent). They did not report more conflicts with parishioners, staff, or other clergy than did the men.

Of the 98 phone interviews we conducted, 27 were with women ministers. The women talked freely about their experiences, and their reports varied regarding whether parish ministry was harder for them than it was for their male counterparts. Of those who said that it was, they most often mentioned that the problems are most troubling for women associate pastors serving under male senior pastors. A Presbyterian woman told us about it:

> I do believe that pastoral ministry is a challenging place to be for a young woman. I have avoided associate pastor positions thus far because I have had so many female colleagues with very negative experiences. At the same time I get *no* interest from congregations as a solo pastor.

Another Presbyterian woman, who left parish ministry at age 32, argued that women need to be better at ministry than men:

> I do feel, when you're starting off, your playing field is not level to begin with. You might have heard it already: women have to be ten times better than a man from the get-go, because people are really watching them and looking for excuses not to like them. Whereas a man can get away with some mediocre performances on certain things, I think it's harder for a woman.

The issue of time pressures for women ministers came up again and again, especially from mothers with children. It was a consensus that more women ministers than men were interested in part-time positions and wished that more of them existed. The Presbyterian woman we just quoted was one of them:

I would return, but only on a part-time basis. I think men still go by a certain model of ministry that's more straightforward, and women, in our understanding of ministry, we're a little more creative in terms of how we see it can happen. And most of the job descriptions today, they require too much for what I can offer in terms of being a mom and all that. There are plenty of church positions for those who are not ordained that can work part-time. But in terms of ordained positions, most all of them that are out there are full-time. I would love to see the church be more open in the future, and recognize that there are a whole bunch of qualified ordained women who would be willing to offer a lot to the church if there were more part-time positions available that recognize their training and their gifts.

The women talked, albeit in guarded tones, about the amount of sexual misconduct by clergy that they have encountered. One woman said "it is pretty rampant." Another agreed:

I've had a number of friends who have experienced sexual harassment in the ministry or sexual misconduct, and a number of them have left or gone elsewhere because the church doesn't want to deal with it. I think a lot of where it's happening is in your multiple staff churches where you do have males and females working together, which is something fairly recent. And usually in the larger churches the pastors at the top of the pile have a significant amount of power. Basically, sexual harassment is a power issue, as opposed to a sexual issue. And what we're told, primarily, is that unless it's really bad, don't do anything about it. Just try to ignore it. Work with it.

We had numerous discussions about whether parishioners treat female pastors differently than they do male ones. Most of the women said yes, they do:

An interesting thing happened a couple of months after I left the church. I was invited to a graduation party of one of the girls I'd been real close to in the senior high youth group. It was the first time I'd been to a social gathering of church members since I'd left, and there were a lot of church members there. And a couple of women came up to me and said, "Oh, you look so great!" Like that was what was important. I don't think they'd have said that to a man, about my appearance. One woman actually said, "Oh gosh, your hair! Just look at that. You wait till you leave the church to start looking really wonderful." And I thought, "What?" But it wasn't like I lost any sleep over it. But I do remember thinking, she'd never have said that if I was a man. It was that kind of stupid stuff. Or people would ask me things about my children that kind of implied, like was I taking good care of them? — because I was working full-time. They'd never have done that if my husband had been the pastor. It was that stuff that I think we all deal with.

A United Methodist woman experienced different treatment while she was a pastor:

I think people feel more free to give women advice and criticism than a man, and I have other female colleagues that have felt that way. Things that they probably would never dare say to a male minister, they would say to a female. And people are more comfortable interrupting women. If I'm working at the office at the church or working at the office at home, people see that as less a barrier to coming in and just sitting down and talking. And some of it irks the daylights out of me [laughs], and some of it, as a pastor, you just have to get past. You say, "Okay, there are things that are advantages to this, and things that are disadvantages."

Such themes were the main ones. It is difficult for us to make any broader generalizations about the feelings of women who left the pastorate, for they were as diverse as their experiences.

Clergy Couples

During our research we talked with numerous members of former clergy couples. We are uncertain exactly how many there were in our sample of 963; we did not ask about it directly in the questionnaire. But seventeen people told us directly that they were part of such a couple, and based on this we think that between 20 and 30 is a reasonable estimate of the total.

To clarify, clergy couples are composed of spouses who are both ministers, but usually not in the same church. The few who do serve the same church (there were three such cases in our sample, all Lutherans) would be referred to as co-pastors. By far the most common pattern among our clergy couples was that husband and wife served different churches within driving distance of each other. In one-third of the cases, one of the two spouses was in specialized rather than local church ministry. The members of clergy couples in our sample were disproportionately women — 12 out of 17 — and they served in only three of the five denominations: Presbyterian, ELCA, and United Methodist. (The other two denominations in our study have few or no women ministers.)

We compared the 17 known members of clergy couples with the rest of the sample and found that they had few complaints about other clergy or about judicatory leaders. They reported more satisfaction with support they received from denominational officials than the others in the sample, and more satisfaction with relationships with other clergy and staff members in their churches. On the other hand, they complained more than others that their work did not permit them to devote adequate time to their children. On average, the members of clergy couples were as happy as others, and possibly happier.

Most relevant here, many said that a major reason they left parish ministry was that their spouse moved for a new job (41 versus 6 percent). That is, in a clergy couple, when one spouse moves to start a new job, there is a probability that the other will leave parish ministry. Our interviews taught us that the decision to leave the pastorate was most often connected to either the spouse's move to another city or the woman pastor's desire to spend more time with her children.

The biggest problem for clergy couples is finding two calls within driving distance of one another. It is a problem for the couples them-

selves, and it is an even bigger problem for denominational officials —
especially in denominations that take responsibility for placing ministers. And if the clergy husband and wife prefer to work as co-pastors
in the same church, it requires some psychological preparation at the
local level, since most churches are not accustomed to co-pastors and
are slow to accept the arrangement. In the interviews we probed to
see if members of clergy couples thought their careers had been hampered, and we found no consensus. We also asked for suggestions for
ways to aid clergy couples and found that people were equally ambivalent. Here, for example, is what a Presbyterian woman told us:

> I think part of the problem is that when you're in that situation,
> from people I've known that have done things as clergy couples,
> usually one person is part-time and one person is full-time. Or else
> [working in the same church] they split a position, and the church
> ends up really getting work like two full-time people when the cou-
> ple are not getting the pay for it. So I think that is a big problem. My
> spouse and I really don't want to do that, so we've always tried to
> maintain our separate places to be and things to do. And that hasn't
> always worked either, because, depending on where you are and the
> type of community, you might not both be able to have full-time
> church employment. So I don't know what the denomination can
> do, other than to help get churches thinking in these ways to know
> what they need to do to support a clergy couple if they call one.
> There's the whole thing of whether you're a clergy couple or just a
> pastor and a spouse, the same thing with the expectations put on a
> pastor's spouse.

Openly Gay and Lesbian Pastors

A distinct subcategory of ex-pastors are those who are openly gay or
lesbian. In our sample we had 27 who were out to us, if not out to everybody. Twenty-one were men and six were women — the same gender proportions as in our overall sample. They had served in four denominations — Presbyterian, ELCA, LCMS, and United Methodist,
with the largest number from the ELCA. Our research indicates that
the vast majority had left the pastorate unwillingly, either because

their denominations forced them out or because of personal circumstances. Most of these ex-pastors were now living with partners in committed, long-term relationships.

All of these persons felt a great deal of anger. Everyone we spoke with was irritated or worse with the institutional church, charging their denominations with evasion, duplicity, and injustice. Most of them had found deep gratification in their years of ministry and fervently wished they could continue. Let us turn to some examples:

Pastor Howard: Coming Out in His Thirties

Pastor Howard was 39 when he left the ELCA pastorate.

> My decision to leave the ministry was based on several things. Primarily, I was in the process of coming out as a gay man. I was married at the time. The whole process of coming to terms with things had really kicked in a depression that was pretty strong, almost disabling at that point. I was basically not functioning very well, career-wise nor as a human being. But I realized that this was not a good fit for me any longer — the Lutheran Church. The ELCA had made it very clear that if you were gay, you needed to be celibate or you were not considered potential for serving in ministry. So I decided, for my own mental health and sanity, I guess, that I had to do some things, which included a career change, which was a source of tremendous grief for me. It sounds very melodramatic, I suppose. It was a lot of losses: my marriage — and I loved my ex-wife very much, but it was just not a fit for either one of us — and I loved my career. My faith is very, very important to me. So there were several losses. I decided to leave. That was seven years ago. Interestingly enough, now I'm back working in a church-related organization. I am serving in a lay capacity at a church working with worship, music, and some counseling. So I've been able to reintegrate that aspect of my life pretty fully, without the privilege of ordination, I guess.
>
> In between time, let me tell you, I hated the church! I would try to go to church and I would sit and cry in the pew when the pastor got up to preach. I'm getting choked up even now thinking about it.

I would just sit there and weep and feel bad. Then I went from there into a kind of rageful phase, where I couldn't even go. The idea of getting up in the morning and going to church was about as remote as possible from my mind. It was just a source of guilt. And then finally, after much time of hassling back and forth, I found this church that I'm a member of now, which is an affirming congregation for gay and lesbian people. But it's not a gay church. I refuse to join a gay church. Come on! From a Christian perspective, this is the family of God! I don't care what you are. This is a very, very good fit for me, but it was a long process in coming. It just took a long time to get the courage to do all those changes, and they all came at once. So if the church were to say, "You can go back into ministry, we're accepting folks who are gay in a committed relationship," in a second I would be saying, "Count me in, I want to go."

A year after Howard left the ministry, a woman from his old bishop's office phoned his ex-wife to solicit information regarding Howard's sexuality. His wife would not answer the woman's questions; she directed her to Howard instead, and told him about the phonecall. Livid, he immediately phoned the woman in the bishop's office and asked her directly what she wanted to know. The woman admitted that she was searching for information for the bishop, and Howard said that yes, if she wanted to know, he was gay and out of the closet. He recounted the conversation to us:

She said, "But people loved you at the church you served. You could still be a pastor as long as you were not in a monogamous relationship at all." I said, "Okay, so what you're saying is, I could go down to [a gay bar] every night of the week I wanted to and bring somebody home, and that would be fine. But if I have one man that I love and am committed to in a relationship of fidelity and monogamy, that's a bad thing." And there was dead silence and she said, "Well, the church has a long way to go on this issue." And I said, "That's right, honey. You won't find me waiting for you when you get there."

I know pastors who are gay who, if that's what you call celibacy, I'll eat my hat. I couldn't lie to myself nor to the people I preached to every Sunday morning. In fact, I even worked on a committee with a female pastor at that time, who was lesbian and was in a relationship and chose not to tell people. She ran away from me like I was a case of the plague, because I was causing conflict for her internally.

Howard told how his sexual urges became undeniable over time, causing depression.

I just became almost non-functioning, the depression was so bad. I was borderline suicidal at that point. I was so conflicted! I knew that I was lying to myself. I was lying to my wife. My life was a lie. That's when I finally decided, enough was enough. I did not come out in the parish, I did not get up and say, "Here's my story and good-bye." But I just decided to move into something else. Also the senior pastor there at the time was clearly aware that I was not functioning well, and he wanted me out of there.

Moving from a series of small-town churches to a large urban congregation made his inner conflict worse.

The big city was more difficult for me from the standpoint of sexuality, because there was more presence of outwardly gay impact there. The homosexual lifestyle was visible. So that in itself just forced me to have to say, "Is this your truth or not? Is this real for you or not?" And I couldn't deny it as easily as I could in the rural, smaller towns where I'd served before. So *that* really was forcing the issue. At that point too, my marriage was pretty well dissolving. As a therapist I saw at one time said, "You could be the straightest man on earth and this marriage would still have ended," because my ex-wife is a very volatile individual and the source of lots of difficulty for me. She would say things and I would have to come around behind and patch things up. She was angry a lot of the time.

When the church became embroiled in conflict over choosing a new senior pastor, Howard became very disillusioned and decided he had to leave. About that time his wife filed for divorce. Today he works in the field of Christian music, and he lives with his partner.

Pastor Jean: Forced Out by the Bishop

Another example is Pastor Jean, a lesbian ELCA pastor who was ousted from parish ministry at the age of 42. She had been living quietly in a relationship with another woman — a relationship that many of her parishioners knew about. But a disapproving person in the church found out and complained to the bishop. Meeting with the bishop, Jean pointed out that some other pastors were not living by the rules on sexuality, and she asserted her right to have a committed relationship. Nevertheless the bishop required her to resign. It was devastating to her, and Jean has been angry about what happened ever since.

> It's been an interesting journey for me. First I had to figure out if I was Christian or Lutheran, because I was so Lutheran I didn't know if I was really Christian without that [*laughs*]. Once I figured out that I could still be a practicing Christian without being Lutheran, that was a huge step for me! I have more respect for people who choose to participate actively in a congregation. Having been outside of the church, I realize how small and petty the church can be. For the 14 years that I was a pastor I was very lucky and very much had a chance to live in the true sanctity of what the church in its goodness is. I really did. I felt very lucky because I had never been a cynic, I'd never had to struggle with faith. I'd never been forced to figure out how to balance reality with a faith, because there was no issue for me in that. It all kind of made sense. The issues came for me when I finally wasn't a part of the organized church and had never been in the world. And all of the sudden it's like, "Oh my God!" And so I respect people who get up and go when they're not being fed on Sundays, so many times.

Jean told how over the years as a pastor she grew to accept her sexuality and how her parishioners loved her.

> I think I got less careful through the years. In a backwards way, I participated in causing the whole blowup. Because you get tired of lying, tired of always having to look behind your back, you get tired of always having to pretend. It just sucks. You have enough on your

plate without having to pretend all the time, and it's not fair. To me, it's a fairness issue. Why should you tell me to be [like a] Catholic priest and sign on the dotted line that I will not be in a relationship? Why do I have to do that when we don't ask anybody else in the church to do that? We don't. We don't ask single people to do that. I don't tell you you're going to hell if you live with somebody and don't get married. I may tell you it would be nice if you got married, and I may question if you're allowed to be a Sunday school teacher, or somebody else will question.

I knew two gay guys in [the area], who lived together in the parsonage. All you have to do is look at them and go, "My God! They're both queens!" But this little tiny church didn't want to see. So they would make their little apple pies for the dinner at the church, and everybody doted on them. They were as obvious as black is on white. I think the church chooses not to see until somebody gets mad, and then they have to. If you're good, the people don't care. It's only when somebody gets mad, then somebody has to care.

I think that being a lesbian also made me a better pastor, because I knew what it was like to be on the outside looking in. When I had couples come in who had to talk about the fact that one of them had cheated on the other one or something, I understood what it meant to live with the constant lie and understood what it meant to worry about if someday you were going to do something stupid. Not because I was cheating on somebody but because I was cheating on the church. I was being faithful to me, but to be faithful to myself meant that I was being unfaithful to the church rules.

Such deep ambivalence was common to all the gay and lesbian ex-pastors we interviewed. An ELCA man who left at age 42 wrote this answer to our question about his feelings when leaving local church ministry:

Resentful, betrayed, unappreciated. Church officials are closed-minded and self-serving. They don't consider the leading of God's Spirit one bit, just their own sense of power.

A Presbyterian man who left at age 46 expressed more sadness than anger:

As a gay person (mostly closeted), it became less and less possible to hope that my denomination would ever change its policies so as to accept and affirm the Christian commitment and ministry of people like me in *all* callings across the church. My congregation was *deeply* supportive — and paid for that support by experiences of ostracism and harassment. My move to a new form of ministry beyond the local church was an attempt to take a step back from the front lines of a struggle that was, and is, breaking my heart.

A Presbyterian woman who left at age 50 felt similarly distant from her denomination:

Primarily I left because it was not safe to be an out lesbian in the Presbyterian Church. Thus I cannot be a pastor in a church without putting myself through hell and a local church through the same thing. There is no place for me.

A man in the LCMS, who left at 38, told us he would not have left at all:

I believe I was a very effective spiritual leader. Laity and staff would agree. I am gay and I was not acting out on my orientation, but a co-worker who was homophobic "blew the whistle on me" by opening my personal e-mail where I was openly addressing my struggle with a confidant.

An ELCA man who left at 41 summed up the distinction many gay and lesbian clergy draw between authentic Christianity and the institutionalized church:

I'm gay, and am celebrating nearly ten years in a committed, monogamous relationship. I refused to live with the institutional church's hypocrisy any longer. I was out to my bishop when he ordained me, out to other staff members and many of my members, who were all very supportive. The vast majority of ELCA leaders know they should support the ordination and committed relationships of gay pastors, but they lack the integrity and courage. They are afraid of losing money and members. I've got no problem with

God or my calling. It's the institutional church that nauseates me as it makes a mockery of its baptismal theology.

It is hard to listen to these stories without reflecting on the conflicts surrounding homosexuality in North American culture today. Same-sex attraction and same-sex relationships are gradually becoming accepted as part of American life. Yet nearly all Protestant denominations are split regarding whether to accept open homosexuality, especially among clergy. The issue will not be resolved soon. Our study can perhaps contribute to the conversation by reporting clearly and openly the feelings of gay and lesbian individuals who at one time served in parish ministry.

Main Findings

1. Women ministers left the pastorate at about the same rate as men.
2. Women associates serving under male senior pastors reported more conflicts among church staff.
3. Women felt more time pressure, and more women would like part-time positions.
4. Openly gay and lesbian ex-pastors feel angry about the way they have been treated by their denominations.

---

12 Thinking about Returning to the Pastorate

I miss preaching. I really, really loved preaching. I miss doing weddings. I miss doing funerals. It sounds strange, but I was good at funerals. Yeah, there are a lot of aspects of it that I miss. I miss serving the people in that way. I don't miss the hierarchy of the church.

A 53-year-old United Methodist woman

We have seen that many dedicated and talented ministers have left parish ministry. How many would like to return? We raised the subject in our interviews and found that many former pastors want to or are at least open to the possibility of returning to parish ministry. We estimate that a third or more of the persons in our sample would come back, given the right circumstances.

Who might return? Mainly two types of persons: those who voluntarily left — either to switch to a specialized ministry or to stay home with children — and those who were forced out against their will due to sexual misconduct, divorce, or fallout with denominational officials. The clearest examples in our sample were the ex-pastors who voluntarily left the ministry to care for family and children. The majority of these persons said that they actively hoped to return to the ministry after their children have left the home. The ex-pastors who voluntarily switched into specialized ministries expressed similar feelings, though they did not have in mind any time frame analogous to that of ministers waiting for their children to leave home. They were open-minded and tentative when talking about their futures. The pastors least interested in returning were those who had gone through dreadful experiences in their last pastorates. These people had by and large given up on ministry; some had also given up on church involvement altogether.

The discussions we had about the possibility of returning to parish ministry taught us several lessons. This chapter explains them by answering two questions: What do the ex-pastors miss about ministry? And under what circumstances would they be ready to return to parish ministry?

What the Ex-Pastors Miss

The majority of the ex-pastors told us that there are at least parts of ministry that they miss. Their accounts were remarkably consistent: they most miss leading worship and being a meaningful part of people's lives. For example, an Assemblies of God man told us he left at age 45 due to stress and now works in business:

> I do love the ministry. The good parts were, I really enjoy working with people. I like taking people, where they think that there is no hope for something, and show them that there's hope. And getting them to look at the other side of the picture in their personal lives, in their spiritual lives, everything. I really got a joy out of doing that. It was fun, it was enjoyable. And I felt that I was really accomplishing what the Lord wanted me to do. And I tried to be down on their level. So many times pastors don't want to take the time, and maybe that's what caused me to get burned out. Someone could call me up any time day or night and I'd be right there, whatever it was, and try to work with them, get through it. I thought that was what a pastor was supposed to do! When I chose to accept what I felt God wanted me to do, that's what I felt: let's do it. So I felt I was giving of myself, and I enjoyed doing that.

We asked an ELCA man who left at age 44 to become a hospital chaplain whether there is anything about parish ministry he misses.

> What I miss is the generational connectedness. I grew up in a community in Philadelphia that, even though that's a big city, it's a big

little town. People at that point didn't move in and out a lot. So there was a lot of generational connectedness. I had gotten to the point in my ministry at that congregation where — there was one young woman, I baptized her, confirmed her, and then officiated at her wedding, and I have buried her grandparents. That is such a richly meaningful thing to me. Even people who are not active in the congregation, five years would pass between Uncle Joe's death and then somebody else would pass away or the family would be in crisis. When I walked in, (a) I was a known quantity; and (b) they didn't have to rehearse the whole family history with me nor hide the dysfunction that we all knew was there. And so there was simply an acceptance that we can almost pick up where we left off. I value those connections.

An ELCA man who left at 39 after coming out as gay expressed his feelings:

I miss the people. [*cries*] Shoot, I thought I was all resolved with this stuff . . . Sorry. I miss the people and having the opportunity to be a part of significant parts of their lives: changes, marriages, losses, needs, celebrations, and doing it in a context of faith. I miss that terribly. I miss the love I felt from people, and I felt so loved as a pastor. And I know that's probably not one of the most healthy reasons for being a pastor, but it certainly is there.

A United Methodist man who left at age 42 in the wake of sexual misconduct said similar things:

I loved being a pastor. I realize, sometimes you have to lose something to realize what you had. I told various people in the last few years that I had the best job in the world. And I lost it. Being a pastor is *very* demanding, but it's also very rewarding, and I miss it. I miss officiating at weddings and funerals and baptisms. I miss worship and I especially miss the preaching. I miss the contact with people in a way that most people in our society don't get on a day-to-day basis. We were real privileged. Maybe clergy don't realize what a privilege that is to be able to be present with people in those troubled times. I miss that. But I don't miss committees. I don't miss the politics.

Another United Methodist man, who left at age 45 after refusing a bishop's placement and now works in computers, missed the feeling of having a call:

This is the first time in my life that I can remember, I don't know where I'm going. I have never in my life just got up and done a job just so that I can make enough money to live. There's always been some greater purpose behind it than that. And I don't have that any more, and that's been very difficult for me. I've often said that God calls people into full-time ministry not because they are great saints but because they're poor saints and they wouldn't do well otherwise. [*laughs*] I feel like I'm proving that, like I need to have church things around me all the time to keep me faithful.

I miss having to pick up my Bible to study for sermons. I loved doing that. I loved sermon prep. I loved the exegesis and studying the Greek and the Hebrew and digging in. I've got thousands of dollars' worth of books in a closet upstairs. I really don't have any reason to keep them any more, but I can't stand to get rid of them. I don't have time to do anything with them any more. I *do* miss that.

A United Methodist woman who left at age 41 for being openly lesbian and now works in family therapy also yearned to feel a call:

I think a part of me has not been able to get away from the fact that I did feel called to the ordained ministry, and there is very definitely a hole in my life, I guess, having walked away from that. Particularly the sacramental pieces, the things involved with worship. I wouldn't say that I was the best preacher, but the entire worship experience, from designing worship to the music, the prayers, the sacraments, those elements are still very important to me. And I think I was gifted in those areas.

There are certainly things that I don't miss. The administrative aspects, attending to buildings and property and those sorts of things, and the financial pieces, needing to be concerned about money. I don't have any interest in maintaining institutions. I have great interest in people's spiritual lives and whether they're connecting with God, and how people perceive God, and are aware or unaware. Just the search for God, I guess, and search for meaning in general. . . . So now I've found myself asking the question a lot after I left: What am I called to now?

An ELCA man who left at 44 due to burnout and is now a teacher missed being deeply involved in worship, especially the sacraments:

I miss a lot of things about it. Most notably, the worship life. I miss leading worship and doing communion. That was the big thing about being dropped from the rolls and the roster, is that I can't serve communion. I could preach but I can't celebrate communion and stuff like that. That was a big blow. I was like, gee, that's the worst, to not be able to be involved in some of that. And like, I've been asked to do weddings of friends now, and I've said, "I can't do them because I'm not officially with the ELCA. I couldn't sign your license, I couldn't do any of that stuff."

And unfortunately, the church I go to here, the worship life really stinks. The organ is bad, the organist is worse. But I don't want to drive fifteen miles [to another ELCA church], and I don't want to go back to my old parish. Right now I'm not a real happy camper, I'm not a good pew-sitter either. I took me about two months to quit writing notes about what was wrong with the service [*laughs*], making notes about what I would change.

We asked a Presbyterian woman who left at age 39 to take care of her children and now works part-time in college administration if she misses the ministry.

Sometimes. I miss the diversity. Ministry is great for diversity, because no two days are alike. [*sniffs*] Oh, I'm getting emotional, I hadn't expected that. . . . I miss people. I miss whole families, whole lives. My job now is desk, computer, and phone. And so it's less satisfying in that way. So yeah, there are things that I miss, relationships primarily.

An ELCA man who left at age 45 because of sexual misconduct singled out the same involvement with people:

It's being a part of the significant events of people's lives. While there are times in pastors' lives when they'll say, "Another wedding? I have to go to another reception and eat more chicken and ham?" But on the other hand, they'll turn right around and say, "Another wedding! Another baptism!" Even "Another funeral!" Because people invite you into the most important, significant events in their lives. I don't miss the council meetings, I don't know any pastors who do. You obviously need business meetings, but you don't miss them. You do miss the significant events where you actually sit down and are able to have an in-depth conversation over a worthwhile issue.

A United Methodist woman who left at 53 due to stress and burnout chose preaching as the thing she missed most:

I miss preaching. I really, really loved preaching. I miss doing weddings. I miss doing funerals. It sounds strange, but I was good at funerals. Yeah, there are a lot of aspects of it that I miss. I miss serving the people in that way. I don't miss the hierarchy of the church. I do miss the public part of it, the speaking, the being able both to use my mind and my ability in that way. I miss putting together sermons, the challenge of that. And that was always fun. And I miss the kids. I loved working with the youth groups and with the kids, and things like that. That's a thing about being a female, you often get shuffled into working with the youth [*laughs*]. "You can do that, you're really good at that." It was something that I enjoyed, as long as they were young. But with teenagers, I had enough of my own.

An LCMS man who left at 33 due to burnout and now works for a church-based association talked about how people in other occupations are different from ministers:

The laity don't understand. Because their world, whether they're farmers or another type of job, they punch in, they punch out. And they don't see you doing that, so they're like, what do you really do? Come on. And my dad joked about that. "What do you really do?" Ha, ha, nudge, nudge. They don't understand. They're like, "That's not a job, what do you mean?" Or when you're working with someone and all of a sudden they take a backwards slide. It's like, "What are you talking about? What's the big deal? You move on." They don't realize the emotion that you invest, your own heart that you're investing, and it can be broken like that. Some will just go, "What's the big deal?" Because they're dealing with business deals or they're dealing with corn crops. "Come on, what's your problem?" They don't realize. Then it's tough to communicate with them outside the pulpit, to be really able to open up and share, because they're in a different world, so to speak.

An ELCA man who left at 51 because of burnout and is now a college administrator told what he misses about ministry:

Oh, I liked the worship and the preaching. And the affirmation, being the center of attention [laughs]. A pastor gets a lot. It's a dangerous place for needy personalities. [laughs] . . . I love worship, I love creating a good worship experience, especially around special days and special events in the church's life. I love pastoral stuff. I miss that. But I don't miss the meetings and I don't miss arguments about money and I don't miss sermon preparation and the politics.

These statements are surprisingly similar in their content. These ex-ministers miss worship, preaching, teaching, involvement with families at significant moments in their lives, and authentic relationships with members of their churches. These experiences are in a very real sense "pearls of great price," worth much of the trouble and sacrifice that are inherently part of parish ministry. We should expect, then, that when the ex-pastors told us the conditions under which they might return, they would entail holding on to the good parts and letting go of the rest.

Conditions for Returning to the Pastorate

We had many opportunities to ask the ex-pastors under what circumstances they would return to the pastorate. A small portion of the pastors, certainly less than half, specified no conditions at all. They said that they would be willing to serve wherever the Lord calls, or that they would be open to any opportunity that might come along. But the others voiced a wide range of conditions for returning. Three of them were mentioned frequently and deserve expression here.

Before doing that, however, we should briefly mention three other stipulations that are noteworthy but less common. First, two or three ex-pastors said that the salary for any position they would consider taking would need to be higher than salaries are now; for example, one said that he would not take a pay cut from his current job as administrator of a social agency. Second, several said they would not agree to move their residence in order to re-enter the ministry; any parish position they might consider would need to be nearby. Third, several said that if they would be convinced that the denomination really needed them and that they could make a difference, and if they felt a strong call from the Lord, they would return to parish ministry. In effect, this third group would be influenced by genuine appeals from church leaders or other pastors.

Having noted these less-frequent conditions, we turn now to the three main themes we encountered when discussing conditions for returning. The first was the most common: the new position would need to be part-time, not full-time. In a few instances pastors told us that the job would need to be specialized — for example, youth ministry or visitation ministry — and they assumed such positions would be part-time. Other pastors did not mention a specialized ministry, but noted instead that they did not want the responsibility and full-time involvement of pastoring a parish.

For example, a Presbyterian man who left at 53 to go into social ministry told about his hope if he re-enters ministry:

My druthers, at this point, would be to be a part-time visitation pastor for a church. Not a senior pastor. Visitation is something I enjoy. I always did an outstanding job at it.

We asked a United Methodist woman, who left at 53 after several conflicts in her church and who now works in business, if she would ever consider going back into ministry:

I have thought about it, off and on, this last couple of years. And I've got to say, obviously there is something still there, because I haven't thrown out all the robes yet [*laughs*]. But I don't think I would go back to this full-time. I realize now that it's a pretty insane life. I'm 57. Having been in this since I was 27 years old, a

whole lifetime of raising kids and moving through this whole process, you don't realize that most people don't live with this. I can
explain. We had a party one night and I looked around, and everybody in the house was either clergy or they were funeral home oper-
ators. This is bizarre. Either clergy, counselors, or funeral home op-
erators. In some ways, you lose contact with the world — if that
makes sense. You're very much trying to speak to it, but you're very
isolated from it. You don't often get invited anywhere except by
other clergy. Your circles become narrower and narrower. Thirty
years ago I started out with a whole collection and group of friends,
and because you move so often, you lose contact.

An LCMS man who left at 50 because of sexual misconduct and now
works in social service described the part-time ministry he would like:

> I would be willing to consider what, I guess, way back in seminary,
> they called a worker-priest approach. . . . I really felt [for] people
> who were out working in the world and, because of their convic-
> tions and faith in the Lord, were wanting to be lay ministers or dea-
> cons or whatever you want to call them. That always had the great-
> est appeal to me, and . . . I wouldn't mind doing that at all. But I
> wouldn't want to do that full-time because I guess I feel sometimes
> the full-time minister gets a pretty narrow focus on life.

A second theme was that the ex-pastors wanted to be free from the
obligations and constraints of denominations. Several told us that they
disliked adhering to the rules and directives of denominational leaders.
They questioned whether managing denominational affairs was really
ministry anyway, and several suggested that denominational affairs actually impede rather than help ministry. We heard this a bit more from
United Methodists than from the others, since the Methodist connec-
tional system demands a greater acceptance of church authority. For
example, a United Methodist man who left at age 56 after a divorce and
then changed denominations did not miss his old one at all:

> I'm not interested in Methodist ministry any more. As a matter of
> fact, I've changed denominations since then. I am now a member of
> a congregation that is as totally un-Methodist as it can get: elder-led

rather than congregation-led. A whole different approach to the way you run an organization. One of the things is that it shows me how much of a pastor's time within the United Methodist Church is spent on promoting the organization. There's just an awful lot of things that United Methodist pastors do that basically are promoting the various programs that this committee or that committee has come up with, or the new quadrennial theme, or on and on and on. Rather than deal with matters of the gospel, you are dealing with matters of the organization. While I was doing it, it never really surfaced clearly in my mind until I got away from it. And then I began to realize that probably something in the neighborhood of 20 percent of your workweek is spent doing just that.

Not just that it's administrative. There's going to be a lot of administrative things no matter what. But it's administrative in the sense that you're promoting this or that part of the connection, the conference, or the district program, whatever that happens to be at the moment. All of these things are good, and all of these things have, in a way, fallout for the local congregation. Within the United Methodist Church there are things called apportionments, which are the local congregation's payment to the conference structure. Of course they want to push that. In addition there is a camping program and there's a mission program and there's a women's program that are larger than the local church, and your time is definitely spent promoting those kinds of things. And if you don't do that, you're kind of considered a renegade in the group, so you don't really have an option about will I or won't I do it.

We talked with an Assemblies of God ex-pastor who left at 44 and now works in banking. He is still smarting from a conflict with denominational officers, and he would like to avoid denominational obligations in the future.

I'm wrestling now with starting a church out of my home. I'm not going to join a denomination. I currently attend a Foursquare Church, and I'm a member there. But I would not become a credentialed minister in the Foursquare Church. I'm a real diehard Assembly, it's just I'm not in the Assemblies anymore. So if I re-enter ministry, it's either going to be a non-denominational church that has Assemblies of God theology, or maybe it's going to be in the Assemblies somehow.

A Presbyterian man who left at 55 in the wake of allegations that he had an affair feels that he had been unjustly treated by the denomination. We asked him if he would consider re-entering ministry:

> Yes, I would. I'm considering what would be the next step for me. Well, that really isn't my choice. That's God's choice. God has been pretty good about leaving me indicators and signs. And if God would say, "I've got a congregation that needs you to come, because these are their needs and you're the best suited," I would go. . . . But the denominational system, the politics and such, I felt like I had really been burned, and that I'd been doing a good job in the ministry I was doing, and I was not welcome to continue to stay there because of how I had violated some ministerial code or some kind of deal. Actually I have applied to some non-denominational churches.

A third feeling we encountered was a strong desire to re-enter ministry in a different denomination or at least in a different geographic location. A few ex-pastors said they wanted to start over with a clean slate, away from the denominational leaders who had been a source of grief for them. Several who were divorced said they wanted to move to a denomination more tolerant of divorce — or at very least they wanted to move to a district in their denomination where the leadership would accept them in spite of the divorce.

Here are two examples of pastors who would consider ministry in different denominations. A United Methodist woman who left at 41 for being openly lesbian chafed at the denomination's stance on sexual orientation:

> I'm not sure that I would be willing to ever go back full-time and let myself be owned, for lack of a better term, by an institution. Especially when I disagree with their stance about who is fit to serve. And that's the piece that I continue to have some struggle with. For a long, long time I was very angry with the denomination's stance. I've moved through some of that and kind of felt a love-hate rela-

tionship with the church, and have sort of struggled to be clear about the difference between God and church, and church as institution and church as community of faith. But I know I need the church in my life. I still worship regularly. I know I can't be a Christian on my own.

An ELCA Lutheran man who left at age 56 after several conflicts told us he misses ministry and would like to return:

But the doors have been closed to me in the Lutheran Church. I really don't know what that means for me down the road. But if someone approached me in another denomination, I would be open to that. Because I really think, given my experience now, I see life totally different. I'm far more gracious. But it doesn't seem like the Lutheran Church sees it that way. Not the people in authority.

These statements from ex-pastors demonstrate that ministry gave meaning and satisfaction to their souls in a way that other occupations — or at least most other occupations — could not. The yearnings in this chapter do much to counterbalance the complaints and frustrations that we heard so often and that we recounted in earlier chapters of this book. Many ex-pastors loved the ministry, and they hold out hope that somehow they can find a way back into it.

Main Findings

1. One-third or more of the ex-pastors would like to return, depending on circumstances.
2. The ex-pastors miss leading worship and being a meaningful part of people's lives.
3. The most common requirement for returning is that the job would need to be part-time.

---

13   Summary and Recommendations from Pastors

Our study has resulted in three major findings regarding why pastors leave local church ministry. First, the main factors pushing pastors away from local church ministry are organizational and interpersonal. It is striking that of the seven main motivations we identified for leaving parish ministry, all fit into one of these two broad categories. We were also struck by some conspicuous absences from the list; we had expected some other reasons to be important, since they are mentioned often in the religious media. Financial and health-related concerns are factors we originally thought might be among the main ones, but in the end they were minor, not major factors. Being openly gay or lesbian, experiencing a loss of faith, or holding different doctrinal stances on such controversial issues as abortion or gay rights turned out similarly to be issues for only a few of the pastors. While much hand-wringing attends these high-profile issues, to keep ministers in local parish ministry requires giving attention principally to more mundane problems, the kind most people deal with day in and day out. Conflict, burnout, feeling unfulfilled, and experiencing family and marriage problems are the main culprits in draining the supply of parish ministers.

The second major finding of our study is that ministers are experiencing a lack of support and support systems, especially when they are coping with conflicts. They are well aware that parish ministry is fraught with conflict, and they expect to deal with a host of different opinions, ideas, and ways of doing things in their congregations. But what they are not prepared for is the lack of support they find when they come under serious attack by congregational factions or families or are falsely accused of misconduct. Some have felt betrayed by a church hierarchy that seems to show favoritism or ignore destructive behavior by other ministers or officials.

The problem of lack of support is complicated. Pastors recognize the need for a personal support system of other ministers, and denominations often foster such relationships. But ministers feel unavoidable competition with each other, which gets in the way of forming healthy support groups. Pastors are reluctant to talk about their problems with other pastors in their denomination who, like themselves, later on will be seeking better churches and denominational promotions. The minister with whom you share your weaknesses today may be your superior a few years from now.

Even when personal support groups of pastors are in place, they are not substitutes for the backing that judicatories can provide. When pastors come under attack or get caught in the crossfire of belligerent congregational factions, they need the support of those in authority. No matter how much a minister is supported by her or his colleagues, those colleagues lack the decision-making power of the denominational officers. Ideally pastors would have a mentor or a superior in the system, to whom they could bring their frustrations, concerns, and fears. But to bring problems to judicatory officers is dangerous for ministers. They are concerned that they will be viewed negatively by staff persons with whom they talk or that they will be branded "problem people." We found that pastors commonly experience mistrust in their relationships with denominational officers and even with their fellow pastors. Frequently they need genuine support and assistance from somewhere outside the denominational power structure.

A third major finding is that it is not just one but rather a combination of stresses and difficulties that influences pastors to leave. Although we were usually able to identify a pastor's primary motivation for leaving, in almost every case there were several motivating factors at work. For example, as we noted in Chapter 6, it was sometimes hard to distinguish between what was primarily a conflict with the congregation and what was a conflict with the denomination, since the two were so often intertwined. Likewise, pastors who left primarily because they were burned out often had been through serious conflicts. Often marriage problems exacerbated, or were exacerbated by, both conflicts and burnout. Even sexual misconduct was sometimes an indirect result of experiences that left pastors emotionally vulnerable. Various stresses and problems build up over time so that what might have been an easily resolvable problem in its early stages becomes a major crisis expelling a pastor from the church.

Denominational Differences

We designed our study to illuminate differences among denominations that would be instructive for everyone. But over the course of our research we were surprised that the differences were smaller than we had anticipated. Still, several came through consistently enough to be mentioned. The United Methodist Church and the Assemblies of God turned out to be the most unique denominations; the Presbyterian Church (U.S.A.), the Evangelical Lutheran Church in America, and the Lutheran Church–Missouri Synod resembled each other in many ways. Of the five denominations, the United Methodist pastors were the most dissatisfied with their ministerial deployment system. They yearned for a greater say in their appointments and for more constructive dialogue with lay leaders in the churches.

The Assemblies of God is unique in that it is a loose association of congregations, a system that accords little authority to denominational offices. Therefore Assemblies pastors feel more on their own than the others. They have fewer expectations of receiving help from district superintendents; thus they rely more on their friendships with fellow clergy. The Assemblies pastors in our study were quickest to remind us that "ministry is tough, and you can't expect anybody to help you if things go bad." The Assemblies is also the most active in planting new churches, and we ran into quite a few Assemblies ex-pastors who had not been able to make their new churches grow. They were a sad group, and they complained about the lack of support they got despite denominational officials' full knowledge that any given church plant had only a modest probability of success.

The ELCA, LCMS, and Presbyterian Church were similar in most respects. Both Lutheran denominations offer their pastors a bit less autonomy in terms of job placement, but those pastors did not com-

Figure 13.1
Recommendations to Denominations

Points of Intervention	*Pastors' Recommendations*
1. Denomination accepts the person as a local church pastor	1. Have seminaries do more to prepare ministers for the practical aspects of ministry
2. Placement in a new church position	2. Improve the call process
3. Period of adjustment to the new church position	3. Provide ongoing support for pastors
4. Emergence of a problem or conflict	4. Provide support for pastors in conflict or crisis

plain more than the Presbyterians about the system. Rather, pastors of all three denominations seemed more troubled by something else. They were perplexed by theological and cultural changes in the membership — the Lutheran and Presbyterian laity. This raised questions about denominational identity and congregational identity. The pastors in these three denominations talked about a problem of knowing really what a pastor is or should be.

Four Points of Intervention for Denominations

Our study identified four points at which denominational leaders can or should intervene in a minister's career; see Figure 13.1 above. In the left column of the figure are the four points, and in the right column are the main recommendations about each point given to us by the pastors. The four possible times of intervention are (1) when a person is accepted to local church ministry by the denomination; (2) when a pastor is placed in a new church position; (3) when he or she is adjusting to the new position; and (4) when a problem or conflict emerges. We will look at the pastors' recommendations for improving the outcome of each.

Recommendations to Denominations

We asked all the ministers for recommendations to help their denominations. Most had definite ideas, and they were happy to share them, hoping that their viewpoints might be communicated more widely through our book. We promised to convey their recommendations as best we could. The recommendations varied widely in content, with ministers suggesting everything from wholesale reconstruction of denominational structures to minute policy changes. But there were four main points on which most agreed.

Recommendation 1: Seminaries should do more to prepare their students for the practical aspects of ministry.

The ministers told us over and over that they wanted to see more training in the nuts-and-bolts of local church ministry. Many felt ill prepared to perform essential pastoral tasks and told us that the realities of parish life were certainly different from what they had expected. Also, a large number recommended better screening of applicants. Here are some examples.

An ELCA man who left at age 42 wished he had had more practical training:

> You go through seminary, and one of the beefs I have with the whole education process for clergy, I mean they spent all this time preparing you theologically around how to be a pastor. But they spent hardly any time around things like the practical issues of ministry: how do you deal with councils; how do you deal with difficult people — alligators in the congregation; how do you foster your own spiritual life? When I was going through seminary, that wasn't even touched on. I just see the seminaries as being self-serving institutions, and this is real cynical, but they're just this huge machine where they have to have so many people coming in one end and going out the other. The people that are teaching have been in those positions for 10, 20, 30 years. When have they been in the pulpit or in a congregation for any length of time? Some of my professors were there one or two years, and then they went right into academia. And these are the people that are teaching me to be a pastor? I mean, that's real frustrating to me.

A former Assemblies of God minister who was 31 years old when he resigned recounted a positive Bible college experience but a lack of practical training:

> You can know the truth, but if you can't present it in a way, and work with people to accept it, you've done no good. And you cause conflict or misunderstandings and stuff. Maybe more practical, more hands-on experience using what we've been taught.

A 45-year-old ELCA pastor thinks seminaries don't teach the importance of pastors' taking care of themselves:

> At the seminary level, there is not enough discussion about the need to do good personal self-care and how to find the support to do that. So one of the ways I talk about that, and I've had the opportunity at the seminary level, is to go in and do some classroom teaching on this. I say that everybody who goes into ministry needs to have three people in their lives before they start: they need a therapist, a mentor, and a pastor, so that there is a therapist that they can go to in confidence with the issues related to personal life, growth type things. They need a mentor, somebody to go to and say, "I don't get this, what am I supposed to do? It's my first funeral." Those types of issues. And you need a pastor, somebody that you can go to as your spiritual advisor. Clergy don't have that and they're not taught how to have that. They're taught the mechanics of theology, but not the practical application of translating what they've learned into what's the reality of parish life like.

A United Methodist minister who left parish ministry when he was 62 noted that ministry is not one-size-fits-all:

> You go to seminary, and they basically teach you how to run a medium-sized church. I suppose they had to tailor-make it that way. They don't really teach you how to run the mega-large church, but they also don't teach you how to run the little single pastorate, the no-staff type of church. And the truth is, for most people, when they come out of seminary, the very first thing that happens is they have anywhere from 10 to 20 years in those kinds of churches. They

haven't taught you how to run a mimeograph machine back in the days that I came on; they haven't taught you to do all of those things. I haven't kept abreast of it, but I bet you there are very few seminaries nowadays that teach computer programming and software and all that kind of stuff that are used in the profession. They don't do those kinds of nuts-and-bolts, nitty-gritty things.

A 50-year-old ELCA former pastor talked about the quality of seminary students:

I chaired the synod's candidacy committee for seven years, I served on it for nine years. And I kept seeing what I considered to be the caliber of the candidates go down and down and down. I finally got so cynical I had to get off the committee. It was more and more being populated by people who had an extraordinary sense of entitlement. And by that I mean, for example, a candidate who lived in [a certain city] who wanted an exception from the ELCA seminary rule, in order to be able to go to the Presbyterian seminary there, get her degree there, do her internship somewhere within a 20-mile radius, and then get a call within that same radius, because her husband was a lawyer and couldn't move his practice. That's a far cry from, "Here am I, send me." I understand that that person's call to ministry came after she had already had a call as a partner and a mother. Oh, and there was an Olympic swimming pool in that mix too, because that candidate had a kid who was a swimmer. And she was a good candidate, intellectually and spiritually, but had some challenges with regard to being inconvenienced.

Other people were, just to use a couple of examples: people in their fourth marriage; physically poor specimens, out of shape, overweight, didn't seem to care a whole lot about themselves or their physical appearance. Or, as one of our committee members put it at one point, when we were talking about using the term "second-career candidates," and he looked at the candidate's dossier and said, "Six jobs in eight years does not constitute a first career." This person was bouncing around from one thing to another, and he finally decided that he wanted to go to seminary.

Recommendation 2: Improve the call process.

This recommendation relates to the second intervention point for ministers: when they are placed in a new position. Many pastors criticized the lack of honesty and forthrightness in the call process. While some thought the process itself needed to be revamped, others asked solely for more forthrightness about problems in churches and better effort to match ministers to churches. A United Methodist man who left at age 46 asked for more consistency and better communication:

> In United Methodism, every conference, every bishop does things differently. I understand there are conferences where every person who is recommended for a church goes and meets with the committee. And they both can go back later and say, "This is a good idea," or "This is not a good idea." I think the era of the imperial bishop needs to go away. For one thing, the bishop can't *know everything*. That means more dialogue, and I know it's going to take more time, and I know it's going to be more trouble. But I think some things are worth it.
>
> There was a cartoon circulated several years ago, where a young pastor was going to the district superintendent or the bishop and saying, "Look, you gave me a challenge, you gave me an opportunity. Can I have a church now?" When they appoint you to a church, they tell you all these wonderful things about where you're going. So we don't listen to it anymore; after the first couple, you know better. But I wish they'd treat us like professionals. If you're a doctor, you tell what's wrong with the patient. I wish they could say, "Look, this is a church in trouble. This is what it needs. We know that you can't levitate it. We recognize that nobody is going to turn this thing around in four years. But try to make it a little better. We understand that you cannot work miracles, but see if you can keep it from getting worse."

A Presbyterian pastor wanted more realism in local church expectations:

> I think overall, as I look at the CIF and PIF forms [Church Information Form and Pastor Information Form, used during hiring] and that kind of situation with the churches, I wish there could be some sort of presbytery-level or General Assembly–level committee that

would be reviewing the kinds of expectations that individual churches are putting on people when they hire. Like a lot of the job applications look like they want to hire God or something. The level of what they expect someone to do is a lot.

An LCMS pastor who left at age 32 spoke about the placement of seminarians:

Seminarians are "placed" in the Missouri Synod, so you're guaranteed a call, but they'll place you. And they ask you about your interests and your abilities and things like that, and then they try to get some of the same input from the congregations, and it probably would be better to have some more thought put into that process. That could be a process to work on: really identifying the congregation's true needs, not just putting down some standard stuff on a call document, that they know the seminary might want to hear. And trying to make the best match. You know, I think arranged marriages work better than our American style of dating and courtship, and [a similar system] could work out great here, but there needs to be a little more thought put into that process.

A United Methodist pastor who left at age 50 criticized the appointment system:

In an effective organization, you want to put your best people where your greatest need is. I had a lesson years ago when I had a little bit of a confrontation about this whole thing with the bishop, and he sat me down and he pulled out this book, it's the appointment book. It's the way that Methodist ministers are appointed. And I thought it was very telling. The way it's arranged is by salary. So the person who is listed number one in the appointment process is the person who is making the highest salary in the conference, and then it goes down from there to the person who is making the lowest. So you've got 300 pastoral charges, say, in the state of Georgia. Well, it's ranked from First Methodist whatever, down to Grace United Methodist Church in Dry Prong, or whatever. Well, the object always is to move up in that system.

It seems to me if that's the basis on which you make appointments, then you have in effect said, "We're not going to necessarily put our best people where our greatest needs are," unless we assume that the larger churches are where our greatest need is, and that may not be true. Some of the greatest needs may be in inner-city churches that need to be revived. But who wants to send somebody there? So I think the whole system needs to be looked at. I just think it says an awful lot that in a church that is based on Christian principles, where Jesus talks about poverty and those kinds of things, the very appointment book itself is arranged in the order of salaries. I can't put those two things together. I've even said that to bishops and district superintendents, that as long as that's the process by which you make appointments, then you've created a system that's really not much different than the way the world does things. And there is that tension in the New Testament about not being conformed to this world.

Recommendation 3: Provide ongoing support for pastors.

The most frequent recommendations we heard had to do with providing support for pastors, both in everyday life and during crises. First we will look at recommendations for ongoing support, both for the newly ordained and for seasoned pastors.

The ex-pastors we interviewed spoke about the difficulty of developing trust with other pastors and with judicatory officers. A United Methodist woman who left parish ministry at age 53 felt this acutely:

The thing that underlies the whole process, and I've seen it in all four of the conferences I've been in, is that the clergy don't trust each other. They're very competitive. I was part of a very close group in one conference, but it was a very small group of clergy that had ties to a local university, basically, either from going to school there for graduate degrees or living in the area. And they were a subgroup within the conference, but the thing is, the rest of the conference didn't trust us and we didn't trust them either. There is just a general distrust of each other among the clergy, and I think it's a real pity. We put on a real camaraderie on the surface, and I think underneath it all, it's pretty much every person for themselves. And I found that very sad.

It's incredibly isolating. There is no place to go for support, unless you have a circle of friends outside the conference. And it's hard to develop that. If you're moving every three to five years, it's pretty hard to maintain friendships. And there is tremendous strain placed on the family, with the kind of movement of clergy that the Methodist church makes.

On the topic of setting boundaries, one Presbyterian woman called for help with assumptions about time:

> The more the denomination can do the better, to help congregations understand the flexible hours piece, supporting pastors' families, in putting boundaries around the job, and doing flex-time. And not having the expectation that he or she will be at her desk 9 to 5, and at my committee meeting on Tuesday nights and in the pulpit Sunday mornings and at the youth retreat on Saturday afternoon. That's a tall order for me to say to [denominational leaders], "Do more about that." I'm not sure how they can do it, about changing congregations' assumptions about what a clergyperson can give them in terms of time. And teaching them how to be respectful and supportive of clergy putting limits around their jobs so they have time for themselves and their family. And in particular for single moms that are pastors, the need for there to be limits.

Another Presbyterian talked about the difficulties single women encounter:

> I would have liked a definition of what's healthy time off. And ministers should be educated to that in the seminary, and people in the church should have some sense that their pastors have time off every week. Granted, emergencies happen. I mean, if someone gets sick and it's my day off, I'm going to go see that person and take a day off some other time.
>
> And some kind of support network for single pastors. Pastors need more support generally and a feeling, at least from the denomination level, that pastors are valued. "You're important" kind of thing. And if you write a letter, at least get it answered. And also the financial. There needs to be a balance between small church and large church salaries.

A Presbyterian minister spoke about mentoring:

I recommend some serious mentoring. Intentionally build that into the program. I think, if not the [presbytery] executive, then certainly that there be people within the district that you can talk nuts-and-bolts things with like housing, housing allowance, buying your own, those kinds of issues, dealing with budgets and compensation. They need to be much more intentional about that.

We need intentional mentoring. I don't care if you're newly ordained or not, when you're moving to a different part of the country you need some solid relationships and you need to have some people as friends, as support. What happened with me was, I was in part of the presbytery where the closest pastor wasn't that far away but he had major health problems shortly after I got there. The closest person that I knew other than the Lutheran pastor was 35 miles away. And he was another 20 miles from the nearest church to him. So that gets to be a difficult kind of thing unless you intentionally build something into the relationship.

An Assemblies of God man who left at age 31 thought having an older pastor as a mentor would be encouraging:

I think maybe an older pastor that had a really good heart, some older people that are encouraging and warm and say, "You know, maybe expectations are too high." You explain some of the things you go through, and someone that's been down the road can tell you, "Hey, you're doing okay, don't worry about it. You're not a success, you're not being measured in numbers. The success is measured in what you do for Christ and your obedience to Him." Something like that.

We need more of a family atmosphere among the ministers. Not just to discuss, you know, how large a church is or whatever, but just to be people with each other, friendships with each other. Encouraging one another, suggesting things.

I think pastors need to learn how to better care for those that are under them and those that are around them. Like I said, just to be a support, an encouragement to each other. Rather than a competition, be an encouragement. Loving support. If someone needs a rebuke, rebuke them in love. If someone needs encouragement because they're discouraged, encourage them. Rather than being all caught up in what they're doing and building their little kingdoms, they need to make sure that others are built up around them.

Recommendation 4: Provide support for pastors in conflict or crisis.

Conflicts are inevitable, and some conflicts become serious. When this happens, pastors need help. Our interviewees repeatedly called for more help in crisis situations. Here are examples, beginning with an Assemblies of God pastor:

> In these little towns out here, like where I'm at now, these guys are out here by themselves. They are out here alone. And the result is, you get pastors like in my dad's church that I alluded to, the guy is here a year and he's gone. The church was hurting, they thought with this guy things were going to be great. Come to find out this pastor has so many problems the church couldn't deal with it, couldn't handle it. And so the church is injured again, this pastor is injured again, and it gets worse. And what is this guy going to do? He's looking for another church. It's bad. The denomination is not addressing this. And it's not that they don't want to. It's that the system that they've built does not allow for it. They have no means of helping these people.

A Presbyterian pastor who remained in local church ministry until his sixties said that pastors need to feel that the denomination supports them and not just the congregation:

> I think one of the things that could be done is that when a minister gets into trouble or has a problem situation, he should have the idea that the presbytery is concerned about him as much as they are concerned about the church. And I didn't have that idea at all. My impression is that ministers often feel that they're kind of out there by themselves. My brother-in-law was a Presbyterian minister too, and he had some of the same feelings. He was in another presbytery. They do things for ministers, they have meetings at campgrounds and things like that. But when push comes to shove time, they sort of leave them alone, and that's not good. I have no idea what the percentage is on how that hurts, but I know there are ministers who hurt.

A United Methodist pastor told us what might have kept him in ministry:

> I think, honestly, had there been a less punitive atmosphere when I went to the bishop the first time and said, "I'm having trouble." First, I went to my district superintendent and said, "Look, I'm having trouble. This is happening in my marriage, my wife is having an affair. And I'm really hurting, I need some time to get myself together." And I was told, "Just go back to work, and be a man. Suck it up." I think the denominational elders need to wake up and say, "Here's a person in trouble. What can we do?" We have to put the same effort into saving our clergy that we put into saving our lay people.

Lack of trust surfaced again and again as pastors discussed their concerns about where to turn in the face of a serious problem. An ELCA pastor described a culture of mistrust and called for support from outside the denominational structure:

> We need supports from outside the denominational structure. It is because of the way the structures are set up. Clergy learn early on, as a matter of fact, most of them learn it somewhere along during the year of internship, not to expect any kind of personal support from the denominational office. I've had students tell me that. They say, "When I was on internship, my supervising pastor said, 'If you have a problem, don't go to the bishop, because someday you might want to have that person get you a call.'" Well, if that's an ingrained method of thinking, unless the role of that person can change and we can re-educate clergy and students to understand that that person now can become that pastor for them, they won't go there anyway.

A United Methodist man who left at age 48 after having marital problems offered a telling comparison:

> The denomination people didn't really know much about it. I mean, can you imagine somebody working for ExxonMobil who is having a marital problem going in to their supervisor and saying, "Look, I got a problem." I know that companies have set up a counseling service that they've contracted with, and a person can go there. But

a man is not going to sit down and have a personal conversation with his supervisor. No. But that's what you're being asked to do in the church.

Recommendations to Congregations

In our interviews we did not ask former pastors directly for their recommendations to congregations because we were mainly interested in denominational systems. Yet in the interviews many ex-pastors talked insightfully about what needs to be said to congregations. They told us that congregations need to be sensitized to the genuine needs of pastors, and lay leaders need to know what they should do, in very concrete terms, to make pastorates successful. Here are the main recommendations they made.

Earlier in this chapter we identified four points in ministers' careers at which denominations might beneficially intervene. Three of the four — placement in a new church position, adjustment to that new position, and emergence of a problem or conflict — are points at which congregations also can have a marked influence. Indeed, both pastors and congregations are more vulnerable and more open to influence at these intervention points. Congregations should be aware of their potential influence — for better or for worse — at these three points. See ex-pastors' recommendations to congregations, summarized in Figure 13.2 on page 213.

Recommendation 1: Articulate genuine congregational goals.

The call process in most denominations is flawed in that it makes negotiating a good match difficult for pastors and congregations. One major problem is insufficient honesty and candor in what is essentially a bargaining process in which each party displays its best side and hides its worst. Indeed, many persons we interviewed said that congregations often did not even know what their goals were or did not have the necessary commitment to attain those goals. Until a congregation has identified clear goals, how can it know what it needs in a pastor? And unless it is committed to attaining the goals it sets, how can it have realistic goals for its pastor? A Presbyterian woman who served as an associate pastor commented on this:

Figure 13.2
Recommendations to Congregations

Points of Intervention	*Pastors' Recommendations*
1. Placement in a new church position	1. Articulate genuine congregational goals
2. Period of adjustment to the new church position	2. Be realistic about expectations
3. Emergence of a problem or conflict	3. Provide relief from workloads when pastors are facing conflict or crisis

One of the things that our leadership board struggled with from the very beginning, from the time I became an associate pastor in 1990 up until after I left, was, what is the identity and mission of this particular congregation? What are our priorities? And how do we assemble a staff and assign them work to do and divide up that work in a way that honors those priorities? And we brought in consultants, we had people making us walk to a blackboard and put little colored labels on lists of things. We had all kinds of exercises that we went through, most of which were very heavily spiritual, involved a lot of prayer and Bible study. We used several different models but we made very little progress. We were at a point in our church and congregational history where we were having great difficulty identifying who we are, what we're here to do, specifically, and what, given that identity and that mission, how the professional staff of the church should be organizing our time to honor those priorities.

She did not think the lack of clarity was because of disagreements:

I think it was more that we didn't know. There were occasionally disagreements too, but it wasn't like there were factions in the church. It wasn't like pro-choice, pro-life; ordination of homosexuals wasn't a big deal for the congregation; abortion wasn't a big deal; nobody was going evolution versus creationists. It wasn't one of those things where there were factions that were fighting each other for control of the church, with well-defined goals which were

in conflict with each other. It was: we don't know what we're supposed to be doing here. And so, as a result, there would be one person complaining because the pastor hadn't visited them, but they
had never told the church or anyone else that they were ill. So it was
more an omission rather than commission.

People didn't know what they were supposed to do and how they
were supposed to do it. And as a result, we pastors were unclear,
despite the fact that we talked about this all the time with the session and with each other, asking, "What are we supposed to be doing?" And then the session would say, "Oh, the pastors have to lead
us." We were all searching for a common vision, for *any* vision, in
fact. And we really didn't find it in a way that made us feel like we
all had a common vision. As a matter of fact, that church is very
busy, very active, and there's a lot of stuff that goes on. They do
marvelous mission and tremendous mission trips so that all the
young people in the community, including those who are not members of the church, clamor to get on this mission trip that we take.
There is great ministry going on there, but we felt that we were
adrift. And that was, I think more than anything else, the biggest
cause of stress and dissatisfaction among both pastors and congregation. I've seen a number of other congregations where that is also
the case. It's not like we were the only ones that didn't know what
we were doing.

At other times what a church says it wants is at variance with
what it is actually willing to support. A former Assemblies of God pastor related his experience:

I had lots of messages about getting outside the walls of the church
and reaching the lost. And not a whole lot of support doing it.

His sermons focused on outreach, and people in the church talked
about the need to reach out:

Yeah, there were a lot of sermons and even within the church itself.
Just seems like there just didn't appear to be a whole lot of authen-
ticity and reality in the church. There were a lot more people interested in keeping the machine going, religion going, than they were
in actually living Christianity.

Several pastors said that parishes seemed unwilling to be truthful about their internal struggles and their real motivations. An LCMS pastor felt that his congregation had asked for help in reaching younger families when its real motive seemed to be saving money by hiring a younger pastor:

> They were saying that they wanted somebody to involve the younger people. In fact, that's one of the things they said on their call documents: We want somebody who will reach out to the middle-aged families in the congregation and get them involved. And that's what I did, and then I got this flak over it, because, you know, I was rocking the boat. And also, it came out later that they wanted a cheap pastor rather than paying more for an experienced pastor, an older pastor, who might have been more of what they were looking for in reality. So yeah, I think there was some, you know, misleading there. And it was more between what they thought they wanted and what they really wanted. I think they really did want to involve the younger people, but they didn't want to make any changes.

Recommendation 2: Be realistic about expectations.

Many former pastors felt overwhelmed by individual and congregational demands on their time and the lack of consideration given to their need for family and personal time. Others found that congregations had unreasonable expectations of what a pastor could accomplish in a given time period. One ELCA former pastor felt pressure to meet both the stated and the unstated expectations of his congregation:

> I think for parish pastors, the hardest part is perceiving the actual expectations of members of the congregation. Because there are spoken expectations and then unspoken expectations. If you're not truly aware of what they are, spoken and unspoken, then I think you get put under a lot of pressure and under a lot of stress.
>
> The first year in a congregation, the honeymoon, it's not necessarily a good time. You're there about four months and one of the ladies says, "Now, the ladies are meeting tonight. You'll come, won't you?" And you say, "Okay, it's on the calendar. Yeah, I'll be there." So you show up for the ladies' meeting and they have some devotion and talk about some business, and then the president looks at you

and says, "And now the pastor has a program." And you're thinking, "Whoa! Whoa! Nobody said anything about this!" And they look at you and they say, "Well, the pastor when he's here, always has the program." Now, if you're quick, you know, the next time you don't come empty-handed. And if you're quick, you make something up on the spot. But it's that kind of unspoken expectation. We know that the pastor is busy and there's lots to do and this congregation has a lot going on. That's said. But then, the unspoken expectation is, "But we expect to see the pastor in our house." If you can't figure that out, if you can't figure out the difference between what people say and what they mean, then I think you're in trouble.

He described how pastors manage to deal with the hidden expectations:

I think some of it is intuitive, I think some people just are able to figure that out. Other people learn. When you don't show up — you said you were going to show up sometimes and you haven't, [you realize] these people are looking for [you]. Pilots have a thing called situational awareness, that they know when they're up in the sky where the ground is and what the situation is. And there just seem to be some clergy, for some reason, [who] don't have that sense in the parish. It's a more reactive kind of thing. And then that sets up tensions. I was lucky. I was with a guy for a long time who is pretty good at this and I learned from him. And I think some of it's intuitive, and some of it's being around the block. When people say one thing, they mean something else, and you just have to figure that out.

An Assemblies of God pastor also found that the often-unstated expectations of his congregation regarding time commitments were impossible to meet.

I think [time] is a big factor and there is no way to make them all happy. There are so many expectations that there is no way you could meet them. You can't visit every parent that's in a nursing home or every person in a 100-member congregation every week. That's impossible. Then you would have no time for anything else. So, if you don't do that and you are meeting some other expectation, you know, spending enough hours in the week on your sermon preparation and your music preparation to pull off a really quality service, then you are not going to do the visitation up to their expectations and just, you know, hundreds of little things. It's just thousands of expectations that some of them you don't even know they expected of you until after they're disappointed.

A United Methodist pastor found that the unrealistic demands on his time were a factor that led to his becoming burned out.

Within the congregation everyone expected you to be the pastor who was available 24 hours a day, seven days a week, including your vacation time. And when you're on vacation, you just carry a pager so they can get in touch with you.

He thought that the congregation did not have a realistic perspective on the extent of the demands they placed on him.

In one sense they did, but in another sense they did have that feeling that you were theirs 24 hours a day, 7 days a week. Almost every one of them would have said, "There will be an occasional time when I will need them." Other than normal working hours. Nobody else should really have to do this. And you ought to be able to have a job, in their mind, that basically works from 9 in the morning to about 10 at night. That is considered, by most people's mind-set, but they'd never sit down and formally say that. But it's true that they really believe you ought to be at work by 9:00 in the morning and they really believe you ought to be available to be at meetings until at about 10:00 at night. But they also believe, at 2:30 or 3:00 in the morning, when they go to the hospital, that you ought to be available for that too.

Recommendation 3: Provide relief from workloads when pastors are facing conflict or crisis.

What happens when a pastor encounters personal or family problems, or when accumulated stress threatens to undermine her or his ability to function? Many of the pastors we talked with wished that congregations would be more sensitive to the limitations of their pastors and would find ways to reduce congregational demands to give them time and energy to address crises. One LCMS pastor, after leaving the ministry, became convinced that churches should give pastors a periodic three-month break.

> I told my wife just last week, "Every pastor needs to get away." If my church realized, if they could just see me now [after leaving]. I actually gained weight, eight or ten pounds. My mom is saying I've never looked happier. She's saying that behind my back to my wife and others, "Obviously he wasn't happy." Every church, if they would just see that and give their pastor a three-month break. "This is what we want to do for you, we want you to recharge, regroup, really think. Think about your call, think about God, think about your own faith, your walk with him, your family. Go do it; this is what we want to do for you." It would benefit an awful lot. So that's the ideal. And then you come back regrouped. In my case, I totally left. Other churches, the minister comes back recharged, hopefully can just come back with better energy and grand vision and help lead the people. So that's the ideal, I would just say. Give those ministers a little break. They don't realize how it can just become such a drain emotionally, they just don't realize it. And then, especially, when you go through a tough economic time, they really don't understand: "Hey, we're all facing it, buddy. Too bad."

One former ELCA pastor described how time and workload pressures led to an episode of depression and how difficult it was to ask for time off.

> The workload was actually about 60 hours a week [for a three-fourths time position]. And that was one of my frustrations, because the synod was saying to the congregation they really needed to look at pastoral salaries and compensation, and that they were expecting more from the pastor than they were willing to provide as far as compensation. And that was one of my frustrations. It did not work to cut back. We tried that, taking two days a week off. That just never was successful. I would get called anyway. And so part of that is my responsibility, I needed to set clearer boundaries on what was appropriate to call the pastor for and what wasn't.

Stress from congregational expectations and from extended family issues exacerbated the pastor's struggle with depression.

> I suffer from clinical depression. And during that time my depression was acting up and we were working with some medications. And so some of those stresses made it very difficult health-wise, and just the professional stress and several in the congregation really not seeming to understand when I needed to take some time off. I was very open with them when the doctors said I needed to take about ten days off for some medication adjustment. And the rumors just spread wildly throughout the community that were very hurtful, that I was alcoholic, and had broken my hip, just weird things that were hurtful to me and my family. We talked about how hurtful that was in the congregation and at council meetings and stuff. And so part of the problem was, I was off for only one Sunday. My stress level was very high and we'd been going through some difficulties with my parents' health. Lots of things all bunched up, seemed to be all at the same time.

Honest communication and sensitivity to the needs of pastors were the overwhelming desires of our interviewees. Pastors, they told us, often find themselves in lonely and thankless positions in which their best efforts fail to meet the expectations of at least some parishioners. Congregations need to share a responsibility for their pastors' success; if they take that risk, they are more likely to find a good match at the time of call, a successful initial adjustment, and a mutually satisfying solution when their pastor is in crisis.

Summary

We have conveyed the seven basic recommendations we heard, each with variations and sub-themes. Former ministers spoke with us candidly, and their concerns need to be heard by officers in all denominations because they are real and they are consequential. The pastors talked with us from their hearts, and they did so hoping that they would be heard.

What is most striking about the recommendations is how often the pastors asked for trust and forthrightness. They too often feel isolated and afraid to confide in their fellow clergy or denominational officers. Both in everyday life and in times of severe conflict, pastors need support systems that will help them cope with the pressures that are inherently part of their vocation. They want very much to minister effectively, and we hope that denominations and congregations will help them to do so.

Main Findings

The pastors made seven recommendations:

1. Seminaries should do more to prepare ministers for the practical aspects of ministry.
2. Denominations should improve the call process.
3. Denominations should provide ongoing support for pastors.
4. Denominations should support pastors in conflict or crisis, offering support from external sources where necessary.
5. Congregations should articulate their genuine goals.
6. Congregations should be realistic about expectations.
7. Congregations should provide relief from workloads when pastors are facing conflict or crisis.

APPENDIX A   *Past Research on Pastors*
Who Left Local Church Ministry

We will summarize nine important studies. (1) Edgar Mills studied 60 male Presbyterian ministers who had made recent job changes of four kinds: a move to secular employment; a return to graduate study; a move into an executive church position; and a move to another pastorate.[1] He interviewed 15 of each; their average age was 34. The men who had left ministry for secular employment were the most unique. They had been in smaller churches and had experienced shorter pastorates. They reported the least enjoyment of ministerial tasks, the most pressures to compromise, and the least clear feedback from laypersons about their level of job performance. Over a third had experienced a serious marital crisis (compared to the other three groups, who reported no marital crises at all).

(2) In 1968, Jud, Mills, and Burch carried out an impressive study of ex-pastors in the United Church of Christ.[2] They sent questionnaires to a random sample of active United Church of Christ clergy and to a sample of ex-pastors from the same denomination. Of the latter, 241 returned the questionnaires and were then invited to one of four regional weekends, at which the authors interviewed 131.

They compared active pastors and ex-pastors on numerous measures and found them to be no different in many respects, including

---

1. Edgar W. Mills, "Career Change in the Protestant Ministry," *Ministry Studies* 3:1 (May 1969): 5-21.
2. Gerald J. Jud, Edgar W. Mills Jr., and Genevieve Walters Burch, *Ex-Pastors: Why Men Leave the Parish Ministry* (Philadelphia: Pilgrim Press, 1970).

age at ordination, seminaries attended, amount of stress reported in their ministry, and strength of faith. But the two groups were different in two ways: (1) the ex-pastors had histories of more frequent church moves and more moving in and out of ministry, and (2) they reported more marital crises and family problems.

An important finding of the study is that whereas the active pastors and ex-pastors had had similar experiences, the ex-pastors had experienced less support and more disillusionment:

> Pastors experience the same system pressures as ex-pastors, with the possible exception of marital discord. It seems likely that pastors differ primarily in still having hope that they can correct the causes of occupational dissonance. If this is so, then crucial support functions should be provided to help the ministers in the nurture of hope and the management of frustration. (p. 107)

Put differently, the crucial difference between pastors and ex-pastors was not in their experiences but in the presence or absence of hope they felt about whether their life as ministers could improve.

(3) A 1994 United Methodist study of women clergy was done by Wiborg and Collier.[3] They carried out a large questionnaire and interview study of women in three categories: clergy in local church ministry, those in other ministries, and those who had left ministry altogether. Women who had surrendered their credentials were not surveyed. Twenty-eight percent of the women had clergy partners. The study found that Methodist women clergy leave local church ministry at a 10 percent higher rate than their male counterparts. Most of the women (about 82 to 86 percent) had entered ministry with hopes of serving local churches, but only 73 percent were serving churches at the time. Single women living in committed relationships (either heterosexual or homosexual) had disproportionately left local church ministry, partly due to decisions by denominational officials and partly due to problems with laity. Also, African American and Asian American women had disproportionately more often left local church ministry for similar reasons.

3. Margaret S. Wiborg and Elizabeth J. Collier, *United Methodist Clergywomen Retention Study*, unbound report (Boston: Boston University School of Theology, 1997).

When the women who had left local church ministry were asked why, the main reason given was a desire for another type of ministry (28 percent of the responses), and second was a lack of support from the denominational system or disillusionment with it (about 25 percent). Other reasons such as family responsibilities, finances, and health, were less important.[4] Unmarried clergywomen complained about the personal isolation, loneliness, and rejection they had experienced in their ministries, especially in small towns.

(4) Zikmund, Lummis, and Chang made a major contribution in their study of men and women ministers in 15 denominations.[5] In 1993-94 they surveyed almost 5,000 men and women clergy and interviewed 248 by phone. Many more women were single than men (38 percent versus 8 percent), and fewer had children under 18 in the home (37 versus 56 percent). On average, women earned 9 percent less than men. Many clergy, especially those early into their careers, felt economic pressures. Married clergy felt these pressures less than single persons, since their families often had second incomes.

The researchers found that women clergy leave church positions more often than men; in their sample, 13 percent of the women and 8 percent of the men had left paid positions in church ministry — either parish ministry or specialized ministry — entirely. (They were in the sample because they still had ordination status.) An additional 12 percent of the women and 11 percent of the men said it was "usually true" that in the last year they thought seriously of leaving.

The research team interviewed women and men who had left and found three important factors. People who had left (a) were not part of a clergy support group, (b) did not believe it would be easy to get a better position, and (c) felt that denominational executives did not recognize their abilities.[6] Zikmund and her associates emphasized problems of "boundary maintenance," that is, keeping private life distinct from ministerial duties. Keeping boundaries in place and juggling multiple demands of family and church were problems often mentioned by the clergy. In addition, clergy in small towns and rural

---

4. Wiborg and Collier, *United Methodist Clergywomen,* p. 70.

5. Barbara Brown Zikmund, Adair T. Lummis, and Patricia Mei Yin Chang, *Clergy Women: An Uphill Calling* (Louisville, Ky.: Westminster John Knox Press, 1998).

6. Zikmund et al., p. 165.

settings were often unhappy due to a lack of contact with other clergy. Single women suffered the most in such settings, feeling as if they lived in a fishbowl. Younger clergy in general had more self-doubt about their abilities than older clergy.

(5) Lummis later analyzed the same data in more detail to assess the determinants of men's and women's decisions to leave the ministry.[7] The strongest determinants for both sexes were not having been a member of a clergy support group, not feeling adequately recognized by denominational executives, and not being confident of being able to get a better church job.

(6) Memming compiled important information on United Methodist ordinands from 1974 to 1994, including what happened during their careers.[8] In 1974, 95 percent of the ordinands were men, compared with 65.5 percent in 1993. The South was the region with the lowest percentage of women clergy. Ordinands in recent years have been older; the median age was 28 in 1974 and 38 in 1993. In the mid-1990s women ordinands were, on average, five years older than men.

Memming was able to see how many ordinands were still in parish ministry after ten years. For the 1974-83 classes, it was 58.5 percent; for the men, 60.3 percent and for the women, 47.5 percent. Retention did not vary by age. For the 1974-83 classes, 7 percent had left ministry totally. For the same 1974-83 classes, the percentage in parish ministry twenty years later was 42.

The Memming study is the only one known to us that measured retention rates precisely; it demonstrates that among the Methodists, more left parish ministry for specialized ministries than left ministry entirely.

(7) The Research Services Office of the Presbyterian Church (U.S.A.) in 1998 surveyed ministers who had been ordained since 1990 and had received at least one call, but who were not presently serving

7. Adair Lummis, "Why Men and Women Leave the Ministry: Hypotheses from Research on Clergy and from Role Exiters of Other Statuses," in *The Power of Gender in Religion*, edited by Georgie Weatherby and Susan Farrell (New York: McGraw-Hill, 1996).

8. Rolf Memming, "United Methodist Ordained Ministry in Transition," in *The People(s) Called Methodist*, edited by William B. Lawrence, Dennis M. Campbell, and Russell E. Richey (Nashville: Abingdon Press, 1998).

in a denominationally recognized ministry.[9] They estimated that about 11 to 13 percent of the 1990-92 ordinands had left Presbyterian ministry.

The questionnaire asked about the principal reasons for leaving the ministry, and the main ones chosen were (1) "I had a sense of completion of my call"; (2) conflict with other staff; (3) a need for more time for children or family; and (4) health problems. The third reason (more time for family) was given only by women. The fourth (health) was given by more women than men.

(8) Smith Sellers carried out nine extended interviews with mainline clergywomen who had been thinking about leaving parish ministry.[10] She found four main themes. First, "Can I be myself and do this?" Some of the women felt a lack of fit between their basic Christian values and working in the church. Second, some questioned ordination and the set-apart status of clergy; they wanted to be faithful to God but not necessarily to their denomination. Third, they had mixed feelings about their loyalty to the church, recognizing the need for some form of institutional structure while feeling disillusioned with the church in its current state. Fourth, they knew of few appealing and meaningful alternatives to their current jobs as ministers. Sellers emphasized the unrest of many women ministers in today's church.

(9) A major interview study in the Lutheran Church–Missouri Synod was done by Klaas and Klaas.[11] Their research team carried out numerous focus groups with pastors, wives of pastors, resigned pastors, seminary students, and children of pastors. They found a high level of burnout among the pastors, estimating that about 30 percent are happy, another 30 percent are ambivalent, 20 percent are well on their way to burnout, and 20 percent are in advanced stages of burnout. Why? Too many pressures, little or no support from denominational leaders or other pastors, no recognition and few successes in

9. Presbyterian Church (U.S.A.) Research Services, "Ministers Ordained in the 1990s: A Look at Clergy Who Have Left the Ministry," unbound report (Louisville, Ky.: Presbyterian Church [U.S.A.], 1999).

10. Karen Smith Sellers, "Crossroads: Clergywomen Thinking Seriously about Leaving Church-Related Ministry" (paper presented at the annual meeting of the Religious Research Association, Boston, Mass., November 1999).

11. Alan C. Klaas and Cheryl D. Klaas, "Clergy Shortage Study," report (St. Louis: Board of Higher Education, Lutheran Church–Missouri Synod, 1999).

their work, too much criticism from laity, low pay, and inadequate seminary preparation. Wives of pastors complained of loneliness, too-frequent residential moves, low family income, and too much stress on their husbands.

The resigned pastors were often victims of mismatches between ministers and congregations (for example, scholarly types in small churches or activists in anti-change churches); the researchers estimated that half of the resignations were due to such mismatches.

The Klaas-Klaas report is the most negative of all the past research. The authors are convinced that things are going badly for clergy in the Lutheran Church–Missouri Synod; the lives of parish pastors are too difficult and unrewarding. Therefore the conditions of parish pastors need to be totally reassessed.

Two other research studies are relevant. McDuff investigated why Protestant women clergy have higher satisfaction than men clergy even though their job positions and pay are less attractive.[12] She found that women receive more subjective, interpersonal rewards, and they have somewhat different occupational values than men — mainly less concern about their total career.

Brunnette-Hill and Finke carried out an important replication of earlier research on how clergy spend their time.[13] They repeated the 1955 Blizzard survey in 1994 and found important changes. Ministers today spend less time with church members, potential members, and religious and civic leaders than they did the past. Clearly they spend less time visiting members and attending local meetings. On the other hand, they spend more time in planning and administration. The total work hours per week declined by over ten hours, from an average of 69 to an average of about 48 to 55. Here is proof of one definite change in ministry over five decades.

---

12. Elaine M. McDuff, "The Gender Paradox in Work Satisfaction and the Protestant Clergy," *Sociology of Religion* 62 (Spring 2001): 1-21. Also see Charles W. Mueller and Elaine M. McDuff, "'Good' Jobs and 'Bad' Jobs: Differences in the Clergy Employment Relationship," *Review of Religious Research* 44 (December 2002): 150-68.

13. Sandi Brunnette-Hill and Roger Finke, "A Time for Every Purpose under Heaven: Updating and Extending Blizzard's Survey on Clergy Time Allocation," *Review of Religious Research* 41 (Fall 1999): 48-64.

Research Method

This study began with a meeting of advisors in Washington, D.C., early in 2001, which included Jackson Carroll, Adair Lummis, Edward White, Jack Marcum, Brooks Faulkner, John Dever, Robert Kohler, and the two co-authors. The main research questions were decided: Why are so many persons leaving local church ministry, and what might be done to reduce those numbers? Are there variations from denomination to denomination? Are there trends in the conditions of ministry since the 1960s that affect the numbers leaving local church ministry?

Since we could find no good opportunities for repeating earlier studies to measure trends, we decided to carry out new surveys. We agreed that new research needed to be a combination of a mail survey and personal interviews by phone. Also, if possible, we should convene focus groups of denominational officials to hear their interpretations of the situation, and we should compare the morale of clergy with the morale of other professional groups such as lawyers, professors, and health care professionals. We envisioned a three-denomination study.

In late summer 2001 we carried out a pretest using 27 names from the Presbyterian Church (U.S.A.), the United Methodist Church, and the Southern Baptist Convention; 12 responded. Jackson Carroll agreed to coordinate our mail survey with his survey of active ministers, providing us with a control group.

Later in 2001 we worked with Presbyterians, United Methodists, and Southern Baptists to see whether they could generate lists of persons who fit our target group definition. Since the Southern Baptist Convention had no suitable lists, we decided to approach the Assemblies of God, and they agreed to take part. Soon afterward the Evangelical Lutheran Church in America and the Lutheran Church–Missouri Synod asked to join the project.

We gathered all existing research, and as an experiment in oral history commissioned four essays by veteran Presbyterian pastors active in denominational affairs, delineating changes over the decades.

At a second planning meeting in January 2002 we made decisions about data collection. We aimed for 150 to 200 cases per denomination. Each denomination agreed to generate a list of persons fitting the target description and to do its own mailing. It was agreed that two waves of questionnaires plus a reminder card would be sent out by denominational offices, and the questionnaires would be returned to us in Washington. No names would be requested, but at the end of the questionnaire we would ask whether respondents would be willing to talk with us by telephone.

1. Sampling and Mailing

The five denominations generated random samples of persons fitting the description. When addresses were missing, denominational staff searched for addresses using the World Wide Web and nationwide CD-ROM telephone directories. It became evident that the lists would be imprecise, so we used two methods of making sure a respondent fit our definition. Included with each questionnaire was a postcard to be returned to the denomination office, whether or not the respondent returned the questionnaire. If the respondent did fill out the questionnaire, the postcard told us not to send a second mailing. If the respondent knew that he or she did not fit, there was a place on the postcard to check one of five possibilities: (1) I am still in local church ministry; (2) I am in a denominational position; (3) I am actively looking for a local church position; (4) I am retired; or (5) other ____. If one was checked, the person was ineligible.

Also the first page of the questionnaire included three questions written to detect persons who did not fit our definition. One asked, "Are you currently serving as pastor or minister of a local church?" The second, "Are you now actively looking for a position as pastor or minister of a local church?" The third, "Are you retired as pastor or minister of a local church?" Any respondent saying yes to any of these was removed from the sample.

A. Presbyterian Church (U.S.A.)

Jack Marcum coordinated the project. He selected 520 ministers for the denominational database who fit the description. The first mailing went out in May 2002. The return rate was lower than expected, so in July the Presbyterian office sent out 72 more to names which had been randomly removed earlier, hence the total number mailed was 592. After two waves of mailings plus a reminder postcard, we received 173 questionnaires from persons who fit the definition and 140 questionnaires or postcards from persons who did not. The return rate of eligible persons was 38 percent.

B. Assemblies of God

Gary Allen coordinated the research, assisted by Barbara Chapman. They assembled a list of 593 persons who fit the description, including both licensed and ordained ministers, and mailed questionnaires to them in April. The return rate was very low, so they added a second random sample of 593. We received 174 good questionnaires from eligible persons, for a completion rate of 19 percent.

C. United Methodist Church

Bob Kohler and Jack Roulier coordinated the mailing. They sent questionnaires to a sample of 1,000 in May and June. From them we received 157 completed questionnaires, and we found that 218 others did not fit the criteria. Later, in April 2003 we discovered that the samples had not included persons who had switched to specialized ministries and that it had included far too many non-ordained persons. Therefore we decided to make a supplementary sample of persons now in specialized ministries and to delete 33 non-ordained non-seminary graduates. We sent questionnaires to 400 persons in specialized ministries in June 2003. The overall responses totalled 219, or 20 percent of all eligible persons.

D. Lutheran Church–Missouri Synod

The research team was led by John O'Hara. In September the team sent out 692 questionnaires but soon discovered that the list with which they were working included many invalid addresses. After finding correct addresses, they sent out a second wave with corrected addresses. Due to inaccuracies in the lists, many persons turned out to be ineligible. From the eligible individuals we received 106 good questionnaires for a response rate of 43 percent.

E. Evangelical Lutheran Church in America

Martin Smith coordinated the research. A mailing went out in September to 719 persons. We received 291 completed questionnaires, for a completion rate of 54 percent.

2. Reflection on the Completion Rates

The completion rates were low, raising the question of what biases were thereby introduced. We have three clues. First, it is possible that our decision to have denominational offices send out the questionnaires was ill advised, since some ex-pastors are unhappy with their denomination and likely to disregard any mailing coming from the denominational office. Second, in the phone interviews we learned that some of the ex-pastors are angry, hurt, and alienated, and we are sure that persons with strong negative feelings were less likely to cooperate with the survey. Third, from the questionnaires we learned that the numbers of ex-pastors who have subsequently left their denominations varies widely. When we asked "What is your *present* denomination or church affiliation?" 30 percent of the former Assemblies of God pastors and 33 percent of the former Methodist pastors had changed denominations. The figures were lower in the other three denominations — whose response rates were higher. This information suggests that unhappiness with the denomination contributed both to the low Assemblies of God and Methodist response rates and also to the high rates of leaving those denominations. We believe that in all five denominations the most alienated persons are underrepresented in our data.

The Control Group of Active Ministers

Jackson Carroll agreed to include in the Duke nationwide survey of active clergy a series of questions about their satisfactions, dissatisfactions, and problems — questions identical to ours. In 2001 he carried out a nationwide phone survey of ministers in numerous denominations. In addition, large mail surveys of congregations were done in three of the denominations we studied — Presbyterian Church (U.S.A.), United Methodist Church, and Evangelical Lutheran Church in America, and the sample methods were identical in the three. (The other two denominations in our studies did not participate.) We were provided data from the mail surveys of the three denominations.

The exact description of the sample of active ministers is important. In each of the three denominations the researchers began with a random sample of congregations. The research group was interested in surveying laity as well as clergy, so they asked the congregations to carry out three tasks: (1) have the "leader" of the congregation fill out a questionnaire on clergy issues, (2) have someone in the congregation fill out a survey about the congregation (size, facilities, programs, services), and (3) have all persons 15 and older attending worship on a specific Sunday complete a survey. For most congregations, fulfilling these requirements was a major commitment in terms of time and effort, and thus only a minority of congregations agreed to participate. Among the Presbyterians, 27 percent agreed to participate, among the Methodists, 22 percent, and among the ELCA Lutherans, 40 percent.

These congregations became the sample to whom questionnaires were then sent. The percentage of their leaders who returned their questionnaires was high — for the Presbyterians, 92 percent; for the United Methodists, 79 percent; and for the ELCA Lutherans, 86 percent. In sum, if a congregation agreed to participate in the larger project, almost always the leader sent back his or her form.

Two clarifications are important. First, the instructions said that the "principal leader of the congregation" should fill out the leader survey. In most cases this was the senior pastor. No respondents were associate ministers or youth ministers except in a few cases where the senior pastor was temporarily absent. Second, the respondents included a few interim or temporary pastors who were serving for a short time while the congregations called permanent pastors; we removed them from the data before analysis. The resulting samples of active ministers included 416 Presbyterians, 171 United Methodists, and 357 ELCA Lutherans. When comparing this control group with our sample of parish-leavers, we looked only at the senior or solo pastors in our sample.

3. Telephone Interviews

The mailed questionnaires included a question at the end: "Would you be willing to be interviewed by telephone about topics in this survey? All phone conversations are confidential." Seventy-eight percent of all the questionnaire respondents said yes. Beginning in September 2002 we phoned a sample of these ministers and interviewed them. We aimed to interview 15 people per denomination, and in the end we interviewed 90 in all five. We make no pretense that they are a random sample. We transcribed most of the interviews, coded them using a 26-part code, and entered them into the computer using a qualitative data program for retrieving topics.

4. Focus Groups of Judicatory Officials

We commissioned focus groups of judicatory officials in all five denominations. The Presbyterians and Methodists convened focus groups in 2001 and 2002. In 2003 the Assemblies of God held two focus groups. The two Lutheran denominations had difficulty scheduling focus groups of bishops and district presidents, so the ELCA researchers mailed questionnaires to bishops (five responded), and the Lutheran Church–Missouri Synod research office furnished us with names of district presidents, five of whom we interviewed by phone. We transcribed the most useful portions of the tapes and interviews.

APPENDIX C *Additional Data Tables*

This appendix includes data tables not mentioned in the text but placed here for further reference.

Table C.1
Personal and Professional History of Sample Members

	UMC (%)	PCUSA (%)	ELCA (%)	LCMS (%)	A/G (%)
Age when began local church ministry					
24 or less	26	11	6	9	54
25-29	30	55	68	44	26
30 or more	44	34	26	48	19
Average (years)	30	30	28	31	25
Age when left local church ministry					
39 or less	28	27	24	31	47
40-49	38	44	49	39	40
50 or more	34	29	27	30	13
Average (years)	45	44	45	45	41
(If ever ordained or credentialed) How many different positions did you serve as a paid local church minister?					
3 or more	72	46	57	37	61
Current marital status					
Never married	8	6	7	6	4
In first marriage	39	64	56	68	82
Divorced or separated	18	11	12	10	4
Widowed	1	2	1	0	1
Remarried	29	15	18	16	4
In a committed relationship	5	3	7	1	6
Any children of any age? Yes	88	82	86	92	96
Any children living at home? Yes	49	61	50	52	73

Table C.2

**Ministerial Experiences of Former and Current Pastors
(Senior and Solo Pastors Only)**

		UMC (%)	PCUSA (%)	ELCA (%)
At the same time did you serve other congregations in addition to this one? Yes	Former	28	10	13
	Current	32	11	17
Do (did) you work at any job other than as minister of that congregation? Yes	Former	19	23	18
	Current	10	11	9
Do (did) you regularly take a day off each week? Yes	Former	78	88	89
	Current	69	78	84
In general, your health is: Excellent or very good	Former	79	72	76
	Current	64	74	74

Which statement best describes your congregation (your last congregation)?

		UMC (%)	PCUSA (%)	ELCA (%)
It has (had) no clear vision, goal, or direction	Former	24	26	17
	Current	7	5	4
It has (had) some ideas but no clear vision	Former	38	42	48
	Current	41	44	46
It has (had) a clear vision but not enough commitment to achieving it	Former	25	18	21
	Current	32	24	26
It has (had) a clear vision and a strong commitment to achieving it	Former	13	13	14
	Current	21	27	24

Table C.3

Reported Feelings When Deciding to Leave Local Church Ministry: Ideas in Open-Ended Comments

	UMC (%)	PCUSA (%)	ELCA (%)	LCMS (%)	A/G (%)
Opportunity came for new ministry	21	33	32	49	24
Denomination not supportive, or conflict with denominational officials	29	26	25	25	23
Burned out, discouraged, stressed, overworked	18	25	26	20	18
Needs of children and family	11	19	8	6	10
Conflicts with church members	8	12	9	6	11
Doctrinal conflicts (service to the poor, homosexuality, women clergy issues, spirituality)	10	9	8	4	6
Domination by senior pastor; conflicts in staff	5	10	8	5	11
Unreasonable expectations from church members	4	11	7	6	7
Marital difficulties or divorce	6	2	5	14	5
Felt constrained by staff or members; church resisted change	6	7	6	7	9
Financial considerations	5	6	4	3	12
Sexual misconduct	4	3	8	8	1
Health issues	5	5	6	1	5
Wished to pursue further education	2	6	4	2	3
Openly gay or lesbian	2	3	4	2	1
Difficulties around co-pastoring with spouse	1	2	0	0	2
Other	23	11	12	10	14

NOTE: Up to three ideas were coded, thus percentages add up to more than 100 percent.

Table C.4

Reason for Leaving Local Church Ministry

How important was each of the following possible reasons why you left your position in local church ministry? (Percent responding "Great importance" or "Somewhat important" to each)

	UMC	PCUSA	ELCA	LCMS	A/G
I felt drained by the demands on me.	53	63	63	47	56
I felt lonely or isolated.	48	49	58	54	45
I was not supported by denominational officials.	54	35	45	37	38
I felt bored or constrained in the position.	44	49	46	39	32
I found a better job outside of congregational work.	40	40	41	38	26
I had marital problems or personal relationship problems.	29	24	29	31	20
I felt doubts about my abilities as a pastoral minister.	17	22	30	34	30
Lay leaders strongly pressured me to leave.	14	22	28	16	18
My spouse or family did not like the congregation.	21	18	19	16	23
I had health problems.	18	18	19	13	13
I moved because my spouse moved for a new job.	5	13	7	0	4
My regional official reassigned me to a different position.	18	0	3	4	2

Table C.5

Feelings about Ministry and Seminary

Do you agree or disagree with these statements?
(Percent responding "Strongly agree" or "Somewhat agree" to each)

	UMC	PCUSA	ELCA	LCMS	A/G
In my last pastoral ministry position . . .					
I felt the demands of laity were unrealistic.	54	58	58	51	43
I felt I could not speak openly and honestly with denominational officials.	63	41	47	40	58
I felt discouraged about being able to find a better ministry job.	31	32	33	27	36
(If married) I was troubled by marital problems.	30	30	32	33	21
My feelings today are . . .					
Training in theological seminary today is not practical and realistic enough.	59	64	55	53	54
Training in theological seminary today is not deep enough spiritually.	55	58	55	53	40
The calling and deployment system of my denomination needs to be reformed.	79	58	60	46	66

Table C.6

Level of Satisfaction in Last Ministry Position

In the final years of your last local church ministry position, what was your level of satisfaction with the following? (Percent responding "Very satisfied")

	UMC	PCUSA	ELCA	LCMS	A/G
Housing or living arrangements	50	62	54	57	54
Your ministry position	38	33	30	37	38
Your overall effectiveness as a pastoral leader in this particular congregation	39	43	33	28	26
Relations with other clergy	28	37	38	23	34
Relations with lay leaders in your congregation	33	40	30	23	34
Your family life	29	30	30	27	42
Your salary and benefits	27	27	29	26	19
Spiritual life	24	23	24	23	36
Support from your denominational officials	10	20	23	19	24
Social life with persons outside of the church	14	17	19	15	22
Ease in maintaining separation between your church duties and your need for private time and family time	11	14	13	8	16

Table C.7
Reason for Not Currently Serving as a Local Church Minister

How important are the following to why you are not currently serving as a local church minister? (Percent saying "Great importance" or "Somewhat important")

	UMC	PCUSA	ELCA	LCMS	A/G
I found another kind of ministry position that I like better.	50	61	49	53	39
I could not get any position that I wanted.	14	22	17	15	19
Clergy or denominational officials here do not want me.	26	13	23	28	12
I decided I do not like local church ministry.	32	31	37	22	21
I am too ill to work at this time.	1	6	3	1	4

Table C.8
Sources of Stress in the Person's Last Ministry Position

In the last year of your last pastoral ministry position, how often: (Percent responding "Very often" or "Fairly often" to each)

	UMC	PCUSA	ELCA	LCMS	A/G
Did you experience stress because of the challenges you faced in that congregation?	63	65	66	57	59
Did you feel lonely and isolated in your work?	60	52	63	57	54
Did you feel that your work in that congregation did not permit you to devote adequate time to your children?	32	31	34	35	28
Did your spouse voice resentment over the amount of time that your ministry took up?	25	24	32	32	27
Did your spouse voice resentment over the financial situation in which you found yourself by being in pastoral ministry?	18	15	17	19	25

Table C.9

Problems and Stressors (Senior and Solo Pastors Only)

Clergy face many problems today. How important are (were) the following to you on a day-to-day basis? (Percent responding "Great problem")

		UMC	PCUSA	ELCA
Finding time for recreation, relaxation, or personal reflection	Former	28	26	23
	Current	20	20	23
Difficulty of having a private life apart from my ministerial role	Former	27	26	27
	Current	10	11	12
Lack of agreement over what the role of a pastor is	Former	26	29	30
	Current	7	9	8
Having people relate to me differently because I'm a pastor	Former	11	11	13
	Current	7	5	4
Relationships with other clergy and staff members in the church	Former	5	12	8
	Current	3	2	2

Table C.10
Conflicts in Last Church

In your last local church ministry position, during the *last two years* of your service, was there any conflict in the congregation? Percent responding "Yes" to each

	UMC	PCUSA	ELCA	LCMS	A/G
Major conflict	37	38	42	42	37

(if a conflict:) What was the conflict about? (check as many as apply)

	UMC	PCUSA	ELCA	LCMS	A/G
Pastoral leadership style	29	41	36	29	42
Finances	30	19	31	25	19
Changes in worship style	24	27	20	29	24
Conflicts between staff and/or clergy	16	21	17	18	18
Issues about new building or renovation	25	15	18	18	18
Changes in music styles	18	20	9	24	20
Lay leadership style	15	15	18	15	9
Changes in other congregation programs	16	14	11	16	16
Doctrines	11	5	6	18	8
Sexual misconduct	6	6	10	6	10
Issues regarding homosexuality	10	11	8	2	1
Racial issues	6	3	4	1	4
Local outreach programs	2	4	4	10	1
Church growth issues	4	3	3	2	4
Other	19	15	11	12	12

Table C.11

Sources of Stress (Senior and Solo Pastors Only)

In the *last five years* of your last pastoral ministry position, how often did you:
(Percent responding "Very often" or "Fairly often")

		UMC	PCUSA	ELCA
Doubt that you are called by God to the ministry?	Former	14	16	17
	Current	8	6	7
Experience stress as a result of dealing with congregation members who are critical of your work?	Former	48	61	50
	Current	33	25	27

In the *last year* of your last pastoral ministry position, how often:
(Percent responding "Very often" or "Fairly often")

		UMC	PCUSA	ELCA
Did you experience stress because of the challenges you faced in that congregation?	Former	63	71	65
	Current	43	49	49
Did you feel lonely and isolated in your work?	Former	62	62	65
	Current	36	32	35
Did you feel that your work in that congregation did not permit you to devote adequate time to your children?	Former	31	31	34
	Current	14	12	19
Did your spouse voice resentment over the amount of time that your ministry took up?	Former	24	28	32
	Current	13	15	21
Did your spouse voice resentment over the financial situation in which you found yourself by being in pastoral ministry?	Former	18	16	18
	Current	10	13	9

My feelings today are:
(Percent responding "Strongly agree" or "Somewhat agree")

		UMC	PCUSA	ELCA
I am really glad that I entered the ministry.	Former	80	84	80
	Current	90	93	91

APPENDIX D   *Helpful Books on*
Problems Facing Pastors

Dobson, Edward G., Speed B. Leas, and Marshall Shelley. *Mastering Conflict and Controversy*. Portland, Ore.: Multnomah Press, 1992.

Faulkner, Brooks R. *Forced Termination: Redemptive Options for Ministers and Churches*. Nashville: Broadman Press, 1986.

————. *Getting on Top of Your Work: A Manual for the 21st-Century Minister*. Nashville: Convention Press, 1999.

Greenfield, Guy. *The Wounded Minister: Healing from and Preventing Personal Attacks*. Grand Rapids: Baker Books, 2001.

Halverstadt, Hugh F. *Managing Church Conflict*. Louisville, Ky.: Westminster John Knox Press, 1991.

Harbaugh, Gary L., William C. Behrens, Jill M. Hudson, and Roy M. Oswald. *Beyond the Boundary: Meeting the Challenge of the First Years of Ministry*. Washington, D.C.: Alban Institute, 1986.

Leas, Speed B. *Discover Your Conflict Management Style*. Washington, D.C.: Alban Institute, 1997.

Lott, David B., editor. *Conflict Management in Congregations*. Washington, D.C.: Alban Institute, 2001.

Oswald, Roy M. *Clergy Self-Care: Finding a Balance for Effective Ministry*. Washington, D.C.: Alban Institute, 1991.

Rediger, C. Lloyd. *Clergy Killers: Guidance for Pastors and Congregations under Attack*. Louisville, Ky.: Westminster/John Knox Press, 1997.

Susek, Ron. *Firestorm: Preventing and Overcoming Church Conflicts*. Grand Rapids: Baker Books, 1999.

References

Aleshire, Daniel O. "Who Is Going to Seminary? A Look at Students in Theological Schools." In *Fact Book on Theological Education 2002-2003*. Pittsburgh: Association of Theological Schools, 2003.

American Bar Association. "Taking a Collective Pulse of the Legal Profession." Report. Chicago: American Bar Association. September 2001.

Ballis, Peter H. *Leaving the Adventist Ministry*. Westport, Conn.: Praeger, 1999.

Beck, John H. "The Effects of the Number of Roles, the Time Spent in Different Roles, and Selected Demographic Variables on Burnout and Job Satisfaction among Iowa Lutheran Clergy." Ph.D. diss., University of Iowa, 1997.

Bennison, Charles E., Jr. *In Praise of Congregations: Leadership in the Local Church Today*. Cambridge, Mass.: Cowley Publications, 1999.

Blanton, Priscilla W., and M. Lane Morris. "Work-Related Predictors of Physical Symptomatology and Emotional Well-Being among Clergy and Spouses." *Review of Religious Research* 40 (June 1999): 331-48.

Blizzard, Samuel W. "The Minister's Dilemma." *Christian Century* 73 (April 25, 1956): 508-10.

————. *The Protestant Parish Minister: A Behavioral Science Interpretation*. Storrs, Conn.: Society for the Scientific Study of Religion, 1985.

Brunnette-Hill, Sandi, and Roger Finke. "A Time for Every Purpose under Heaven: Updating and Extending Blizzard's Survey on Clergy Time Allocation." *Review of Religious Research* 41 (Fall 1999): 48-64.

Caplow, Theodore, Louis Hicks, and Ben J. Wattenberg. *The First Measured Century*. Washington, D.C.: American Enterprise Press, 2001.

Carper, Eugene C. "The Recruitment and Conservation of the Ministry in the Church of the Brethren." Th.D. diss., Boston University School of Theology, 1962.

Carroll, Jackson W. *Mainline to the Future: Congregations for the 21st Century.* Louisville, Ky.: Westminster John Knox Press, 2000.

——. *As One with Authority: Reflective Leadership in Ministry.* Louisville, Ky.: Westminster John Knox Press, 1991.

Carroll, Jackson W., Barbara Hargrove, and Adair T. Lummis. *Women of the Cloth: A New Opportunity for Churches.* New York: Harper & Row, 1983.

Chang, Patricia Mei Yin. *Assessing the Clergy Supply in the 21st Century. Pulpit & Pew* Research Report. Dunham, N.C.: Duke University, 2004.

——. "Pulpit Supply: A Clergy Shortage?" *Christian Century* (November 29, 2003): 28-32.

Chaves, Mark. *Ordaining Women: Culture and Conflict in Religious Organizations.* Cambridge, Mass.: Harvard University Press, 1997.

Cherniss, Cary. *Beyond Burnout: Helping Teachers, Nurses, Therapists, and Lawyers Recover from Stress and Disillusionment.* New York: Routledge, 1995.

Coalter, Milton, John M. Mulder, and Louis B. Weeks. *Vital Signs: The Promise of Mainstream Protestantism.* Grand Rapids: Eerdmans, 1996.

Dworkin, Ronald W. "Why Doctors Are Down." *Commentary* 111 (May 2001): 43-47.

Evangelical Lutheran Church in America, Division for Ministry. *Ministry Needs and Resources in the 21st Century.* Report. Chicago: Evangelical Lutheran Church in America, 2000.

Finke, Roger, and Rodney Stark. *The Churching of America, 1776-1900: Winners and Losers in Our Religious Economy.* New Brunswick, N.J.: Rutgers University Press, 1992.

Heinz, John P., Kathleen E. Hull, and Ava A. Harter. "Lawyers and Their Discontents: Findings from a Survey of the Chicago Bar." *Indiana Law Journal* 74 (1999): 735-59.

Hoge, Dean R., Charles Zech, Patrick McNamara, and Michael J. Donahue. *Money Matters: Personal Giving in American Churches.* Louisville, Ky.: Westminster John Knox Press, 1996.

Jud, Gerald J., Edgar W. Mills Jr., and Genevieve Walters Burch. *Ex-Pastors: Why Men Leave the Parish Ministry.* Philadelphia: Pilgrim Press, 1970.

Klaas, Alan C., and Cheryl D. Klaas. "Clergy Shortage Study." Report to the Board of Higher Education, The Lutheran Church–Missouri Synod. St. Louis, 1999.

Krause, Neal, Christopher G. Ellison, and Keith M. Wulff. "Church-Based Emotional Support, Negative Interaction, and Psychological Well-Being: Findings from a National Sample of Presbyterians." *Journal for the Scientific Study of Religion* 37 (1998): 725-41.

Lee, Cameron. "Specifying Intrusive Demands and Their Outcomes in Congregational Ministry: A Report on the Ministry Demands Inventory." *Journal for the Scientific Study of Religion* 38 (1999): 477-89.

Lehman, Edward C., Jr. *Gender and Work: The Case of the Clergy*. Albany, N.Y.: State University of New York Press, 1993.

——. *Women's Path into Ministry: Six Major Studies*. Durham, N.C.: Duke University Pulpit and Pew Project, 2002.

Linzer, Mark, et al. "Managed Care, Time Pressure, and Physician Job Satisfaction: Results from the Physician Worklife Study." *Journal of General Internal Medicine* 15 (July 2000): 441-50.

Lloyd, Chris, Robert King, and Lesley Chenoweth. "Social Work, Stress and Burnout: A Review." *Journal of Mental Health* 11:3 (2002): 255-65.

Lummis, Adair. *What Do Lay People Want in Pastors? Answers from Lay Search Committee Chairs and Regional Judicatory Leaders*. Durham, N.C.: Duke Divinity School, 2003.

——. "Why Men and Women Leave the Ministry: Hypotheses from Research on Clergy and from Role Exiters of Other Statuses." In *The Power of Gender in Religion*, edited by Georgie Weatherby and Susan Farrell. New York: McGraw-Hill, 1996.

McDuff, Elaine M. "The Gender Paradox in Work Satisfaction and the Protestant Clergy." *Sociology of Religion* 62 (2001): 1-21.

Mascum, Jack. "Parsing the Pastor 'Shortage.'" *Monday Morning* (September 3, 2001): 1-3.

Memming, Rolf. "United Methodist Ordained Ministry in Transition." In *The People(s) Called Methodist*, edited by William B. Lawrence, Dennis M. Campbell, and Russell E. Richey. Nashville: Abingdon Press, 1998.

Miller, Donald E. *Reinventing American Protestantism*. Berkeley: University of California Press, 1997.

Mills, Edgar W. "Career Change in the Protestant Ministry." *Ministry Studies* 3:1 (May 1969): 5-21.

——. "The Sacred in Ministry Studies." In *The Sacred in a Secular Age*, edited by Phillip E. Hammond. Berkeley: University of California Press, 1985.

Mills, Edgar W., and Garry W. Hesser. "A Contemporary Portrait of Clergymen." In *Confusion and Hope: Clergy, Laity, and the Church in Transition*, edited by Glenn R. Bucher and Patricia R. Hill. Philadelphia: Fortress Press, 1974.

Mills, Edgar W., and John P. Koval. *Stress in the Ministry*. Washington, D.C.: Ministry Studies Board, 1971.

Morin, Richard, and Dan Balz. "Americans Losing Trust in Each Other and Institutions." *Washington Post*, January 28, 1996, pp. A1, A6.

Nesbitt, Paula D. *Feminization of the Clergy in America: Occupational and Organizational Perspectives*. New York: Oxford University Press, 1997.

Pathman, Donald E., et al. "Physician Job Satisfaction, Job Dissatisfaction, and Physician Turnover." *The Journal of Family Practice* 51 (July 2002): 1-9.

Poulin, John E. "Job Task and Organizational Predictors of Social Worker Job Satisfaction Change: A Panel Study." *Administration in Social Work* 18:1 (1994): 21-38.

Presbyterian Church (U.S.A.) Research Services. "Ministers Ordained in the 1990s: A Look at Clergy Who Have Left the Ministry." Unbound report. Louisville, Ky.: Presbyterian Church (U.S.A.), July 1999.

Putnam, Robert D. *Bowling Alone: The Collapse and Revival of American Community*. New York: Simon & Schuster, 2000.

Rayburn, Carole A. "Counseling Depressed Female Religious Professionals: Nuns and Clergywomen." *Counseling and Values* 35 (January 1991): 136-48.

Rhode, Deborah L. *Balanced Lives: Changing the Culture of Legal Practice*. Report, Commission on Women in the Profession. Chicago: American Bar Association, 2001.

Robert Wood Johnson Foundation. "Study of Career Satisfaction among Practicing Physicians." National Program Project Report. Princeton, N.J., 2002. Available online at http://www.rwjf.org/reports/grr/027069.htm.

Sargeant, Kimon H. *Seeker Churches*. New Brunswick, N.J.: Rutgers University Press, 2000.

Schiltz, Patrick J. "On Being a Happy, Healthy, and Ethical Member of an Unhappy, Unhealthy, and Unethical Profession." *Vanderbilt Law Review* 52 (May 1999): 871-951.

Schneider, C. J., and D. Schneider. *In Their Own Right: The History of American Clergywomen*. New York: Crossroad, 1997.

Smith, Christian. *American Evangelicalism: Embattled and Thriving.* Chicago: University of Chicago Press, 1998.

Smith Sellers, Karen. "Crossroads: Clergywomen Thinking Seriously about Leaving Church-Related Ministry." Paper presented at the annual meeting of the Religious Research Association, Boston, Mass., November 1999.

Soderfeldt, Marit, Bjorn Soderfeldt, and Lars-Erik Warg. "Burnout in Social Work." *Social Work* 40:5 (1995): 638-46.

Swanson, V., K. G. Power, and R. J. Simpson. "Occupational Stress and Family Life: A Comparison of Male and Female Doctors." *Journal of Occupational and Organizational Psychology* 71 (September 1998): 237-60.

Wertheimer, Jack. "The Rabbi Crisis." *Commentary* (May 2003): 35-39.

Wheeler, Barbara G. "Fit for Ministry? A New Profile of Seminarians." *Christian Century* (April 11, 2001): 16-23.

Wiborg, Margaret S., and Elizabeth J. Collier. *United Methodist Clergywomen Retention Study.* Report. Boston: Anna Howard Shaw Center, Boston University School of Theology, 1997.

Wicai, Hillary. "Clergy by the Numbers: Statistics Show It's Not a Youthful Picture." *Congregations* (March-April 2001): 6-9.

Wuthnow, Robert. *The Restructuring of American Religion: Society and Faith since World War II.* Princeton, N.J.: Princeton University Press, 1988.

———. *The Struggle for America's Soul: Evangelicals, Liberals, and Secularism.* Grand Rapids: Eerdmans, 1989.

Zikmund, Barbara Brown, Adair T. Lummis, and Patricia Mei Yin Chang. *Clergy Women: An Uphill Calling.* Louisville, Ky.: Westminster John Knox Press, 1998.

Index